Decorative and Sculptural Ironwork

Tools, Techniques, Inspiration

2nd Edition

Dona Z. Meilach

Consultants:
George Martin, Ph.D.
E. A. Chase, Sculptor
Theodore Davidson, Ph.D.

Schiffer Publishing Ltd

4880 Lower Valley Road, Atglen, PA 19310 USA

Dedicated to My Dedicated Consultants:

George Martin

E. A. Chase

Ted Davidson

"There is a sense of reassurance knowing that one has a direct linkage with a past, that this knowledge, which is a gift, has been passed on, person to person, an individualized kind of history spoken with the hand."
Christopher Ray, 1976

All photos not otherwise credited have been taken by Mel and Dona Meilach.

Title Page: BUSH BOWIE BLADE. Daryl Meier. Damascus steel knife with images of 13 flags; presented to President George Bush. 18" long with 13" blade. 1992. *Photo, Weyer Intl.*

Back Cover: ASP PILLOW DAGGER, Virgil England, Damascus steel, gold, mammoth ivory handle. 7 1/2" long. *Photo, Weyer Intl.*

Library of Congress Cataloging-in-Publication Data

Meilach, Dona Z.
    Decorative and sculptural ironwork: tools, techniques, inspiration/Dona Z. Meilach.
    --2nd ed.
        p. cm.
    Includes bibliographical references and index.
    ISBN: 978-0-7643-0790-4 (pbk.)
    1. Blacksmithing. 2. Ironwork. I. Title
TT220.M4   1999   98-53076
739.4--dc21

Designed by "Sue"
Type set in TypoUpright BT/Zurich BT

ISBN: 978-0-7643-0790-4
Printed in China

Schiffer Books are available at special discounts for bulk purchases for sales promotions or premiums. Special editions, including personalized covers, corporate imprints, and excerpts can be created in large quantities for special needs. For more information contact the publisher:

Published by Schiffer Publishing Ltd.
4880 Lower Valley Road
Atglen, PA 19310
Phone: (610) 593-1777;
Fax: (610) 593-2002
E-mail: Info@schifferbooks.com

For the largest selection of fine reference books on this and related subjects, please visit our web site at:
www.schifferbooks.com
We are always looking for people to write books on new and related subjects. If you have an idea for a book please contact us at the above address.

This book may be purchased from the publisher.
Include $5.00 for shipping.
Please try your bookstore first.
You may write for a free catalog.

In Europe, Schiffer books are distributed by
Bushwood Books
6 Marksbury Ave.
Kew Gardens
Surrey TW9 4JF England
Phone: 44 (0) 20 8392 8585;
Fax: 44 (0) 20 8392 9876
E-mail: info@bushwoodbooks.co.uk
Website: www.bushwoodbooks.co.uk

Acknowledgments

If I were to write a sequel to this book, it would most likely be titled *Blacksmiths I Have Met: How Great and Interesting They Are.* When I began the research for this project, I knew a modern chapter to black-smithing was unfolding; but I never anticipated the zest, quality, and quantity of the response I received.

The warmth (both from the forges and from the men working them), invitations to visit, to photograph, to talk about smithing from people in unsuspected corners and crannies of the country has been an unforgetta-ble experience.

Everyone was willing and eager to share his techniques, discoveries, and knowledge and to learn what others were doing. Those who demon-strated their methods never hesitated to light their forges while we set up cameras and lighting. Their names accompany their demonstrations.

I am grateful to the smiths who sent in photos of their work, and some who shipped their work or traveled miles to bring it to be photo-graphed; to the industries that cooperated by sending photos, research, booklets, charts, graphs, and anything else I asked for; and to the mu-seums that permitted me to photograph work or that supplied photos of objects I felt would underscore the historical aspects of ironwork.

I especially want to thank my three consultants for their time and effort in developing specific written portions and for carefully checking the final manuscript: George Martin of Creative Metal Crafts and the University of California, Los Angeles; E. A. Chase, sculptor, from Santa Cruz, Calif.; and Ted Davidson, materials scientist from Rochester, N.Y. I am especially grateful to Stephen Bondi who, by marvelous chance, became my European correspondent and researcher. When he was work-ing in the Benetton Studios in Treviso, Italy, during a sabbatical from his teaching position in Washington, D.C., he encouraged Simon Benetton to contact me . . . resulting in a wealth of dramatic examples. He also photo-graphed several historical pieces in the Victoria and Albert Museum, London.

I must thank the Philadelphia contingent of ironworkers: Bill Leth, Christopher Ray, Anita Riley, Max Segal, and Jack Andrews for their courtesy and hospitality. And especially, Harvey Yellin for allowing me free access to his father's valuable collection . . . and for his help when extra hands were needed to hold lights and photographic paraphernalia.

A visit to Southern Illinois University at Carbondale uncovered an incredible hotbed of forging activity. Professor L. Brent Kington and his talented and enthusiastic graduate students demonstrated several tech-niques. Robert Griffith, Daryl Meier, and Jim Wallace volunteered to develop the entire chapter on Damascus steel, using material they were researching for their Master's theses. Assembling it for this book bene-fited everyone; they worked at a feverish pace, and the result of more than four hundred man-hours is evident in chapter 11.

My vote for highest energy-enthusiasm level goes to David LaPlantz, Humboldt State University, Arcata, Calif., for his intensive and thorough demonstration on angle raising in chapter 12 and to his wife, Shereen, for the excellent photographs of the series.

I must acknowledge the cooperation on every level from my husband, Dr. Melvin Meilach, who often traveled with me, relieving me of the driving and map reading on country back roads, arranging schedules, helping with the photography and note-taking, and enduring erratic meal and sleeping schedules during the actual organization and writing of the book.

Thanks, too, to Collette Russell, who helped keep the correspondence and photographs organized, and to Marilyn Regula for her typing of the final manuscript.

Dona Z. Meilach

Acknowledgments for the 2nd Edition

In the 21 years since the first edition of *Decorative and Sculptural Ironwork* was published, much has changed and much has not. The greatest change has been the numbers of people now involved in forging and metalwork and the advanced state of the art. What has not changed is the sense of spirit, giving and sharing. When I announced this forthcoming edition and additions, the response was overwhelming along with notes that the original book (reportedly dog-eared and dirty) had been the catalyst for a career or a lifelong foray into blacksmithing.

This new edition wouldn't have happened without Norman Larson's and Jock Dempsey's constant prodding to republish the book and Nancy Schiffer's foresight in realizing its value. My thanks to Stephen Bondi, George Martin, Daryl Meier, Richard Schrader, James A. Wallace, and the staff at the Artist-Blacksmith's Association of North America (ABANA) for their help.

I appreciate the effort taken by each person who responded to my call for photos. I only wish space would permit publishing all their work. Possibly, in a new book at a later date.

Dona Z. Meilach
Carlsbad, CA.
November, 1998

Foreword

With a subject as vast and ancient as forging and blacksmithing, it was necessary to adhere to a specific direction for the scope of this new volume. It seemed pointless to cover ground that has already been adequately written about in other reliable works, old and new.

Therefore, the scope of *Decorative and Sculptural Ironwork* deals with the activity that is emerging as a renaissance in an art form that appeared to be dying but instead has been steadily smoldering. It is not so concerned with the history or romance of the blacksmith, with a preservation of antique styles, or the making of tools. Rather, it presents a no-nonsense adaptation of the smith's techniques to the expressive output of the contemporary artist-craftsman. It offers the best available examples by people working today whether they are creating objects for personal expression as sculpture, for functional use as gates, grilles, hinges, weather vanes, utensils, and myriad other items, or a combination of functional-sculptural pieces.

The concern is with the trend, how it is growing, where it appears to be moving; to introduce the reader to the potential of forging techniques and how they may be adapted to his own work.

For those who may never plan to heat up a forge, it offers a stimulating source of ideas for work in other media and a continuing study into the potential of metals in art for the collector, gallery director, and museum curator.

Dona Meilach, 1977

Foreword for the 2nd Edition

In the two decades since the first publication of *Decorative and Sculptural Ironwork*, the public has endorsed the craft in a magnitude that was completely unanticipated. Original concerns that blacksmithing was an endangered and impracticable trade have proven groundless. Forged steel has flourished in architectural, sculptural and decorative uses. The Artists-Blacksmith's Association of North America (ABANA), that began in the mid-1970s with a nucleus of several hundred members, now boasts over four thousand members and other professional blacksmithing organizations exist around the globe on every continent. The guarded optimism expressed in the book's first edition, that blacksmithing was on the verge of a renaissance, is, indeed, history. It has happened.

The field virtually exploded once it was no longer confined to historical reenactment or economically tied to strictly functional or industrial products. Almost every major city in the United States has at least one smithy offering custom design and forging services. Some specialize in architectural works, others restrict themselves to furniture, lighting or other interior accessories, utilitarian objects, and still others concentrate on sculpture. Individual artistic design sensitivities have become as diverse as the nation itself. In these past twenty years, a definite sense of regionalism has emerged and contemporary versions of historic styles have further pushed an already rich visual vocabulary.

The physics of forging steel remain unchanged and many smiths adhere to traditional methods of joinery or styles, but the blacksmithing community as a whole has embraced modern technology. They use modern welding equipment such as MIG and TIG machines, plasma arc cutting equipment that is making new design concepts possible, along with an exploration into the world of nonferrous metals. Computer imaging has entered the otherwise smoky din of the smithy. Forged iron concepts are being translated into bronze and aluminum and painted surfaces aren't just black any longer.

The future of blacksmithing is exciting. We have witnessed its rediscovery and evolution into a contemporary medium capable of speaking in both the decorative and fine arts. This second edition of *Decorative and Sculptural Ironwork* continues to provide an exploration of techniques and concepts and a glimpse into the new trends.

James A. Wallace, Director
National Ornamental Metal Museum
Memphis, Tennessee

Contents

Daryl Meier has overheated the iron to create sparks for a dramatic visual photographic effect.

Photo, Bob Davis

1

New Creativity with Metal Forging

SINCE the beginning of the twentieth century, references have relegated the ironworker to a more poetic than productive position. The image of the muscular blacksmith pounding on his anvil, the ringing of the hammer blow, and the smell of the forge became a romanticized vision of the past. Objects once carefully and lovingly wrought by the smith were mass-produced of cast iron by industry which could make them cheaper and faster.

What happened to the brawny village smithy that Henry Wadsworth Longfellow immortalized in his famous poem? Did he close himself up in a small garage only to sharpen plows and make horseshoes? Many did. But there were exceptions. Through them, the art of iron forging has been quietly glowing like an ember and appears ready to burst into a brightly burning flame. There is incredible activity and interest in working iron by individual metalworkers and sculptors. Evidence heartily supports the fact that the prestigious *Encyclopaedia Britannica* will have to revise the definition of blacksmith in its 1974 edition. It states: "The chief work of the blacksmith today is to shoe horses and to repair simple wrought iron objects."

Throughout the country, blacksmiths working at forges or with other heat sources are shaping hot iron into myriad creative forms that are functional and beautiful. They are a new breed of blacksmith, men and women, who are rediscovering the inherent beauty and the malleability of the heated black metal as a medium for contemporary artistic statements.

The ironworkers are rediscovering what generations of smiths knew long ago—that iron has remarkable properties. It is a metal which can be drawn out, formed, machined, cast, laminated, hammered, inlaid, etched, punched, split, rolled, bent, chased, spun, welded, riveted, collared, and more. The plasticity of hot iron invites spontaneity . . . a kind of direct action among man, fire, hammer, and metal.

The reasons for the rising generation of blacksmiths to pick up hammer and tongs vary. Some are interested in the nostalgia of smithing

A wrought-iron hanging bracket for street lighting is one of hundreds of objects for which blacksmithing techniques are used. The widened and curved scroll endings are made by heating and hammering to shape.
Photographed in Florence, Italy,
Mel Meilach

and turn their hand towards the re-creation of historical objects: to emulate hinges, locks, hooks, weapons, armor, and tools of earlier cultures. Others are seeking new forms for the age-old materials and techniques. It is basically the second approach that is being explored in this book.

Before we discuss the background of blacksmithing and the current activity, it is essential to understand a few definitions and conditions of the medium.

1 • Blacksmithing

Blacksmithing, traditionally, deals with the shaping and forging of iron, hence "black = iron" and "smith = a worker in metals." Those who shape silver are called silversmiths; those who work with gold are goldsmiths. Often anyone who worked in tin and any metal other than iron was called a "whitesmith." The smith who made horseshoes was called a farrier.

2 • Wrought Iron

There is confusion about the term "wrought iron." We tend to call anything made of black metal today wrought iron. But there are two meanings to the words.

A. Wrought iron (as a noun) refers to a material which is difficult to buy today, but one which a century ago was the most available form of malleable iron. It is a commercial form of iron with a characteristic fibrous structure that is malleable and relatively soft; it contains less than 0.05 percent and usually less than 0.03 percent carbon. Because iron with this low carbon content is scarce today, most smiths use steels containing various combinations of iron with a higher percentage of carbon. Therefore, when we talk of wrought iron, today, we generally mean steel.

B. Wrought iron also means metal that has been worked, formed, and

Shield and helmet from sheet metal, sword
from tool steel; a re-creation of objects
from the Norman period. By Beau Hickory.
Photo, Larsen

shaped by some means such as beating, twisting, bending, or embellishing.

3 • Forge

The term "forge" also has two meanings. (A) The forge is a furnace or shop where metal is heated and worked; (B) to forge means to form metal by heating or hammering.

4 • The Ancient Blacksmith

In reality, today's blacksmith uses methods and techniques not too different from those of his ancient ancestors. However, he does not revel in the same magical and supernatural powers that some were endowed with. The blacksmith of early Greek mythology had almost uncanny abilities; he was pictured as taming fire to his will and turning the ores of the earth into magic to make invincible weapons or simple tools. To the ancient Greeks, the god Hephaestus, the son of Zeus and Hera, forged thunderbolts which were hurled in anger from Olympus to tame and rule a world occupied by rebellious peoples.

Among the Romans, he was named Vulcan who did marvelous things. He caught Venus and her lover, Ares, in a net of iron. He made the weapons of the gods. Stories tell us he was served in his home by maidens he had fashioned from gold and who were able to move, talk, and think. Vulcan's name still has many derivatives in our own language referring to heat-processed items with superabundant strength. He was Osiris of Egypt and Thor in Norse myth. He turned, eventually, into a whole race of demigods—giant Cyclops or dwarf Nibelungs—having mystical skills in ironwork.

The more human blacksmiths of ancient times were essential to the progress and life of the peoples. When the use of iron spread from the Middle East to Europe in the last millennium and gave birth to the Iron Age, the blacksmith equipped the warrior with swords, daggers, and spearheads. He gave the farmer the first efficient axe and ploughshare and provided the craftsmen with better tools than those fashioned from stone or bronze.

By Howard Keyser (Keyser Brothers). Detail of the top of a gate in the Washington Cathedral, Washington, D.C. The basic iron forging procedures are used: carving, splitting, drawing out, twisting, collaring, etching, and fabrication.

Courtesy, artist

Though iron was known to have been extracted from ores by prehistoric man and used by the Egyptians almost nine thousand years ago, archaeologists date the beginning of the Iron Age about 1200 B.C., the time when early peoples learned to use it. The biblical reference of beating swords into ploughshares is one of many clues that ancient man knew how to work these metals to objects of war and peace.

Italian artistry with ironwork has been outstanding for centuries. One authority maintains that when invaders swept across Italy about 1000 B.C. they brought with them techniques for working iron and used them to reduce the earlier population to slavery. There was a demand for chains and instruments of torture. The museums of Italy, and especially the National Museum of the Villa Giulia at Rome, support this observation. Here one will find the myriad objects needed for the inhabitants of a growing civilization; utensils, tools, weapons, and objects for adornment and furnishings. The iron and copper which the Etruscans had at their disposal enabled them to forge superior items which facilitated their wars of expansion and conquest.

Despite the early usage of metals, where, when, and how it was discovered, it was not until the European Middle Ages, with the introduction of the iron cannon that iron actually overtook copper and bronze to achieve first place among metals in use. And, despite its widespread application in other parts of the world, iron remained relatively unknown in the Americas until the arrival of Columbus.

The blacksmith of early cultures was essential to the development and progress of the society. His output was more often deemed a trade, rather than an art. No matter how artistic and talented a smith was, his products, being useful, were not viewed and critiqued as an art in the same vein as the work of the sculptor, painter, or architect. Yet, the

embellishments created by medieval, Renaissance, and seventeenth and eighteenth century blacksmiths that appear as gates, grilles, locks, torch brackets, lanterns, iron posts, banisters, balustrades, fireplace screens, weather vanes, door hardware, containers, candle holders, chains, armor, guns, knives and swords, doorframes, boxes, keys—the list is endless—are so intricately and artistically integrated that, looking back, one can only marvel at their ability and ingenuity. The pages of Henri René D'Allemagne's collection in his volume *Decorative Antique Ironwork* underscore the infinite variety blacksmiths achieved in their art along with the unlimited potential of iron as a medium for artistic expression.

Style in decorative ironwork has varied throughout the years but for the most part it is the finest practical embodiment of a linear idea. According to Otto Höver's "Style in Decorative Wrought-Iron Work" in *The Encyclopaedia of Ironwork*, "All the many possibilities for the designs of artistically wrought iron lead back to a basic linear element: the iron bar. ... Grillwork is the ultimate object of all the technical and artistic work done by the masters of the guild of smiths."

Höver emphasizes that the undisputed peaks of decorative wrought-iron work had their inherent stylistic characteristics dictated by the three main forms of the bar: the flat, round, and square. During the beginning and middle of the Gothic period the flat wrought-iron bar, in parts narrow and in parts wide, was favored. The round bar dominated the late Gothic period and, in northern Europe, continued into the Renaissance. In Italy and the south, during the Renaissance, the use of square bars dominated.

Höver also points out that the decorative art of the smith has always been taken from "graphic" examples. Ornamentation in iron appeared secondary to the inventiveness of artists and illuminators. At the begin-

The artistry in functional iron objects is better appreciated when one becomes involved with and learns the differences between hand-forged and mass-produced objects. The creativity of the blacksmith's occupation becomes apparent in this detail from a gate at the Washington Cathedral, Washington, D.C. By Samuel Yellin. 1928.

Four views of the Yellin Museum, Philadelphia, Pa. The museum is a veritable storehouse of ironwork detailing. Hundreds of duplicate pieces from many of Samuel Yellin's commissions are displayed. When specific structural and technical problems were solved in a job, details were re-created for study and future reference. These are a legacy in the history of ironwork.

6

Dogon. Africa. A standing *nommo* figure illustrates the technical skill of the African blacksmith in the shaped bar, split legs, fabricated arms, carved features, and body design. 8¼" high.

From the Wunderman Collection, N.Y.
Photo, Lester Wunderman

ning and middle of the Gothic period one can see counterparts of the designs in the borders of illuminated manuscripts. The mountings on the west portal of Notre Dame in Paris are a direct offshoot of manuscript drawings as seen in the spiral forms, leaf, and rosettelike terminations that appear on the panels.

During the seventeenth and eighteenth centuries, in France, the smith's patterns leaned heavily on the engravings, which were highly ornamental and linear. Gates, porticos, balustrades, all echoed the ribbonlike swells and curves, the flowing lines gathered together frankly with intricately engraved collars and straps.

Throughout European history, grillwork echoed the styles and tastes of the countries and times and emulated work in other media; stone carving, painting, graphics, furniture, and even clothing styles . . . all of which set the tastes for the various arts. A study of many time periods will reveal the obvious and subtle differences between them. For example, the German idea of form in the late baroque and early rococo period can be identified by dynamic winged decorations as opposed to a static and structural form used in Italy and France during the same period.

IRONWORK OF THE LATE 1900S

Jumping to a more contemporary history, it is fascinating to note the influence of the Eiffel Tower built in France in 1889 as a structural and decorative statement that set new standards for ironwork. It negated the ornamentation of the rococo; it expressed visually and structurally the strength and beauty of iron and steel.

Another influential factor on the direction of decorative ironwork began in England in the late 1800s with the Arts and Crafts Movement guided by William Morris who was artistically multifaceted. He was an architect, painter, interior decorator, illustrator, poet, essayist, and Socialist. Morris, who aimed to revive arts and crafts for the masses, to take it out of the realm of tradition and privileged rich classes, inspired a new set of aesthetic standards. His teachings worked a profound influence on matters relating to architecture and the applied arts. The greatest success of the movement was a revival of printing as an art form in the 1890s. With the smith's dependency upon graphics for linear design elements, ironwork of the period also took on a new elegance and moved in a new direction. It culminated in the Art Nouveau style.

Art Nouveau was an international movement of new art characterized by certain recurrent stylistic elements, particularly by two dimensional linear design and the use of sinuous, often plantlike arabesques. Each country used its own sources for inspiring the Art Nouveau look, and much of it appeared in their iron grillwork, gates, and door hardware of the period beginning at the turn of the twentieth century. English exponents drew on Celtic Art, the Spanish architect Antonio Gaudí formed his own unique interpretation based on Moorish antecedents. The linear influence of medieval manuscripts, Japanese prints, Gothic art and forms from animal and vegetable kingdoms were all variously used. Victor Horta's name stands out as the designer in this period. His boldly styled interiors integrated the curving, sinuous ironwork banisters and supporting columns with graceful staircases; foliating designs were woven into the rugs, painted on walls, and created in furniture. So successful and striking are the ironwork examples of this period that many

Ironwork from seventeenth- and eighteenth-century England and France illustrates sculptural detailing within the functional context. *Left:* Detail from a grille with carved lions and chiseled designs. *Below:* A door knocker with a carved animal head and twisted neck. From the Victoria and Albert Museum, London, England.
Photo, Stephen Bondi

of the smiths working today relate to Art Nouveau for their inspirations. You will see this in the gates by Jim Hubbell, Tom Markuson, and Albert Paley, especially.

EARLY AMERICAN IRONWORK

The Europeans who settled in America followed the precedents of their homeland countries in the design of the architectural ironwork used in gates and balconies. Gerald K. Geerling's excellent historical survey, *Wrought Iron in Architecture* published in 1929 states: "It would be of interest to know whether America came to be termed 'the melting pot' of the world because of her ironwork . . . the immigrant craftsman could render existing favorites which were within more limited means of forging at his command over here, yet the completed work has all the peculiar qualities which any product might be expected to have on being 'melted down.'"

Weather vane. By Glen Gardner. 1974.
Mild plate and bar steel forged and riveted.
The openwork is accomplished by piercing
with a cold chisel. 36" wide, 24" high.
Courtesy, artist

The colonial blacksmith, however, intent on creating the necessities of a new society, appeared for the most part untouched by and disassociated from the stylistic vogues that occurred on the continent. An indication of the activity and necessity of the smith in America can still be felt by driving through Pennsylvania, Virginia, and Georgia where many towns bear the name of the forge that had been built there.

The style of the colonial American blacksmith was simple, direct, utilitarian with little embellishment. Lanterns, locks, and candle holders were essentially unadorned with any kind of surface detailing. The drawn-out member of a candlestick could as easily have been the tine of a spading fork. The demands for objects were so great that a smith might spend an entire winter making only a few tools and nails. In the early years of the Jamestown colony, land was so plentiful and nails so scarce that they would burn down the building on abandoned land to salvage nails for reuse, but this practice was forbidden by law in 1644.

Actually nails were more often made by the blacksmith's apprentice and one source estimates that eight boys could turn out 25,000 nails in a week provided there was enough iron rod.

The colonial blacksmith made axes for felling trees, matlocks, wagon wheel rims, sleigh runners, chains, and ploughs and all the iron fittings for frame houses and schooners, and objects for use in the home. It was the blacksmith who hammered out Benjamin Franklin's lightning rods and the guns for the Minutemen. In the nineteenth and twentieth centuries the American blacksmith lost most of his traditional importance because of the growth of large-scale industry; however the common surname "Smith" is a reminder that every village had a blacksmith.

THE TWENTIETH CENTURY

Although general literature and the trends of the times point to the demise of blacksmithing as a craft, there was still work to be done by the individual who could custom-design for specific clients and for architectural commissions. Probably the best known in America was Samuel Yellin, who was born in Poland in 1885 and began working in a Russian forge when he was only seven years old. During his apprenticeship years, young Yellin learned a variety of techniques from making a nail to forging an elaborate piece of armor. By the age of seventeen he was a master craftsman and ready to earn his way with his skills. He left Russia and spent three years in Belgium reproducing Gothic ironwork, and two years in England where he again studied and emulated the ornamental designs that had been created by generations of his predecessors.

He came to America in 1906 and settled in Philadelphia where he worked and taught ornamental ironwork techniques during the brief crafts revival in this country that followed on the heels of the European Arts and Crafts movement. Eventually, Yellin opened a studio which became so well known that by the 1920s he had about three hundred blacksmiths who produced small and monumental ironworks for many buildings on the east coast, and a few on the west coast. So well known are Yellin's works, so outstanding in their detailing, that contemporary smiths visit and study the detailing in Yellin's gates wherever they are still in use—in banks of New York and churches of Philadelphia and elsewhere. A visit to the Yellin museum in Philadelphia, maintained by his son, Harvey Yellin, offers a veritable encyclopedic resource of exciting approaches to the blacksmith's problems and solutions for them.

Samuel Yellin's ironwork and that created by the craftsmen he attracted to his shop from the 1920s to the mid-1930s won numerous architectural awards. He executed much hardware and many of the gates and other iron embellishments in the Washington Cathedral, Washington, D.C.

There are still men living who worked in Yellin's Arch Street Metal Workers' Studio during its busiest years. Most had already known blacksmithing in their native countries, and Yellin found them at the docks and brought them to Philadelphia, gave them jobs, and a welcome entree into their new world. Their expertise and Yellin's ability to design and execute large commissions all combined to make his name outstanding in the field.

There were other people, too, whose work was commissioned by the Washington Cathedral in the lean years of the depression. Howard Keyser of Keyser Brothers was able to discuss and document several of the commissions in which he was involved. Still active as a blacksmith, he has passed his knowledge and techniques on to sculptors whose work appears in this book. Christopher Ray and Anita Riley learned from Mr. Keyser the fundamentals of blacksmithing. He encouraged them to use their experiences as sculptors for approaching iron and steel with a contemporary artistic awareness.

The work of Fritz Kühn and Fritz Ulrich of Germany has exercised a profound influence on traditional ironwork. Fritz Kühn's gates and grilles that are ingeniously and meticulously crafted may be viewed in the handsome volumes that he has written. They contain drawings of his working procedures and photographs of a wealth of details.

A contemporary approach to Italian ironwork, completely divorced from the traditional idiom associated with the Renaissance and baroque grilles and gates can be found in the work of Allesandro Mazzucotelli and that of Toni and Simon Benetton. The Benetton studios have been and still are prime innovators in that country, and it is with great pleasure that their work is shown in various sections in this book.

A door knocker from the Washington Cathedral, Washington, D.C., of flattened and pierced iron bar with a wrapped coil of iron attached to a backplate. By Samuel Yellin. 1927.

A contemporary barbeque set by Eric Moebius utilizes basic traditional blacksmithing techniques, splitting, drawing out, shaping, twisting, and riveting.

AFRICAN IRONWORK

Of more recent historic interest is the activity in ironwork practiced by the African blacksmith who holds a unique status in the society. Metals are highly regarded by the Africans and used for jewelry, sheaths, arrows, breastplates, candle holders, farming implements, ceremonial objects, furniture and many other vital things. The person who can fashion the metals into these objects has such a powerful status that he can cross tribal lines, marry royalty, and even rule as king in some tribes. With all his power and responsibility, he has retained a simplicity of form that is refreshing when compared to the ornate qualities of ironwork elsewhere.

When African masks, woodwork, and other objects were brought to France, early in the twentieth century, they inspired painters such as Pablo Picasso and Paul Cézanne to alter the direction of their visual images. The same response was felt among sculptors working in various media; Constantin Brancusi's wood and stone sculptures exhibit an economy of form. Alberto Giacometti's lean long figures were a response to the African craftsman's influence, and many of the people working with the Bauhaus school in the first quarter of the twentieth century speak of African art as a catalyst for new designs. This same influence had long-reaching effects, and still has, on the artist and craftsmen working as directly with the metal in our society as in the African culture.

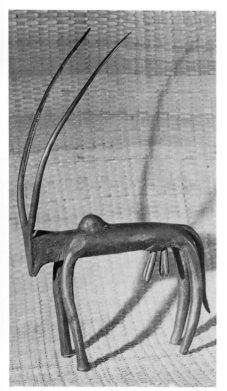

A Bakuba antelope sculpture, Africa. The simplicity and elemental gesture of African ironwork was an inspiration for sculptors in many media at the turn of the century and still is.

Collection, Linden-Museum, Stuttgart, Germany

HEAD. Julio Gonzalez. 1935 (?). Wrought iron. 17¾" high, 15¼" wide.

Collection, The Museum of Modern Art, New York

TWENTIETH-CENTURY SCULPTURE

The use of iron and steel for three-dimensional expressive sculpture is a phenomenon of this century. The material possesses little art history in the fine arts milieu . . . it has all been in the realm of utilitarian objects, grillwork, gates, and architectural decor. The use of steels for sculpture grew hand in hand with the application of modern industrial equipment to sculptural form.

Until early in the twentieth century, the vast majority of three-dimensional metal sculptures were made by the lost wax casting process, and any serious piece of work was created in bronze. Casting methods are still used today, but the entire scope of metal sculpture has radically changed since the early 1900s. Of importance to this discussion is the fact that often the sculptor has emulated many blacksmithing techniques. Although he has not called himself a blacksmith, he has used the essential equipment and procedures. Today, many sculptors are researching blacksmithing methods so they can continue to select the procedures needed for the forms they visualize. "It's not important what we call ourselves, or what we use," emphasizes one artist, "so long as we achieve the forms we want. If heating iron over a coal forge is more efficient than working with an oxyacetylene torch, then we'll set up a forge." And many have. From San Diego to Boston, and across the ocean, ironworkers, or sculptors, or however they deem themselves, are pounding and shaping iron hot and cold to result in exciting changes in style and approach.

The earliest application of steels and other metals used directly (as opposed to casting) appear to be the work of Pablo Gargallo. Gargallo (1891–1934), a Spanish sculptor born in Mailla, Aragon, studied in Barcelona and Paris. His early pieces created in 1911 and 1912 are mostly masks imitating the work of the primitive African artist that appeared in Europe about that time. He also sculpted naturalistic works showing the influence of Auguste Rodin and Aristide Maillol. The best of these, made of iron, is the *Portrait of Picasso* (1912). He created an interplay of voids and solids with the iron that he shaped by hammering while hot or by cold bending. He achieved abstract volumes and, by the use of convex, concave, and flat planes, created a piece that was both abstract and natural. By the 1920s, he had so pioneered the technique that, along with Julio Gonzalez, he is considered one of the innovators and most influential artists of direct metal techniques.

Julio Gonzalez (1876–1942), born in Barcelona, had a background as a goldsmith: he studied painting in Paris but returned to metalwork about 1910. He, too, was inspired by the Africans' artistry and created a series of silver and bronze portrait masks. He turned to sculpture in 1926 and worked first in the cubist style and later in a more individualistic style. Gonzalez, inspired by Picasso, also influenced Picasso. It was he who taught Picasso to weld, which resulted in the latter's pieces made from industrial steel scrap. Gonzalez's use of iron for his abstract works and his application of the medium for enclosing positive space as a design element have had a considerable influence on twentieth century sculpture.

By the 1930s, several young American artists with experience in metalwork from other disciplines, began to apply their knowledge and the tools of industry to sculpture. David Smith (1906–1965), born in Decatur, Indiana, was disenchanted with formal approaches to art education through his college curriculum. He continually experimented on his own, developing a series of different styles during his life. He learned to weld during the summers of 1925 and 1927 at the Studebaker automobile factory in South Bend, Indiana. Smith moved to New York where he

TANKTOTEM #1. David Smith. 1952. Sheet and bar steel hammered and drawn. *Courtesy, The Art Institute of Chicago*

WHALER OF NANTUCKET. Theodore J. Roszak. Steel overlaid with nickel and silver. 34" high, 45" wide, 25" deep.

Courtesy, The Art Institute of Chicago

studied painting and was strongly influenced by cubist painters, an important factor in studying his sculptures which often require frontal viewing.

In 1930 Smith saw photographs of Picasso's first welded metal constructions and realized the possibilities of creating art from metal, a material he had previously associated only with labor and industry. When he bought his first set of welding equipment in 1933 the landlord of his apartment building was afraid he would burn things down. The beginning of his forays into iron sculpture began when Smith walked along the navy pier and saw a ramshackle-looking structure with the sign Terminal Iron Works. Next morning he walked in and said, "I'm an artist, I have a welding outfit. I'd like to work here." "Hell! yes—move in" was the response. And Smith set about learning all he could about ironwork, tools, and methods. In 1934 he exhibited his first two iron sculptures. He continued to explore the union of painting and sculpture, and by the 1940s he was working mainly with steel and using both gas and arc welding along with coke forging. He preferred working with steel, he said, because ... "steel can be stainless, painted, lacquered, waxed, processed and electroplated. It can be cast. Steel has multiple possibilities which have never been used. It has high tensile strength. Pinions can support masses, soft steel can bend cold, both with and across its grain, yet have a tensile strength of 50,000 to 60,000 pounds to one square inch. It can be drawn, cupped, spun and forged, cut and patinaed by acetylene gas and oxygen and welded both electrically and by the acetylene oxygen process. It can be chiseled, ground, filed and polished. Welds can possess greater strength than the parent metal." Having worked with other materials such as aluminum, stone, brass, and wood, Smith realized the inadequacy of their strength when trying to make them conform, and, as a result, he turned to steel.

CHIEN MOQUER. David Hayes. 1964. Forged steel. Steel plate formed and shaped in the same fashion that armor was made in ancient times. Seams can now be welded with gas and electric equipment so that large shaped pieces of metal are easier to fabricate than in medieval times. 23" high.

Collection, Mr. & Mrs. Jon Martin, Jr.
Courtesy, Willard Gallery, N.Y.

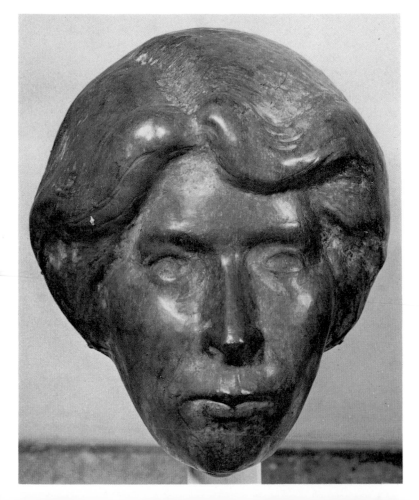

PORTRAIT OF NOLA. Julio Gonzalez. 1920s. Brass and copper repoussé. The general techniques of metalsmithing often overlap those of the blacksmith, and similar results can be achieved within the confines of a particular metal's limitations.

Courtesy, National Museum Service, Paris

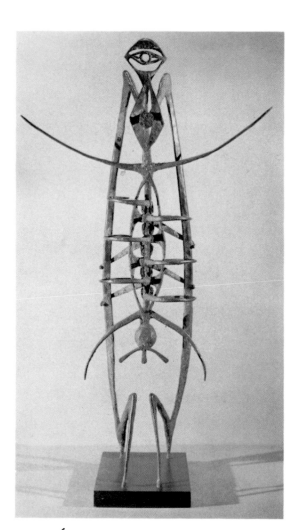

AUTO-DA-FÉ II. Lindsay Decker. 1955.
Forged and brazed steel, 43" high.
Courtesy, Detroit Institute of Arts,
Michigan

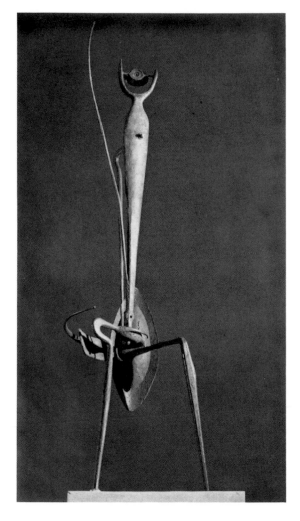

WOMAN. Reg Butler. 1949. Forged iron.
Courtesy, The Tate Gallery, London

COMPOSITION #5. Mauro De Biasio. 1975. 20", high.

Courtesy, artist

Theodore Roszak, another iron sculpture innovator, was also work-ing in New York during the 1930s, but as a painter and lithographer influenced by the Cubism movement. During World War II he was em-ployed in an airplane factory and acquired the metalworking techniques that he later applied to produce his first Constructivist sculpture. By the 1940s he experimented more and more with iron and steel. Art critics of the time and soon art historians, because of the work of Gonzalez, Smith, and Roszak, began to dub the early 1940s the Iron Age. And indeed it was. It evolved into the entire concept of direct metal sculpture. Roszak experimented with various metals and finally achieved the effects he desired by overlaying hammered steel with nickel and silver or with other metals.

By the end of World War II, with nations again at peace, and more people familiar with and able to secure industrial equipment, direct metal sculpture bloomed. With steel, artists could digress from the solidity of traditional shapes and create more open areas and frankly organic forms. The openness and thin, delicate-looking structural innovations possible with direct metal are not feasible in the casting process. With iron and steel, one can draw out a thin member and thereby pierce space and volume in ways that were unattainable previously.

It is impossible to state how many of the new artists utilized a coal forge, nor is it important. Because of the popularity and ease of gas and electric welding equipment, and the ability to cut large pieces of metals with the torch, the blacksmith's fire lay relatively dormant and isolated during this time.

ROCKING HORSE. L. Brent Kington. 1972.
Steel, forged, chiseled, and chased. The
object as sculptural form. 44" long.
                    Courtesy, artist

In the United States at the end of the 1960s a new wave of interest
swept the country. It was deemed "nostalgia." Young people, particularly, began a movement back to the ways of our forefathers. They established communes in the country and began to recapture living modes of
the early land settlers. Among the trends revived was making your necessities by hand. The young people learned wood carving, weaving, sewing,
and metalworking, including traditional forging, and they produced these
things on a small scale having nothing to do with industry. Among the
metalworkers, farmers discovered a new market for their old anvils, their
rusty hearths, their weather- and work-worn trip-hammers. Rusty and
mud-caked tongs were considered "finds" to the energetic ponytailed,
bearded, new crop of frontiersmen. At the same time, the interest in
blacksmithing was being sparked by these same young people attending

IRON SCULPTURES AND DRAWINGS. By Joe Nyiri. A sketch drawn to small scale suggests the general composition, proportion, silhouette, and design harmony for the visual interpretation of iron to sculptural idea.

Courtesy, artist

college art classes. Available books on blacksmithing were minimal, most having been printed scores of years ago and being out of print. As interest at the college level increased, metalworkers who had studied jewelry making found that steel could be handled in similar ways .to copper, brass, and silver but that it offered potential for large work and more exploration.

In 1964, L. Brent Kington, professor of art at Southern Illinois University, Carbondale, became interested in the potential of iron at a meeting of the World Craft Council in New York. At the same time, he was awed by the collection of arms and armor at the Metropolitan Museum and also by C. S. Smith's book on metallography with its discussion of Damascus steel.

He returned to Carbondale and bought three pieces of equipment to set up a shop in his backyard. He found a local blacksmith to teach him how to build a fire. He experimented through late 1967. With his background in jewelry and metals, Kington began to explore enthusiastically the possibilities of using nonferrous metal techniques with ferrous metals. In 1969, he had his first showing of ironwork in the Objects U.S.A. show and in a showing of the Society of North American Goldsmiths. These were "objects," but with the sculptural aspects achieved by a master craftsman. "The difficulties at that time," explains Kington, "were learning to scale up 3 1/2-inch pieces to 5–6 feet." His main concern was not so much in making the object, per se, as it was in putting together information about techniques that he could pass on to students. As he worked out the problems of construction and spatial concepts, he says, "I went back to school in my backyard shop. I interviewed local smiths, farmers, anyone who had ever forged iron."

In May 1970 Kington organized a "Blacksmith/70" conference at Southern Illinois University. Alex Bealer who had recently authored a book on his favorite hobby, blacksmithing, appeared and the students really began to get involved. In October 1970, Shop One, a gallery in Rochester, N.Y., had an exhibit of about forty iron objects made by craftsmen working in individual studios across the country. Few of the exhibitors realized that others were so committed to the idiom. Soon a consciousness about iron as a medium for nontraditional exploration permeated the art-craft community. Articles about ironwork and reviews of shows with iron objects appeared in issues of *Craft Horizons,* the magazine of the American Craft Council.

In 1973, Albert Paley and Tom Markuson, jewelers who had taken up smithing, organized a show at Brockport College in Brockport, N.Y. Kington gave a workshop there which attracted seventy-five conferees; people from California through Maine; engineers, artists, psychologists, businessmen. From this emerged and grew an organization titled The Artist-Blacksmiths Association of North America (ABANA), which held its first conference in Lumpkin, Georgia, in 1973, followed by a second one March 1974 and a third at Southern Illinois University in October 1976. The enthusiasm for working with forges, anvils, and hammers was so great that their sounds seem to have been carried by the air to distant places. Since then, blacksmithing activity has emerged across the country. Schools for teaching blacksmithing have been established and many colleges are integrating smithing courses in their art curricula.

Research interviews with craftsmen indicate a necessity for sharing the knowledge that each person discovers from his own experience and by talking with others. There is no doubt that blacksmithing, though an ancient craft, is new, vital, and open to infinite exploration in our contemporary context.

Opposite:

Detail of a door (see page 285 for the total piece). By the Benetton Studios, Treviso, Italy. The surface treatment, edges, and feeling of fluidity illustrate the malleability and plasticity that can be achieved with iron worked on a large scale.
Courtesy, Simon Benetton

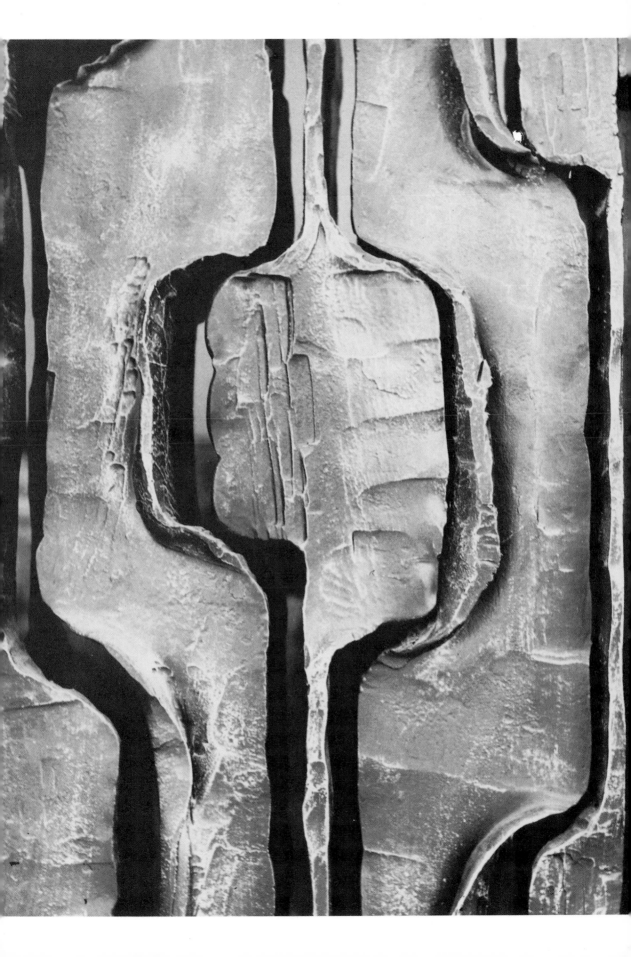

The Shop, the Forge and the Tools

THE contemporary blacksmith's shop is not much different from the romanticized, literary version of it harbored in most of our minds. The equipment is essentially the same as that used by our smithy ancestors, with the addition of several modern machine tools in most shops. Traveling about, meeting with and interviewing today's ironworkers, underscored one essential fact: given the motivation, a person can work iron almost anywhere (although a home basement workshop is not recommended because of the amount of smoke that might be produced).

The majority of ironworkers set up shop in a portion of a garage, or a factory building, in their backyards, in a barn or shack, in or behind the studios of a college art department . . . and even in a specially designed tent. I have photographed contemporary smiths working from a garage behind a gas station in Philadelphia, to an old barn in northern Wisconsin, to an open air lean-to overlooking the beach at Santa Barbara.

No matter what the environment, the equipment is essentially the same; one needs a forge for the heat source. This consists of a *hearth*, to hold the fire and the *tuyere*, the nozzle through which the air blast is brought to the heated coals, and the *blower* which delivers the air blast. The designs, sizes, and shapes of these basic items vary considerably as you will note in the illustrations that follow. But the basic principles remain the same: the hearth, sometimes brick or stone, but usually cast iron or sheet metal with a ventilation hood, holds the coals. The blower, which may be a bellows, or a hand- or rheostat-controlled fan system, helps achieve the necessary draft to fan the fire.

Other equipment, all analyzed for their function and type, are discussed in this chapter and in chapter 5. You will need the anvil mounted to a proper working height, anvil tools, hammer, tongs, punches, and chisels. One also needs a container for fuel, large wood or metal buckets for water for cooling the iron and quenching tools. The water is also there to quench any out-of-hand fires. A modern fire extinguisher should be an essential piece of shop safety equipment.

Larry Mann of Lexington, Va., working on a small knife in his blacksmith shop. The anvil should be placed close to the forge so that heat loss of the iron is minimal; tools should be located for convenience; water buckets nearby for efficiency and safety.

Photo, Sally Mann

23

Placement of the anvil and tools in relation to the forge is important. Usually the anvil is placed in front of the forge and slightly to one side so that as you move from forge to anvil, you will have a free, unobstructed path, yet be close enough so you do not lose too much heat from the iron before you begin to work it. Hammers and tongs should be placed closeby for easy access. They may be stored on a specially designed rack which can be improvised from barrels and crates and/or hung in a slotted area on a heavy tool bench. The slot can be made by protruding an extra piece of wood out from the bench with a space properly designed to accommodate the hammer handles when they are dropped in. These can also hold the anvil tools. The photos of various shop setups will suggest possible ideas for organizing your own work area and tool storage.

The lighting in the workshop is also an essential consideration. This is one time where modern electricity and floodlighting is not suggested. Working out of direct light is considered the optimum condition, possibly keeping the forge in a dark area of the shop. The reason? The smith must observe carefully the color of the iron as it is heated. The color, which depends upon the amount of heat given and the size of the fire used, determines the workability of the iron. It can be dissipated in an overlit situation and the smith will have difficulty judging the amount of heat in the metal.

A nearby sturdy workbench holds the necessary vises in which the smith must clamp the iron for shaping and bending. The vises must be securely mounted and away from a wall to allow easy access with long and short pieces of iron. Generally, the workbench should be kept free for laying out patterns and working; it does tend to accumulate assorted items in a day's work, so keeping it straightened daily is a good habit. Ideally, the workbench should be designed for your height with the top coming up about one-third of the distance between your wrist and elbow.

Used blacksmith's equipment is not so easy to find today; new items are available but many are expensive. The ironworker becomes almost as inventive at finding his tools as he is about the objects he makes. Used equipment can be found if one hunts in likely places, and watches ads in newspapers and ironworkers' magazines. Farmers in rural areas are a prime source for old equipment and tools. Many worthwhile anvils, tongs, and hammers have been bought reasonably in small town garage sales and flea markets. They can also be found around mining towns. Trip-hammers can often be gleaned from used-machinery dealers found in the classified telephone book of large cities. Fifty- to two-hundred-pound hammers are not so much used industrially today because they do not conform to industrial safety standards, so many dealers are anxious to move them off their floors for a minimal price and your willingness to take them away.

Chisels, anvil tools, and tongs are often made by the smith who knows exactly what he wants, how the items should be balanced, and so forth. Toolmaking is not covered in this book; but you can find instructions for fashioning all kinds of tools from early and recent books dealing with traditional blacksmithing listed in the bibliography.

Manually operated portable bellows and forge at the First Southern Illinois Arts and Crafts Festival held at DuQuoin State Fair Grounds, DuQuoin, Ill., 1970.
Photo, Terry Nelms

Hearth for a coke fire has a Champion electric motor-driven blower with rheostat for air control. It also has a clinker breaker and counterbalanced ash door.
Photographed at the forge of Eric Moebius, Mazomanie, Wis.

Jack Andrews of Paoli, Pa., built a hearth of sheet metal into a wooden workbench and placed a rotary blower beneath.

VARIOUS TYPES OF HEARTHS AND FORGE SETUPS

Right: At Turley's Forge in Santa Fe, N. Mex., hearths and anvils for six students are placed in a converted barn. Frank Turley demonstrates a proper working position for drawing out a piece of bar stock.
Courtesy, Bethlehem Steel Corp.

Below left: An Indian tepee made of sailcloth with an ample opening at the top for ventilation is the forge for Jack Andrews, Paoli, Pa. An extra inner piece of cloth attached about shoulder height within the tent creates necessary airflow. Jack carefully studied the American Indian methods of working iron within their tents before he re-created his own. It is engineered, as are the Indians', so that rainwater will work its way along the posts and not fall within the tent.

Below right: Ben Dial, Palos Verdes Estates, Calif., uses a portable forge on wheels that can be quickly moved about. Portable forges are available in sizes from 18" to 3' in diameter and from 3" to 5 1/2" in depth.

Tom Bredlow, Tucson, Arizona, uses a cast-iron hearth with a tall chimney pipe, hooded ventilation, and an electric rheostat-controlled blast. Hoods and chimneys are not needed when working out of doors.

Christopher Ray's forge in Philadelphia, Pa., is located in a factory building. In addition to the forge, tools, and iron storage racks shown, Chris has modern power tools and welding equipment. The setup was purchased from Howard Keyser, an old-time ironworker, who taught him the techniques he applies so ably to sculptures (chapter 13) and gates (chapter 8).
Photo, courtesy, Howard Keyser

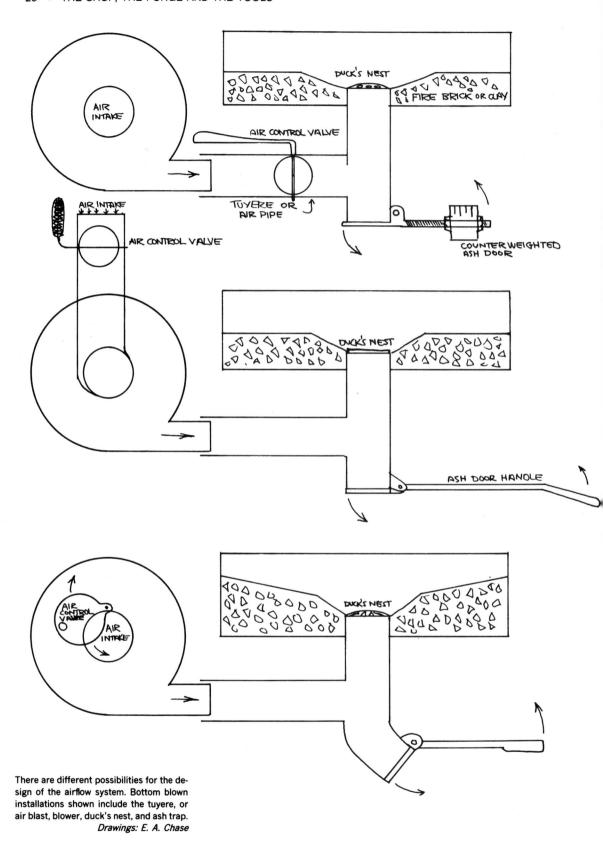

DUCK'S NEST

FIRE BRICK OR CLAY

AIR INTAKE

AIR CONTROL VALVE

TUYERE OR AIR PIPE

COUNTERWEIGHTED ASH DOOR

AIR INTAKE

AIR CONTROL VALVE

DUCK'S NEST

ASH DOOR HANDLE

AIR CONTROL VALVE

AIR INTAKE

DUCK'S NEST

There are different possibilities for the design of the airflow system. Bottom blown installations shown include the tuyere, or air blast, blower, duck's nest, and ash trap.
Drawings: E. A. Chase

THE AIRFLOW SYSTEM

An important feature of the hearth is the *tuyere* (pronounced twē-yer), or air pipe, called the *tue iron*. It is the air supply duct for the forge which routes the air from its source to the fire grate, or *duck's nest*. In modern forges the tuyere is generally made of steel or cast-iron pipe or tubing. Somewhere along the length of the tuyere, at a location convenient to the smith, a butterfly valve is usually found that can regulate the air supply to the fire. If a centrifugal blower is part of the system, the air valve may be adapted to the exhaust or intake side of the blower. With a bellows system, a crank-operated blower or an electrical blower with a rheostat control is used, and then a separate air valve is usually not necessary.

Regulation of the airflow is very important because of the effect of the quantity of oxygen delivered to the fire and the iron being heated. Too little air will "starve" the fire, thus reducing its heat potential. Too much will cause the fire to burn beyond its usefulness. The iron will overheat, oxidize, and form excessive slag. The latter condition will make it impossible to forge weld, will reduce the overall dimensions of sound metal, leave a pocked surface, and possibly ruin the steel if its carbon content is critical. Experience is necessary to determine the proper air supply for the given size fire and function.

An ash trap should be somewhere below the junction between the air pipe and the duck's nest (see illustration). Here the ashes collect as the fire burns. The ash release door is usually either counterweighted or provided with a handle for ash removal; the illustration shows different possible setups. It is best to have sufficient area for the ash to settle below the tuyere to avoid catching this residue in the air turbulence.

E. A. CHASE

CENTRIFUGAL BLOWERS

Some smiths still use air bellows for their forges with great satisfaction, contending that air regulation can thus be finely controlled and that the device itself is aesthetically pleasing. Most smithies, however, use either a hand-crank-operated or an electrically powered blower of a centrifugal design. This design has a very high focused air volume potential for its size, making it possible to supply a large forge with plentiful air from a small blower. Small forges may even be successfully operated with a common electric hair dryer with the heating element removed.

The choice between a hand-crank and an electric power blower is an individual matter. A hand-crank system requires no electricity and provides fine control of the air input. The crank design utilizes the impeller as a flywheel; when the desired cranking speed has been attained, the weight of the impeller in centrifugal motion will continue its rotation long enough for a normal "heat" without further cranking.

A major disadvantage of the hand-crank system is that one hand must be used to crank: this can be awkward if the smith is handling a heavy piece of iron. The blower location must be high enough to be accessible for cranking, which means it is usually above the firepot.

The advantage of the electric blower is that it can be located below the firepot, out of the way and both hands may be used for handling tools and hot iron.

Criticism of the electric blower generally centers on the control of air feed which, without proper control, can be indiscriminate. It is essential to regulate the air supply by means of either a butterfly valve (see illustrations) or by a rheostat switch that can be hand-, foot- or knee-operated. The electric blower does, of course, require a power source which may not always be available to outdoor forges.

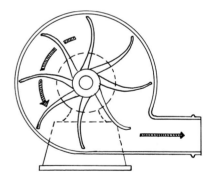

Cross section of centrifugal blower case, showing impeller blades.

The modern blacksmith may use heat sources other than the traditional coal fire. An oxyacetylene torch used within a brick hearth can be easily improvised for small pieces.
Photographed at Virginia Commonwealth University, Richmond

Other Heat Sources for Forging

The modern smithy has more options for heat sources than ever before. For many centuries huge quantities of wood were heated to make a special low sulfur coal for the smith's fire and many forests were consumed for this purpose. This low sulfur coal, called "blacksmith's coal," burned longer and with greater heat potential than regular coal. In addition to blacksmith's coal (discussed in chapter 3) the contemporary ironworker can use gas (liquid, propane, natural, or acetylene) charged either with forced air or pure oxygen. Most commonly, liquid propane or natural gas are used with forced air for large capacity burners. Pure oxygen is used with acetylene or liquid propane gas for handheld torches of lower capacity but higher temperatures.

Although coal is still the most popular source for heat, other heat sources are advantageous in certain conditions and specific procedures. A gas-fired forge has many desirable features. Combustion of gas is very complete, so there are no heavy smoke pollutants although gaseous by-products are hazardous in confined areas. Depending on whether the smith uses natural piped gas or bottled propane fuel, storage and availability problems associated with blacksmith's coal are virtually eliminated. The forging heat is almost instantly available with direct flame gas burners although great heat waste also results. The more cumbersome but efficient firebrick-lined gas forges require some heat-up time, but provide a great area of uniform heat.

The greatest disadvantage of the gas forge is its relative inaccessibility for heating the metal. Firepots of refractory lined gas forges cannot allow close visual contact with the heating metal because of their enclosed design. Freestanding gas burners provide good visual contact, but they, too, waste heat.

The oxyacetylene or oxypropane torches have some usefulness to the smith for localized heating on large iron sheet, or for heating small metal pieces where rapid heat dissipation is a problem. They cannot economically replace the high BTU output of either a coal or gas forge, or where there is a need for continuous heavy forging. For most iron heating, the torch is less desirable than the gas or coal forge. Its volume of heat is low and its burning temperature is higher than that of an air-fed forge.

Oxygen gas torches are relatively expensive to operate for heating, especially if large tips are used. Often they can be more efficiently used for cutting and welding than similar operations in the coal forge so that most modern blacksmithing shops do have torch equipment.

There is no question that oxyacetylene equipment is more expensive to operate for large forging jobs than gas or coal. It is difficult to predict if gas or coal is, or will continue to be, more economical. Much depends on our national energy crises, where one lives in relation to sources for the material. Currently, a coal forge will produce more BTUs per dollar than a gas forge, if used properly.

E. A. CHASE

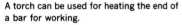

A torch can be used for heating the end of a bar for working.

Gas forge at George Martin's Creative Metal Crafts, Santa Monica, Calif. The air is supplied by a rotary blower and natural gas into an Eclipse mixer nozzle.

Table model gas forge used at the Sculpture House, New York, for heating metal blanks to make wood-carving tools. The same type of forge is employed by Michael Malpass at Pratt Institute, Brooklyn, N.Y., for his sculptures of animals.

ANVILS

The anvil, the tool on which to strike the iron, is the blacksmith's workbench. A flat rock was used by early smiths and still is employed by ironworkers in primitive cultures. Ingenious and elaborate decorative ironwork, tools, and weapons have been forged on such a rock. However, a rock has drawbacks; it may spall under the influence of impact and/or heat and it is difficult to maintain a smooth surface . . . a necessity for producing good work.

The first report of metal anvils replacing stone comes from the Bronze Age. These early metal anvils consisted of a spike opposite the flat face; the spike was driven into a suitable wooden mounting block. Spike anvils are still in use by farriers in Europe for reshaping sickles and scythe blades during the harvest.

Iron anvils replaced bronze with the advent of the Iron Age. Illustrations from Greek and Roman workshops show blacksmiths and locksmiths using anvils substantially the same shape as those of stone. However, since the fourth century A.D. an anvil shaped similarly to our modern anvil has existed.

Basically, the blacksmith's anvil has a solid base with a smooth face on top and round or square arms extending horizontally from the base. The proportions of the face and the shape of the horns, or bicks, depends on the special job for which the anvil might be used. The London pattern anvil is most popular today. Generally, it is 12 to 15 inches high with the length of the horn about 12 inches.

The weight of the anvil is chosen to suit the size of the work to be performed. An anvil weighing 150–200 pounds would be suitable for general work on sections up to and about three-quarters of an inch

THE LONDON PATTERN ANVIL

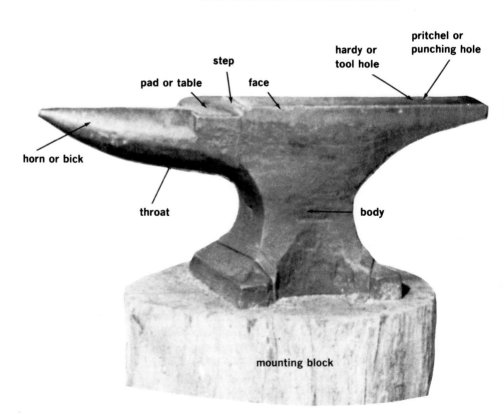

pritchel or punching hole

hardy or tool hole

step

pad or table   face

horn or bick

throat   body

mounting block

square. For light work, such as silver or coppersmithing, a 100-pound anvil may be adequate. A 300–400-pound anvil is recommended for any work using sledgehammers. Even for smaller work a heavier anvil will give a more solid "feel" and may reduce working time.

During the last century, the best anvils were made from forged steel. Today, the better anvils are made from cast steel and the cheaper ones from cast iron. A good steel anvil is made from steel containing perhaps 0.3 percent carbon and is heat-treated so that the body is in the annealed (soft) condition and the face in the hardened and tempered condition. In some less costly cast-iron and steel anvils, a separate face plate of tempered steel is brazed or welded to the body.

Two holes appear in the face of the anvil. A round hole, called the pritchel hole, or punching hole, is 3/8–5/8 inch in diameter; a 1–1 1/2-inch square is the hardy hole. The pritchel hole is a legacy of the horseshoeing anvil where that hole is used to form pritchels, or studs, inserted in some horseshoes. The hardy hole accommodates a variety of auxiliary tools used for specialized operations.

In front of the face is a short pad, or table, of unhardened steel or iron used to support material to be cut with a chisel. The face of the anvil should never be used to cut metals with a chisel because the hardened chisel would leave marks and ruin the smooth surface; therefore one should also use the pad for cutting. The horn, generally made in an unhardened condition, is used for shaping.

An anvil must be mounted on a solid base for optimum effectiveness. Traditionally a hardwood stump such as oak or elm is used and bound with iron hoops to prevent splitting. The wood grain should be arrayed vertically. Softwood stumps are suitable, but tend to split so they *must* be bound with metal strapping. An effective base can also be made from a steel drum filled with sand to the required height. It is essential to mount the anvil so that the face is horizontally level and to secure the anvil to its base so it will not "walk" under the influence of hammer blows. It should not be bolted down so rigidly that no play or bounce exists at all. It may be secured with U-shaped nails or metal strapping.

The height of the anvil face from the floor should be such that the smith standing beside the anvil with his fist lightly curled should be able just to touch the face with his knuckles. An anvil placed too high or too low for an individual smith will result in hammer blows striking the work at an angle to the face instead of parallel with it.

The first consideration in choosing an anvil is the work to be performed on it. A well-cared-for anvil loses little of its value with age, and there is no virtue in fighting an old dented anvil to produce good work. Used anvils, often available from industry and farmers, should be checked for dents and broken or worn edges. A useful check to determine the quality of a used and a new anvil is the ring produced when the anvil is struck with a hammer. A light and clear ringing will indicate a sound steel anvil. Cast iron responds with a dull thunk and the presence of cracks in the anvil would also be indicated by a dull sound. Even new anvils can be badly heat-treated and contain severe cracks which may result in major fractures when used. Small blowholes in cast steel anvils are generally not too objectionable. Provided the face is not struck with sharp-edged hardened tools, a good anvil will give years of service with minimum care and maintenance.

Refacing a worn anvil is possible, but a considerable project. The worn face must be ground down and replaced either with a layer of hard-facing alloy applied by an electric arc method or by a heat-treated steel plate brazed or welded to the anvil body. In each case the entire anvil must be preheated to 800° to 1000° F and slowly cooled after facing. The hard facing alloy must be ground smooth after application; the steel plate can be left as is.

GEORGE MARTIN

Double bick anvil.

A spike anvil can be fashioned easily by the smith. A split in the center holds two inserted pieces that are scrolled to prevent the spike from further penetrating the block each time the work is hit on the face.
Collection, Peter Boiger, Berkeley, Calif.

Ben Dial protects his anvil under a house on wheels which also makes potential intruders think a watchdog is on the premises.

A top and bottom swage with the stem of a tenon between. The swage is used to shape and finish the shank when hot.

George Martin

ANVIL VARIATIONS AND ANVIL TOOLS

For special procedures, the anvil may be modified with a number of loose tools that are inserted into the holes. These are often fashioned by the smith himself. A modified anvil with a double horn (page 33), useful for chain making or scrollwork, has longer and more slender horns than the London pattern anvil.

Probably the most important anvil tool is the *hardy,* a wedge-shaped tool placed in the hardy hole and used as a hot chisel to split iron or cut off lengths. *Fullers* are like chisels and sets but with rounded noses. They are used for making a longitudinal half-round depression or groove in metal. A bottom fuller is placed in the hardy hole and used to form shoulders or collars; they are also used for grooving, spreading metals, fluting, drawing down, necking, and making concave shapes.

Swages are top and bottom tools made in various sizes and diameters for finishing metal rods in convex shapes. Top and bottom swages are used in conjunction with each other; the bottom swage is placed in the hardy hole and the top one is held over the metal being shaped. Swages can be fashioned by the smith in any form desired and should be made of medium carbon tool steel.

An *Anvil stake* can be used either on the face or over the edge of the anvil for drawing out and rounding up small intricate curves, rings, and collars.

Both the pritchel hole and the hardy hole may be used for attaching various improvised hold-down gadgets which may provide a third hand so frequently required. Other anvil tools may be created for fashioning specialized scrolls or leaves, for ball shapes, bending angle iron, supporting dies for work such as punching holes, or other operations that the individual requires. Throughout the book, the use of these various tools should be observed carefully in various demonstrations.

George Martin

Swage blocks, made of cast iron or steel in weights from 50 to 600 pounds, have various surface patterns, perforations, grooves, and depressions used for shaping or punching hot or cold steel. The block may be set on the ground or mounted on a stand or stump grooved to accommodate the swage.

A wedge-shaped hardy, forged from a compressed-air chisel tool, is used to cut off a tenon that was shaped in the swage. The hot metal is placed on the hardy edge, rotated, and hammered until it breaks off.
George Martin

Bruce Newell organizes tool storage within a narrow wooden shelf with a space into which the handles are dropped.

A leg vise is mounted on a workbench with the post against the floor and bench. The spring below the jaws forces the right jaw outward. It is mounted so it is easily accessible from at least three sides. At Christopher Ray's.

VISES

Mass, rigidity, and capacity are the requirements for a blacksmith's vise. These criteria may be summed up in one word . . . BIG. A vise is used as an anvil for forming clamped work, for hot and cold bending, holding forming stakes and anvils, and whatever special torture an individual smithy can visit with his hammers. For use in a blacksmith's shop a vise should be at least thirty-five pounds . . . preferably larger. A heavy vise should be properly mounted or its merits will be defeated. It should be solidly posted to the ground to minimize energy dissipation of the hammer blow.

The traditional blacksmith's vise, called a "leg vise" or a "box vise," has an integral steel post which supports it to endure heavy pounding. It is designed on a pivot point from which the two pivoting members close pincerlike via a heavy-duty acme-type screw. The leg, or post, which projects to the floor is an extension of the back jaw. A plate, collared on the back post, is used to mount the vise to the bench but extending away from it sufficiently to permit the worker to approach the vise from three sides.

The jaw design of the leg vise is not very efficient because the closed jaws are on an angle rather than parallel to one another. The main use of the tool is for bending and holding jobs. The comparatively slender design of the vise is made possible by the use of cast steel which has higher tensile strength and shock resistance than the cast iron used for most other types of vises. The bigger, the better, applies to a leg vise.

Leg vises are available in weights of 40 to 120 pounds. Such vises are relatively hard to find today because they have become items valued by antique collectors as well as by the blacksmith.

A *machinist's,* or *bench, vise* is so named because the design provides great clamping power and rigidity, making it an excellent choice for working machine parts. These same features make it extremely suitable for blacksmith work.

The machinist's vise is usually heavy cast iron or steel. One jaw moves parallel to a stationary jaw on an acme-screw-driven slide with the result that the jaws are always parallel to each other and are extremely rigid. The parallel design gives some advantages over the leg vise for clamping thick and off-center work. In a good vise, the screw post runs through the slide, a feature that centers the stress of heavy clamping to prevent distortion or breakage. Beware of cheap versions of machinist's vises where the screw post does not run through the guide or where the slide and the way are not machined to fit. They are not suitable for the heavy pounding a blacksmith's vise must endure.

A machinist's vise, or bench vise, of over 50 pounds, preferably 150 pounds, is recommended although they are available in weights of 30 to 200 pounds. The essential function of a vise is to grip a part rigidly. They are either fixed or of a swivel type to allow access from all sides.

Ideally, the bench vise should be supported from base to floor, preferably projecting off of a heavy workbench or freestanding. One method is to mount it in front of the bench on its own post and secure it as an extra fourth leg. Another mounting method is to put the vise on a solid freestanding pole. Either method permits great accessibility. In any vise having serrated jaws, the jaws should be lined with soft steel if you wish to avoid marking hot metal held between them.

Heavy machinist's vises are hard to find and expensive on the used tool market. They are still being made by domestic and foreign manufacturers. Quality and size are important.

Utility vises are designed like the machinist's vise in a superficial way. They are not really suitable for heavy work. Usually they are of exposed screw design with rigidity supplied by remote slides. They are comparatively inexpensive and not manufactured in large sizes required for smithing. Generally, they are not a good choice.

E. A. CHASE

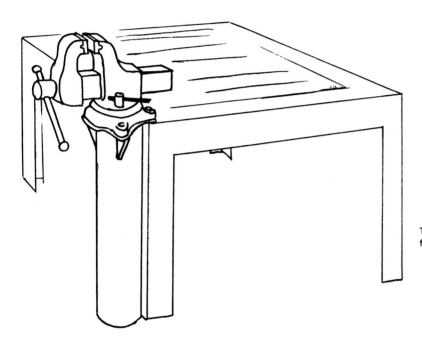

The machinist's vise mounted as an extra fourth leg. Note three-sided access.
Drawing: E. A. Chase

Tools used for smithing lightweight bars and rounds; 50-pound anvil, stump, machinist's vise, oxyacetylene torch, and assorted tools.
Photographed at Virginia Commonwealth University, Richmond

cross peen   sledgehammer

set hammer   flatter

The set hammer has a smooth, flat face about 1¼" square and is used to make square corners and shoulders by placing it on the work and then striking the top with a hammer or sledge. The flatter is used for the same work as the set hammer except that it has a flatter, larger face.

HAMMERS AND THEIR USES

The well-equipped smith owns a dazzling assortment of hammers which he has either bought or made himself. They have varying weights and shapes and are used directly on the metal or to drive another tool such as a chisel, punch, or flatter. Observe the hammers throughout the various demonstrations and how they are used.

The *cross peen hammer* (*in use, opposite*) is one of the basic blacksmith's tools. It is a square or octagonal-shaped piece with a slightly rounded face on one end and a wedge on the other and fitted through the center with a hickory or ash handle. The cross peen is available in weights ranging from 1 pound 4 ounces to 4 pounds with the 2 and 4 pound weights most preferred. The cross peen hammer is used to draw out, stretch, and flatten, and within these three operations lie the vast specialties of the smith.

The *ball peen hammer* (*opposite below*) is an excellent all around tool for hollowing, rounding, riveting, peening, and scarfing; the face is used for upsetting, drawing, shaping, and hammering. One end is slightly rounded, and the other more severly tapered. It is also a machinist's tool and the easy-to-buy hammers range in weight from about 1 1/2 to 3 1/2 pounds. The shapes and roundness of the ends will vary.

Any working hammer should feel like an extension of your arm. It should feel comfortable and be balanced to suit you. Generally, the hammer handle should be held about two-thirds of its length from the end. You should stand at the anvil with your legs spread enough to brace yourself firmly. Your head should be bent slightly to one side so you don't hit yourself with the hammer as it is raised. To begin, raise the hammer about shoulder level, then drive downward using the whole arm . . . with the elbow (not the wrist) doing most of the driving. Actually, the anvil should be allowed to do much of the work as it forces the hammer to bounce back with each blow.

The type of hammer blow depends on the piece being hammered and how the smith wishes to spread the hot metal . . . to draw out, stretch, or flatten. The work is moved rather than the hammer's changing position each time it is dropped. This assures a constant, accurate stroke with less waste of motion than if the smith moved the hammer around the anvil at each blow. When the smith taps his hammer on the anvil, he is not beating out a tune, rather he alternates, hitting his work and the face of the anvil, achieving an offbeat while he turns the work and/or rests his arm. It is a rhythm that is attained by practice.

Sledgehammers weigh 6 to 20 pounds and have a handle about 30 inches long. They are used by the smith's helper, or striker, and swung with two hands while the smith holds the iron or a tool to be driven by the sledge.

Rawhide mallets, brass hammers, and carpenter's claw hammers may also be among the smith's tools. They are used as the smithy sees fit for various particular operations of his own invention. Softer hammers of rawhide, brass, or even wood are used for straightening or shaping where hammer marks are not desired.

Assorted hammers include a German or American pattern cross peen, English pattern cross peen, French pattern cross peen, Martin's straight peen, engineer's ball peen (*left to right*).

George Martin

The flat and wedged edges of the cross peen hammer have different functions. The flat face can safely be used to draw out thin steel. On thick steel the wedged edge can be used to concentrate blows on a small area with the blows at a right angle to the direction the metal is being extended. Sometimes the hammer is turned in midair so that both edges are used ·alternately.

Photographed at Turley's Forge

Christopher Ray demonstrates the proper position for raising the hammer as he applies the face of the ball peen to a metal bar being shaped over a special tool placed in the anvil hardy hole.

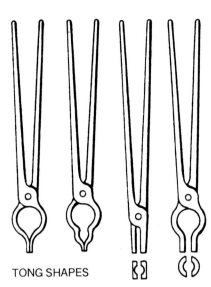

TONG SHAPES

Left to right:
single pickup
double pickup
straight lip
curved lip

TONGS

Tongs are the indispensable smith's tools for holding metal that is too hot to handle. The most common shaped tongs are shown at left and include those with straight and curved lips, single and double pickup jaws. The photos, below, will give you a better idea of the wide variety of jaw shapes in an individual smith's tool rack. The smith often makes a pair of tongs to fit the individual job.

Early ironworkers owned only a few tong shapes, but, as their work became more sophisticated and diversified, they made tongs for each specific job; one pair may have been shaped as spoke pullers, another for holding large tires while being heated, cupped jaw tongs were made for holding horseshoes and so forth. H. R. Bradley Smith's book *Blacksmiths' and Farriers' Tools at Shelburne Museum* illustrates fifty-six different-shaped tongs and states, "It is safe to say that if a skilled blacksmith were asked to identify all of the museum's tongs, he would not be able to give every one a positive label. If a man did not actually make or use a particular shaped tong, he could not necessarily state with certainty what the tong was used for."

The tongs should fit the iron they must grasp. While this may seem an obvious oversimplified statement, the beginner does not always think of using straight lip tongs for a straight piece of iron . . . rather he may grab curved tongs and discover that the iron will slip and twist. If it slips it is dangerous. It is even more dangerous to hold the poorly grasped hot metal on the anvil and to hit it with the hammer. It can elude the tongs, bounce up, and hit one in the face. A ring or link may be slipped over the handles to hold them firmly.

Never leave the tongs in the fire with the work.

The old-time blacksmith did not have the advantage of the modern vise-grip self-locking pliers which many workers use for holding hot and cold metal. They are available with double curved jaws for holding round stock, with straight jaws for flat stock, and in different lengths and weights.

Varied shapes of tong jaws . . . most are created by the smith for specific purposes.
George Martin

Tongs are usually kept near the forge on a rack along with or close to the hardies, swages, and fullers.

Tongs are relatively easy to fashion from 7/8-inch square bar stock by heating the ends, shaping them over the anvil edge or horn, as desired, and riveting the two arms together. Details for making tongs can be found in early books on blacksmithing and in the book *The Blacksmith's Craft,* lesson 37 (see bibliography), published by the Council for Small Industries in Rural Areas (CoSira).

Tongs arranged on a wheeled rack for portability and efficiency at Ben Dial's.

Vise-grip self-locking pliers, also called locking plier wrenches, can replace tongs for many holding jobs.

proper ring   improper

Straight lip properly holding a straight bar of hot iron.

A set punch is driven by a cross peen.

PUNCHES — CHISELS

Punches and chisels are used for punching holes of various sizes and for cutting, splitting, and carving iron. The tools are made either hand held or set (handled). The hand-held punches (*shown at left*) are usually about 2 feet long, so that the portion grasped by the hand is far away from the heated end. Ends are shaped differently to achieve a variety of shaped holes and are tapered so they will withdraw from the hole readily. Handled punches look like pointed hammers or chisels. Punching and chiseling procedures spread the iron; none of the material is lost as in wood cutting and drilling.

Cold chisels are usually hand held. Hot chisels, like punches, may be either hand held or set. Set chisels are designed specifically for either hot or cold work. They are placed on the metal to be cut and then struck with a hammer or sledge by the smith or his striker. The hot chisel usually has about a 30° angle edge bevel while the cold chisel has about a 60° edge bevel.

A cold chisel is used only for cutting cold metal and is wider and heavier than the hot chisel. Because hot metal is soft, the cutting edge of the hot chisel does not need to be as heavy as that of the cold chisel.

When cutting hot metals, the edge of the punch and chisel will become hot and should be cooled frequently to protect the tool. When heads of tools become battered from hammering, the ends can be trimmed and reshaped on the anvil. If ends are permitted to splay, they can chip off under the hammer blows and cause splinters that may fly into the face or eye (a valid reason for wearing safety masks when performing these operations).

A relative to punches and chisels is *drifts.* These are pieces of steel with a long taper at one end and a short taper at the other; they are driven through punched holes to enlarge, shape, and smooth them. They may be square, round, oblong, and other shapes. A square drift would be sharp on all four sides, a round one sharp all around its circumference. Drifts are not used in today's shop as much as they were because modern power equipment such as drills and lathes can often do the job more quickly and efficiently.

In addition to the traditional tools already discussed, the smith will have files and rasps, hacksaws and hand pliers for a variety of finishing procedures.

The hot set chisel is driven with a sledge-hammer or hafted as a hammer and used for splitting and cutting. Observe that the bar iron is held in the jaws of a leg vise.
Christopher Ray

Wood and wire shafted cold and hot chisels; wire shafted square and round punches.

George Martin

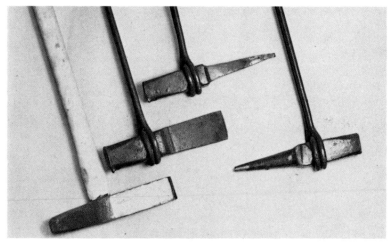

TRIP-HAMMERS

A trip-hammer is actually an ancient invention. Early hammers consisted of a water wheel with a long pole weighted on one end which was dropped down on the anvil and, because of the dropping action, it was also called a drop hammer.

With the onset of steam and the Industrial Revolution, the hammer became a self-contained machine using either a steam piston or a cam drive lifting the hammer and throwing the hammer down. At slow speeds the hammer's jaws never close. The upper hammer is suspended on a spring so that the faster the hammer is lifted, the more inertia builds in the hammer jaw to close it.

The modern trip-hammer allows the smith to be a one-man operation. When the smith places his iron on the bottom hammer jaw, the top one can be dropped down to do the shaping . . . thereby replacing the role of the striker or apprentice.

Trip-hammers today range in weight from twenty-five to one hundred pounds for small units to several tons in large forging mills. The small units of twenty-five to fifty pounds can handle capacities up to 3 inches square. An experienced smith can use them for very delicate quarter-inch or smaller forgings . . . even tapering to needle-sharp points. Such machines employ either a clutch, a slip belt, or a valve system drive engaged by foot pressure, thus freeing both of the smith's hands to direct the iron.

The trip-hammer has sets of interchangeable jaws to accommodate a variety of dies for fullering, swaging, tapering, and so forth. It can also be used with an assistant holding a tool under the upper jaw and over the work.

Trip-hammers are available new and used. They should be mounted on heavy wood or concrete slabs.

WILLIAM E. LETH

Left:
Daryl Meier works an electric powered trip-hammer on a piece of hot iron.

Right:
A smaller model hammer is used to draw out a piece of stock for a woodworking tool at the Sculpture House, New York.

MACHINE TOOLS

The modern ironworker has a choice that his antecedents did not. He has at his disposal a wealth of hand and electrically powered machine tools to assist him in achieving the finished product he visualizes. The intelligent integration of modern and traditional tools and techniques is partially responsible for the renewed interest in blacksmithing as an answer to artistic creativity. While some ironworkers are intrigued by the old method of working for the sake of technique, the modern metalworker views techniques and tools as a means to an end. The object made, as opposed to the technique itself, is the reason for working.

Therefore, the modern ironworker adapts available machine tools to his needs; and it is more usual than not to find grinders, cut-off units, sophisticated welding equipment, drill presses, lathes, sanders, and buffers on a tool bench easily accessible to the forge and anvil.

Generally, the equipment should be arranged to allow adequate working space around them for the size of the ironwork to be accomplished. Portable grinders and buffers that can be brought to large pieces of work are invaluable. Nonportable tools should be bolted down onto heavy (not flimsy) workbenches braced against a strong wall where possible. When an individual worker does not have space for or cannot afford such equipment, the facilities of a local shop may be rented in off hours. Classes at adult education programs can benefit the metalworker, for he has the use of the school's workroom and equipment for his own projects.

The drill press is used for boring holes in iron. In this procedure iron is actually scarfed, or removed, as opposed to making holes with a punch which cuts and spreads the metal.

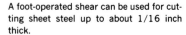

A hand-operated shear makes quick work of round and square bar stock.

A foot-operated shear can be used for cutting sheet steel up to about 1/16 inch thick.

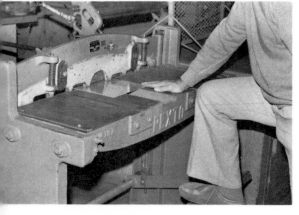

Hardened steel pieces can be cut with an abrasive metal cutoff saw.

Portable grinding wheels are invaluable for rapid metal removal. Always be sure the object to be ground is securely fastened to the workbench with clamps or held in a vise. Note the vise-grip welding clamp, which is ideal for deep or complex clamping jobs.

Abrasive sanders with different dimensions and paper grits may be used for finishing almost any shape metal surface. *At left,* the sanding wheel is used to finish the compound-curved interior of a bowl. *Right,* it conforms to the bend of a hollow-shaped rod.

Courtesy, Merit Abrasive Products, Inc.

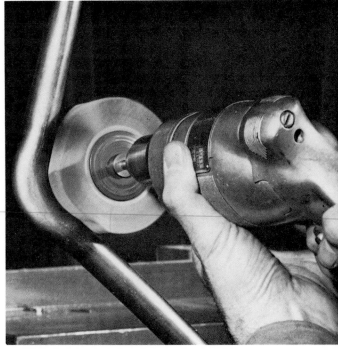

WELDING

Traditionally, the blacksmith joins two pieces of metal by *pressing* them together . . . a process referred to as forge or pressure welding which is discussed in chapters 5 and 11. Briefly, it involves heating the two pieces of metal to be joined, then hammering them together. Forge welding may still be indicated for many procedures, but in recent years faster welding processes have become available.

Modern welding methods are usually referred to as *fusion* welding. A heat source generates sufficient heat to create and maintain a molten pool of the metal. The heat may be supplied by a gas flame or by electricity. Many aesthetic possibilities exist when forging and fusion welding are combined for texturing and fabricating forms.

History of Welding

Actually heat for brazing and soldering was used in the Bronze Age (about 700 to 100 B.C.) for jewelry and domestic articles. Welding did not evolve until the smith worked with iron and learned to heat and hammer it together sometime prior to the Middle Ages. The most renowned was the use of welding for the Damascus blades about that time (discussed in chapter 11).

Some gas welding appeared at the end of the nineteenth century, but the first wide scale use of gas welding with oxyacetylene equipment was during World War I. It completely revolutionized the metalworking industry. Arc welding, using a consumable electrode, was also introduced in this period but the wires used produced brittle, unsatisfactory welds. The solution of wrapping the bare wire with asbestos and an entwined aluminum wire made the system workable. During World War II, arc welding became universally used.

Since then, other welding methods have been developed. In the 1940s the tungsten–inert gas process, using a nonconsumable tungsten electrode, was introduced. More recently, a gas-shielded process, using a wire electrode that is consumed in the weld, was developed, followed by assorted other welding techniques that are usually not available to the individual craftsman.

Which Equipment to Use, for What

Aside from aesthetics and availability, the decision of which welding method to use depends upon 1) metal type and thickness, 2) economy, and 3) distortion or warpage.

Oxyacetylene is the most common form of gas welding, producing a fusion weld. The heat produced by burning acetylene gas with oxygen gas gives a temperature of about 6000° F. But the volume of heat (BTUs) is dissipated by the conduction of the metal and the surrounding air. Therefore the thickness and conductivity of the metal greatly affects the efficiency of gas welding. For thin-gauge sheet steel, some copper alloys, and some aluminum, Monel Metal, and stainless steels gas welding can be efficient and economical. Thicker metals of aluminum, stainless steel, and copper alloys are most efficiently welded with the electric arc or tungsten–inert gas systems . . . usually over ⅛ inch for ferrous alloys, except where the artist may wish the special puddling control afforded by gas welding.

The oxyacetylene torch is also used for cutting by replacing the welding tips with a cutting tip. The common term "cutting" with the torch is only partially true. Actually, the torch supplies a stream of pure oxygen to the heated ferrous metal which oxidizes at a rapid rate. The process depends on an affinity for oxygen with the metal so only rapidly oxidizing ferrous alloys are thus cuttable. Stainless steel, aluminum, and copper alloys cannot be cut with the torch. Cast iron cannot be successfully

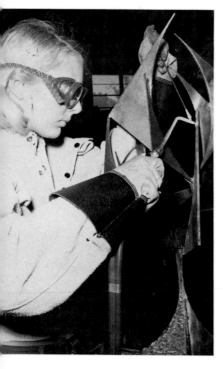

Oxyacetylene welding utilizes a welding filler rod. Protective gloves and clothing should be worn along with goggles with colored lenses. Always wear enclosed shoes and cotton or wool (not synthetic) fabrics where clothing is exposed. Long hair should be tied back.

Courtesy, Hobart Brothers

torch-cut either because of the layers of graphite in the metal which act as an insulator. Cutting of these metals is better done with power cut-off equipment or sometimes with a special cutting electrode of the electric arc.

The *electric arc welder* produces an instant 10,000° F heat at the metal surface, so welding is instantaneous. Arc welding is cheaper in time and material than gas welding. Electricity as a source of energy is more available and less expensive. Coated electrodes (called consumable electrodes because they supply the filler metal for the weld) are required for arc welding. They are bought in sizes from 1/16 inch to 3/8 inch and in different alloy coating combinations. Though arc welding electrodes are expensive for ordinary varieties, the overall cost per foot of weld bead for arc welding is far cheaper than the overall cost of gas and welding rods for gas welding.

Tungsten–inert gas (TIG) is another method of electric welding offering control almost as fine as gas welding. This method uses a semipermanent tungsten electrode (nonmelting) to supply an arc flame into which filler metal of the proper alloy is fed much as with gas welding. While the welding is in process a blanket of inert gas (usually Freon) covers the weld area to exclude atmospheric oxygen. The gas "blanket" eliminates the need for fluxes. Although this method can produce varied textures in the weld melt, it shares with the "stick" electrode process the need for a full face mask with extremely dark protective lenses. The dark lenses allow good observation of the weld area once the arc is "struck," but the surrounding area is in darkness. This can interfere with the sense of "wholeness" of the piece being worked. Eye protection for gas welding is essential but less critical since the intensity of light is lower and there are no ultraviolet rays. The lighter lenses used allow good general visibility of the whole piece.

The Metal Inert Gas (MIG) is a system involving metal arc welding. Instead of a rod, a wire is fed through the handle. The arc is maintained between the end of the wire and the work either manually or automatically. It is also called a micro-wire semiautomatic process. The simplicity of wire welding keeps the artist's concentration on aesthetic problems, rather than on the welding procedure itself.

Torch cutting divides iron quickly. The angle at which the cutting torch is held determines the type of cut. Cutting speed is important: moving too slowly may cause the metal to re-fuse behind the torch resulting in a slag that is more resistant to heat and recutting than the original.

Distortion and Warpage

Warpage and distortion of the metal is a problem with any welding technique. It is more severe with gas welding. Thermal stresses created by the welding heat and the metal deposition must be controlled by careful clamping and bracing of the object to be welded. Proper preheating can also reduce cracks and internal stresses built up during heating and subsequent cooling. Arc welding techniques produce faster welds than gas so the consequent heat dissipation is less and the warpage is less. The thicker the metal, the more difficult it is to control warpage.

E. A. Chase

Shown is a gas-driven generator-type arc welder used where portability is necessary and expense is a secondary consideration. An electric transformer-type arc welder is a relatively small unit, now in the $100 to $200 range, making it feasible for the individual workshop. (*Not illustrated.*)

Courtesy, Hobart Brothers Co.

When using an arc welder, you must wear a full face shield with dark lens to protect against dangerous ultraviolet light. The electric rod is placed in the handpiece, and the arc started by torching the work. The arc melts the metals to be welded, and the weld is fast and deep.

*J. Guadalupe Benitez,
Muñoz Furniture Factory,
Tijuana, Mexico*

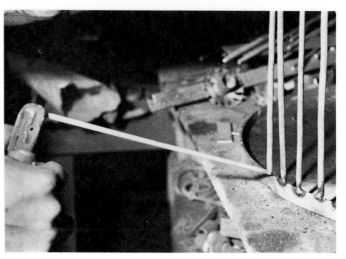

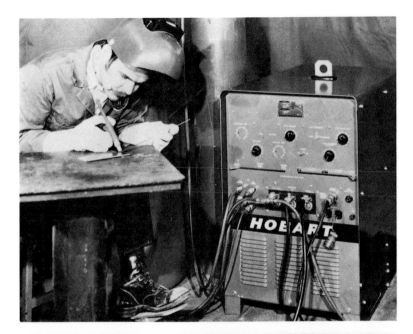

In the tungsten arc welder (TIG), the arc is struck between a hand-held insulated tungsten rod, and oxidation is prevented by a cover of inert gas such as argon or helium.

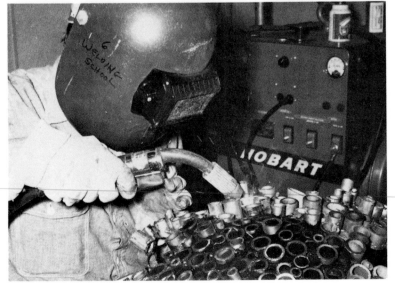

In the metal-inert gas (MIG), a wire is continually fed through the handle, and the arc is maintained between the wire end and the work, either manually or automatically.

Photos, Courtesy, Hobart Brothers Co.

The Fire, the Fuel, and the Heat

AMONG the important facilities the blacksmith has in his shop is the fire that heats the iron to its various stages of malleability. Therefore, the fire, the type of fuel used, and the kind of heat generated become essential knowledge for the smith. The beginning smith is hard put to know, by sight and definition, the best kind of fuel for his needs. He often begins with what he can find and becomes frustrated trying to achieve an efficient, workable fire.

Blacksmith's coal, the general fuel for forging, is a select grade of bituminous soft coal with a low sulfur and phosphorous content and is low in inorganic materials which contribute to ash. If high concentrations of sulfur are present, they may combine with the metal being forged and tend to embrittle it; they also pollute the atmosphere. Good coal yields a minimum of ash particles and a low residue of incombustible materials that produce undesirable clinkers.

Optimally, the coal should be composed of lumps about the size of the first joint of your little finger plus some smaller pieces and some coal dust, called "fines."

Scientifically, such coal breaks down into the following proportions:

Carbon	(high)	55 – 65 percent
Moisture	(low)	2.5 – 3 percent
Ash	(low)	3 – 8 percent
Sulfur	(low)	1 – 2 percent
Volatility	(high)	30 – 40 percent
BTU	(high)	13,500 – 14,500

Soft coal contains a relatively high content of volatile substances which produce a smoky fire in the early stages but assist in binding coal so it can coalesce and convert into coke. Coke is a lightweight porous product, the result of dry distillation of coal, which is the hot burning fuel you want to work iron.

Steel mills make coke in huge ovens; blacksmiths produce it on the hearths of their forges. Sometimes coke itself is used for continuous work and can be purchased instead of coal. It may be available from large coal companies or electric generating stations. Fire is more difficult to start with coke, so coal is used at the start; then the first fire is maintained with coke. Crushed or broken-up boiler coke or furnace coke is *not* suitable for a forging fire.

Unfortunately, as blacksmithing disappeared, so did the supply of blacksmithing coal. While there are still ample quantities within the earth, coal companies are not commonly making it available to smiths in small amounts. Large steel companies own the mines and supply it in carloads

L. Brent Kington cleans out the box within the brick forge he designed and built. The blower is at the right rear. The suspended hood and chimney permit access to the fire from all around. Note the handmade fire tools, a shovel, poker, and rake, and the handle for the ash trap door.

1) Bits of fine coke are placed in the box. Depending on the fuel, some wood chips and paper can be placed beneath the coke.

2) Pieces of coal are added about halfway up the box.

3) The coals are lit with the flame of an oxyacetylene torch. A piece of wadded paper, lit with a match and poked down into the coals, will start the fire also.

to metallurgical and industrial buyers. In some areas though, one can buy blacksmiths' coal in 100 pound sacks from hardware stores and coal dealers; much depends on demand and supply.

Where blacksmiths' coal is hard to secure, a suggestion from the Artist-Blacksmiths Association of North America might be helpful. Smiths in one area may combine their resources and, if feasible, order a carload of coal or coke at one time (the only way it may be available) until better sources for small amounts open up. You will have to research suppliers by contacting local coal companies and steel mills. Freight costs are also a factor and must be considered in the price.

Charcoal (the same that one uses for backyard barbecuing) is available at builders' stores and the supermarket. This is the original blacksmith fuel, but the cost is prohibitive unless you can locate a wholesale source where it is available at quantity prices. Charcoal is a clean-burning fuel and, with a forced draft, it will make a hot fire. It burns up faster than coke, however, and tends to produce considerable ash and sparks.

Generous ventilation is a must for your forge! Large volumes of odorless, deadly carbon monoxide may be generated by the fire and will be lethal in a poorly ventilated enclosure. This is true for *all* the fuels listed, even gas. With coal, the smoke alone will make the need for a hood and tall chimney apparent if you have a roof over the forge. Outdoors they may not be needed.

THE FIRE

While many books detail the "best" way to begin and maintain a fire, each smith seems to have a personal preference for the shape of the coals, the size of the fire, and how to maintain it. Therefore, basic instructions are offered and, when you become experienced in working the iron in the fire, you will determine what is best for your kind of work.

Basically, one can build an *open* or a *hollow* fire. In an *open* fire, combustion occurs on top of the heap over the tuyere; while in the *hollow* fire, the combustion takes place in the center with the coal being roofed over the fire, igloo fashion, with a hole in the front to receive the iron. The hollow fire is hotter than an open fire because it radiates heat all around.

To Build the Fire

Clean out and remove any clinkers or ash from the receptacle, especially around the tuyere. For a coal fire, add some crumpled paper; for a coke fire, you may need wood chips or paper in front of the tuyere. Add some coke from an earlier fire broken up into small pea-size lumps. Additional fuel should be placed on the hearth surface around the block as a ready supply to be raked into the going fire. Keep a sprinkler can filled with water handy to wet down the fuel so the fire will not spread out larger than needed.

To Light the Fire

Use a piece of newspaper crumpled into a fairly tight ball, light it with a match and hold it flame downward on the prepared dry fuel and poke it in with the fire poker. (Or use an oxyacetylene torch if available as does Brent Kington in the accompanying demonstration.) Simultaneously gently crank the blower until the flame is burning well, then crank more vigorously. On a rheostat-equipped unit, adjust the air valves to achieve a similar result. Then reduce the air blast as the fire catches and the smoke begins to dissipate. Rake some fresh coal onto the fire a little at a time. Keep adding fuel until you are confident that the fire is burning. Eventually, the coal will turn into a gray spongy coke which smokes very little. This coke can be used to give your fire a fresh start each day.

4) The fire catches on and begins to flame, additional fuel is shoveled over the smoldering coals . . .

To Maintain the Fire

Your fire will not continue to burn exactly the way you want it to. It must be maintained by working the draft and adding fuel. In a bottom blown forge, new fuel should never be heaped on top of the fire, but always worked in from the outside so that impurities in the coal are burnt away before it comes in contact with the metal. The fire will build up to its best, maintain this condition according to the fuel and the work, then die down. Good fuel will produce a fire that may last all day on rough work, but poor fuel may be dead in an hour even if used on fine work.

Always strive to work with a clean fire which is achieved by turning the tuyere lever or poking your poker down to the bottom of the fire to avoid clinkers. Whenever you leave the fire, open the ash trap to prevent gases from backing up and possibly causing explosions.

Clinkers

Clinkers are the blacksmith's bugaboo. A clinker is produced from the ash in the coal congealing together with iron scale. As the fuel burns, clinkers are formed in a molten state and work down to the bottom of the fire in front of the blast hole causing an obstruction. Bits are blown upward and will stick to the hot metal as globs. Metal with clinkers cannot be welded, and clinker particles may be hammered into the metal's surface or spurt out and burn the hands.

5) . . . until the flame is burning properly. This is an "open" fire compared to a "hollow" fire where the flames are contained within an igloolike buildup of fuel.

Demonstration by L. Brent Kington

Knowing when a clinker forms, locating and removing it, takes experience and practiced judgment. Sometimes the clinker does not form into a large enough lump to remove it from the fire with the hooked tip of the poker and without disturbing the fire. You will suspect that clinkers have formed if the heat of the fire drops noticeably. Hot clinker pieces may be recognized because they are a brighter red than the glowing fuel, have a smooth surface, and, when cool, have a characteristic "clink" sound when hit with the fire poker.

WHERE TO PLACE THE IRON

The metal being heated should be placed in the heart of the hot part of the fire over a good bed of fuel, *not* on top of the flame's surface. By keeping the iron within the flame, it is protected from excess air and the fire is hotter.

A blacksmith's stand adjustable to different heights is sometimes called a "second man." It supports extralong stock that protrudes over the edge of the forge while being heated. Many forges have an adjustable U-shaped support attached on the side for holding long stock. (At George Martin's.) Note that this is a side-blown forge, air comes in from the left and right and not from the bottom.

Small portable forges are not generally designed for long pieces of stock. Ben Dial improvised his and cut a small door in the side of the hearth, which he hinged. The stock lies flat in the heart of the fire and is supported by the edge of the forge.

A water dipper–sprinkler can be made from an aluminum beer can with a handle of metal or wood fashioned to hold it. It is used to sprinkle water on the coals around the fire, and to cool portions of hot steel as needed. (At Ben Dial's.)

FIRE TOOLS

Management of the fire is accomplished by tools the smith often makes for himself: a poker, a shovel, and a rake. The poker is used to loosen the fire, stir the hot coals, and pierce clinkers. The rake's function is to pull out clinkers, bring together separate pieces of coal, and clean out old coal beds. The shovel is used to add coal to a fire and to remove ashes.

Another helpful item is a water dipper-sprinkler, for keeping the surrounding coal dampened. This can be made from a coffee or beer can attached to or nailed onto a handle made of wood or metal (*shown at right*). Holes are punched around one end of the can and the other end is left solid. The can is dipped in the water bucket, and then it is used as a sieve for slowly sprinkling water on the coals around the fire or for cooling down a part of the hot steel that sticks out if it is to be handled.

THE WATER BUCKET OR QUENCHING TUB

Standing water in a bucket made of wood, a steel oil drum, or metal garbage container is always placed next to the forge for cooling the metal and for several purposes. Such containers should be sturdy and can be anywhere from 5 to 50 gallon size. They should not be plastic because hot metal dropped into the bucket can rapidly disintegrate the plastic.

Water is an excellent cooling medium for soft hot steel, but it must not be used to cool many tool or high carbon steels. This process of cooling, called "quenching," transfers the heat out of the metal at varying rates and, in the case of tool steels, also determines the hardness and microstructure of the finished piece.

A bucket of water is also kept close to the forge for safety reasons.

SAFETY

The subject of safety in the blacksmith shop often is taken too casually . . . until after an accident occurs. The value of a bucket of water and a fire extinguisher has already been mentioned. Burn ointments are also suggested. Other fire/heat-oriented hazards might be dropping a piece of hot iron on a pet or on a child . . . both of which should be kept away from the working area. Iron should *always* be picked up with proper-shaped tongs, never with the bare hands should any heat be left in an unattended piece. Coping with accidental fires and burns is only part of the safety picture.

Blacksmiths do not pay enough attention to protection of their faces and eyes. It doesn't take much to become blinded by a small particle of scale that bounces off the anvil, or to chip the end of a punch or a hot cut that blows up onto your face. A proper pair of safety glasses or a face mask is indispensable regardless of the arguments that safety glasses limit one's vision and are uncomfortable. It's easier to become accustomed to safety glasses than to impaired sight or no sight at all. Ordinary tempered prescription glasses simply will not resist the impact of a chunk of steel flying off a grinding wheel or hot off the anvil's face. Extended exposure to heat may cause eye cataracts, an occupational disease of workers exposed to infrared radiation over many years. Infrared absorbing glass exists and can be ground into prescription lenses.

Another major hazard is present from the toxic vapors produced at the forge so that proper ventilation is mandatory. Any fire at all produces quantities of carbon monoxide gas. In an area where ventilation is limited, you may be building up potentially lethal concentrations of carbon monoxide. Always work with an adequate draft, a chimney or hood over your forge, and ventilation—whether it's a fan or an open doorway. The best safety is to work out in the open completely.

Proper use of power tools has been covered at length in every reputable book on machine shop practice, but it bears reiterating. Always have power tools in optimum working condition. Use proper electrical cords and ground the equipment with double insulated wiring . . . especially where the working area gets damp. A ground fault interrupter is a nice thing to have on your workshop electrical circuit.

TED DAVIDSON

A high-impact plastic face shield should be worn to protect the eyes and face from sparks and flying bits of metal during hammering, chiseling, and grinding procedures.

Courtesy, Merit Abrasive Products, Inc.

Tom Bredlow uses the traditional fire tools to begin and maintain his fire. The rack below his elbow may be extended to accommodate long stock. Tongs are held on a rack at the front of the forge.

HEATING THE IRON

With the equipment ready for use and the fire lit, the smith is ready to heat a bar of iron. As the iron gets progressively hotter, it will pass through several color changes. Learning to observe these color changes and their accompanying temperature range is essential to knowing how the metal can be worked. Color should be determined in dim light, not in bright sun. If necessary, keep a shielded heavy wood keg or metal box nearby to thrust the metal into so you can observe the color changes.

The hotter the metal, the more plastic it is and the easier to shape. Yet metal can be overheated and burn affecting its basic structure so that it cannot be worked. Each time the metal is made red-hot, the smith refers to the procedure as a "heat." Different procedures require different "heats," and these can best be learned by actually working with the metal. The colors of heated metal and the resulting temperature range can be compared by consulting the photo in the last page of the color section titled *Heat Colors.* These range from a warm heat in the blue red range to a hot or near welding heat in the yellow range. Metal that is heated beyond a white stage gives off showers of sparks and is too hot for welding or any other use. The following, in conjunction with the color chart, will serve as a guide:

WARM HEAT—The metal is passed slowly through the fire until it is too hot to be touched with the hands. You cannot forge at this low temperature.

BLACK HEAT—Still not used for forging but can be used for giving linseed oil rubbed ironwork a mat finish.

DULL RED or BLOOD RED—This temperature is used mainly for forging and hardening high carbon steel and will be discussed in chapters 4, 10, and 11.

BRIGHT RED or CHERRY RED—For light forging procedures on mild steel and for forging most carbon steel. It is the proper heat for bending, twisting, bending over the anvil, light punching, and hot chiseling. High carbon steel must not be heated any higher.

BRIGHT YELLOW or NEAR WELDING HEAT—The correct temperature for most forging operations. Use heat for mild steel and wrought iron.

FULL WELDING HEAT—If the fire and blast are working optimally, a few white bursting sparks will appear among the red sparks, indicating a correct temperature for welding most mild steel. At the upper range the metal is too hot and can begin to melt and burn. At the thin margin between these two ranges, the metal is the proper state which permits two pieces brought together to be hammered and welded to one another.

All procedures are described and demonstrated in chapter 5.

PHASE PRESENT IN ANNEALED CARBON ALLOYS AT VARIOUS TEMPERATURES

The following chart, used in conjunction with the color chart, will help you determine the workability of metal at the varying temperature ranges.

UPPER CRITICAL TEMPERATURE (A)—Above this temperature the structure consists of *austenite*, which coarsens with increasing time and temperature. Upper critical temperature is lowered as carbon increases to 0.85 percent.

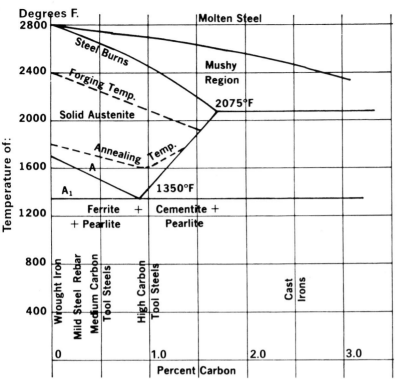

**Diagram of Phases
Present in Annealed Iron
Carbon Alloys at Various
Temperatures**
Courtesy, George Martin

ANNEALING consists of heating steels to slightly above A_1, holding for austenite to form, then slowly cooling in order to produce small grain size, softness, good ductility, and other properties. On cooling slowly the austenite transforms to *ferrite* and *pearlite.*

FORGING RANGE extends to several hundred degrees above the upper critical temperature.

BURNING RANGE is above the forging range. Burned steel *cannot be cured* except by remelting.

STRESS RELIEVING consists of heating to a range definitely below the lower critical temperature, A_1, holding for one hour or more per inch of thickness, then slowly cooling. Purpose is to allow the steel to relieve itself of locked-up stress.

BLUE BRITTLE RANGE occurs approximately at 300° to 700°F, in which range steels are more brittle than above or below this range. Peening or working of steel should not be done in this range.

FERRITE is practically pure iron (in plain carbon steels), existing below the lower critical temperature. It is magnetic and has very slight solid solubility for carbon.

AUSTENITE is the nonmagnetic form of iron and has the power to dissolve carbon and alloying elements.

CEMENTITE, or iron carbide, is a chemical compound of iron and carbon, Fe_3C.

PEARLITE is a mechanical mixture of ferrite and cementite.

MARTENSITE is an extremely hard phase of steel, formed from austenite, which is cooled or quenched very rapidly. It is too hard and brittle for use and must be tempered, or toughened, by reheating to a temperature well below the lower critical temperature.

Copper vessel with forged iron legs. By Larry Jones. The contemporary artist-craftsman may combine steel with other metals.

Courtesy, artist

4

The Smith's Materials: Iron, Steel, Alloys

METAL, the basic material of the smith, has myriad ramifications and can lead the craftsman along many new paths and levels of learning about materials. One can easily buy a piece of steel and begin working it until he discovers what he can and cannot do with it. He may try his hand on scrap pieces of steel and find, by trial and error, that some steels are more malleable than others, that one piece will develop into the object he wants to make, but another will crack and fracture. One can continue working with only an empirical approach to materials, find one source and type of metal that does what he wants it to and continue happily beating out his objects with that metal. Or one can become familiar with the structure of iron and steel and with their basic properties. With that knowledge, the smith is better equipped to work iron, steel, and the various alloys alone and in combination with one another.

Metallurgy, the science and technology of metals, includes the structure and various processes of working metals by hand and industrially. For those seeking in-depth information about specific metals under varying circumstances, a list of books dealing with metallurgy is offered in the Appendix. For forging as practiced by the artists-craftsmen, the following information along with the practical applications throughout the book will serve as a foundation.

WROUGHT IRON

Wrought iron is essentially almost pure iron with very little carbon. Wrought iron was developed during the Industrial Revolution in the seventeenth and eighteenth centuries when there was an increasing demand for an easily workable iron. The first process to meet this requirement was developed by Cort in England in the eighteenth century. Called "the Puddling Process," it was suitable for refining scrap or pig iron obtained by smelting iron ore into a highly refined, very malleable product in sufficient quantities for existing industries. The puddling process utilized a furnace containing a shallow hearth capable of producing approximately five hundred pounds of iron every three hours. The last mill producing wrought iron suspended operation in 1975. Only small stocks remain and may be hard to find. Whenever wrought iron is available new, or from scrap, it should be used judiciously for high-class smithing and ornamental ironwork.

Wrought iron conforming to Specification A-186 of the American Society of Testing and Materials is characterized by a very low carbon content (less than 0.03 percent) and a pronounced fibrous structure. The slag inclusions are so fine that a square inch may contain up to 250,000 particles which give the material its strong directional properties and ductility in the direction of these fibers. It is corrosion resistant —compared to mild steels—and, therefore, a sought-after metal for marine, seawater, and outdoor installations. When exposed to moist air, wrought iron develops a patina of bronze-colored oxides which protect it against further attack. (Mild steels develop rust, which eats into the surface.) Wrought iron, because it is almost pure iron, can be heated to a high temperature in which it becomes very plastic and can then be formed into intricate shapes by blacksmiths more easily than steels.

GEORGE MARTIN

The structure of wrought iron magnified 320 times.

Courtesy, George Martin

A puddling furnace as used until 1975 contains a shallow hearth capable of holding approximately 500 pounds of pig iron or cast iron. Heat is generated by a coal fire, and the iron is stirred for about three hours by two operators. The resulting lump is forged into a billet and rolled into bars.
Courtesy, Thomas Walmsley and Sons, Ltd., England

STEELS

Plain carbon steel is a family of alloys composed of iron plus various amounts of carbon with minor amounts of silicon, manganese, phosphorus, and sulfur. When a piece of plain carbon steel is broken, the fracture resembles crystals or an appearance like the break in a lump of sugar. The various amounts of carbon added to iron to create steel are controlled to yield specific properties resulting in three subfamilies termed low, medium, and high carbon. In addition, other metals such as chromium, molybdenum, nickel, tungsten, and vanadium may be added to make special alloy steels that are harder, tougher, and stronger than plain carbon steels. Steels are available from steel supply houses in various lengths, shapes, and sections based on weight. (See Appendix.)

Some understanding of how iron is made into steel is helpful and interesting. Iron-bearing ores, mined from the earth, are typically oxides or mixtures of oxides; an example is hematite: Fe_2O_3. Iron is produced by chemically reducing the ore from its oxide state to iron metal. This process is carried out at high temperatures in the blast furnace by reactions among coke, limestone, and iron ore. The result is "pig iron" containing 94 percent iron, 4 percent carbon, 1 percent silicon, and minor amounts of elements such as manganese, phosphorus and sulfur. The conversion of pig iron to steel involves a second refinement to control the carbon content and, when needed, to adjust or add alloying ingredients as in the making of tool or stainless steel. This second refinement may be accomplished by a variety of processes: open hearth, Bessemer converter, basic oxygen, or electric furnace; the net result is steel of a particular grade or composition. The United States uses about 100 million tons of iron and steel annually.

Properties of Steel

Carbon is the most important alloying element of steel. Carbon added to iron imparts strength and hardness to the resulting steel and allows it to be heat-treated. Only small variations in the amount of carbon result in large changes in properties as can be seen in the accompanying chart showing the relation of mechanical properties and structure to carbon content. Properties are affected by heat treatment and mechanical treatment as well as composition. For example, forging affects the size of the crystal aggregates (grains) in metals. The composition of the steel determines what can be accomplished with it. Thermomechanical treatment determines the structure and properties which are achieved. Plain carbon steel is the logical choice for the smith whose main concern is a metal that can be shaped to a desired form.

Low Carbon Steel

Low carbon steel, also known as machine steel and mild steel, contains about 0.05 to .30 percent carbon and is used for all general work that does not require special properties. It is not hardenable by heat treatment and can be welded easily.

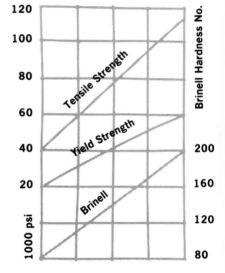

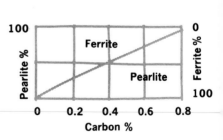

Relation of Mechanical Properties and Structure to Carbon Content of Slowly Cooled Carbon Steels

When strength and hardness are *not* the prime considerations, low carbon steel is the obvious choice for ease of fabrication and low cost. Low carbon steel appears in auto bodies (0.1 percent carbon), "tin" cans (0.08 percent); structural steel (0.1 to 0.15 percent carbon) such as beams, girders, channels, and angles, and Rebar (0.3 percent carbon) for concrete reinforcement.

Medium Carbon Steel

Medium carbon steel is stronger than low carbon steel. It contains about 0.30 to 0.60 percent carbon. The medium carbon steels are hardenable by heat treatment and are commonly employed in this condition. There is a decrease in ductility and toughness in steel as the carbon content and hardness increase. One uses the lowest carbon content necessary to achieve the required hardness and wear resistance. Typical uses of this range are tools subject to impact such as hammers, cold chisels, dies, etc. Railroad rails have carbon contents from 0.55 to 0.75 percent. Medium carbon steel is more difficult to bend, weld, and machine than low carbon steel.

High Carbon Steel

High carbon steel, also known as drill rod and high carbon tool steel, contains about 0.60 to 1.5 percent carbon. The *more carbon* the steel contains the harder it becomes. Tool steel is used for drills, taps, dies, reamers, files, and knives. It is hard to bend, weld, and cut. Before cutting, it must be annealed, or softened, to make it workable. As drill rod, it is available in bars having a very smooth finish and accurate size.

Hot Rolled Steel

The result of the steelmaking process is used either for steel castings or for large blocks called ingots. These ingots are rolled while hot between heavy, powerful steel rolls, each about two to three feet in diameter in much the same way that clothes are squeezed through a clothes wringer. The hot steel is rolled between several sets of rolls, which may have contoured surfaces and consecutively smaller gaps. When finished, this steel is called "hot rolled" because it was rolled while it was hot. Work that must be bent or twisted cold may be made of hot rolled steel.

The ingots may be put through a variety of rolls to yield different shapes and sizes. Some are rolled into rounds and flats and some into thin sheets about 3/16" for sheet steel, or thicker for plate steel. Pipe and tubing are made by drawing steel strip through a funnel-shaped ring. After cooling, hot rolled steel has a thin, black, hard skin or crust of scale.

Cold Rolled Steel

Cold rolled steel is made from hot rolled steel; that is, steel that was rolled while hot is rolled again when cold. The hot rolled steel is a little larger than the final size of the cold rolled steel; it is reduced only a small amount by the cold rolling.

The bars or rods of hot rolled steel, when cold, are first put into an acid pickling solution to remove the scale from the surface of the steel. The acid is washed off by dipping the bars in pure water and then in lime water. When dry, the bars are rolled while cold between highly finished rollers under great pressure. This gives them a smooth, bright finish and a very exact size. Cold rolled steel is often used without any more finishing or machining.

Using Scrap Steel

Any metal scrap pile is a fascinating source of potential raw materials. It is difficult to identify a particular grade of steel by appearance only. Therefore, it is important for the craftsman-blacksmith to have some means of identifying and testing scrap steel. Initial identification can be made by knowing what a found object was used for previously and then judging its steel and probable carbon content on that basis. The chart below will serve as a guide.

Additional means for testing the probable content of steel are shown in the chart: Identification of Metals. The most often used and reliable is the "spark test," also known as the "emery-wheel test." Different kinds of iron and steel will give off different sparks when the metal is held lightly against the grinding wheel. In judging, one should look for (1) the color of the spark, (2) the shape of the spark as it leaves the grinding wheel after it explodes, (3) the quantity of sparks, and (4) the distance the sparks shoot from the grinding wheel.

One way to judge the amount of carbon by the spark test is to compare the sparks with those of a piece of steel with a known alloy and carbon content.

CARBON STEELS AND THEIR USES

Percent of Carbon in Steel	Uses
Low-Carbon:	
0.05–0.20	Automobile bodies, buildings, pipes, chains, rivets, screws, nails.
0.20–0.30	Gears, shafts, bolts, forgings, bridges, buildings.
Medium-Carbon:	
0.30–0.40	Connecting rods, crank pins, axles, drop forgings.
0.40–0.50	Car axles, crankshafts, rails, boilers, auger bits, screwdrivers.
0.50–0.60	Hammers, sledges.
High-Carbon:	
0.60–0.70	Stamping and pressing dies, drop-forging dies, drop forgings, screwdrivers, blacksmiths' hammers, table knives, setscrews.
0.70–0.80	Punches, cold chisels, hammers, sledges, shear blades, table knives, drop-forging dies, anvil faces, wrenches, vise jaws, band saws, crowbars, lathe centers, rivet sets.
0.80–0.90	Punches, rivet sets, large taps, threading dies, drop-forging dies, shear blades, table knives, saws, hammers, cold chisels, woodworking chisels, rock drills, axes, springs.
0.90–1.00	Taps, small punches, threading dies, needles, knives, springs, machinists' hammers, screwdrivers, drills, milling cutters, axes, reamers, rock drills, chisels, lathe centers, hacksaw blades.
1.00–1.10	Axes, chisels, small taps, hand reamers, lathe centers, mandrels, threading dies, milling cutters, springs, turning and planing tools, knives, drills.
1.10–1.20	Milling cutters, reamers, woodworking tools, saws, knives, ball bearings, cold cutting dies, threading dies, taps, twist drills, pipe cutters, lathe centers, hatchets, turning and planing tools.
1.20–1.30	Turning and planning tools, twist drills, scythes, files, circular cutters, engravers' tools, surgical cutlery, saws for cutting metals, tools for turning brass and wood, reamers.
1.30–1.40	Small twist drills, razors, small engravers' tools, surgical instruments, knives, boring tools, wire drawing dies, tools for turning hard metals, files, woodworking chisels.
1.40–1.50	Razors, saws for cutting steel, wire drawing dies, fine cutters.

While many smiths successfully use materials gleaned from earlier usage, the practice can have drawbacks. It is not unusual to attempt to make something from a piece of scrap metal and discover that the tools you have will not work . . . sometimes to the detriment of your tools and their cutting edges. George Martin cites the experience of a student who tried to save money by using scrap steel. He ruined $30 worth of saw blades and carbide drills. If he had used new steel to begin with, he would have had little problem creating the objects he wanted to make; and he would not have wasted an inordinate amount of time, effort, and tools.

Cast iron, because of its brittle nature due to high carbon content, cannot be forged. A little practice spotting objects with casting seams and raised lettering will help identify cast scrap. Drainpipe, steam radiators, and fire hydrants are examples. Reinforcing rod for concrete is also not worth bringing home. It is often "hot short" (breaks off at orange heat when being forged), and ridges are difficult to remove.

Heat Treatment

It has already been pointed out that high carbon steels are used for tools, knives, and other objects where a certain hardness, strength, and toughness are desirable. To bring about these conditions, the steel is heated and then cooled in different ways . . . a process called heat treatment. Chapters 10 and 11 delve further into the use of tool steel and the treatment of steels for cutting instruments.

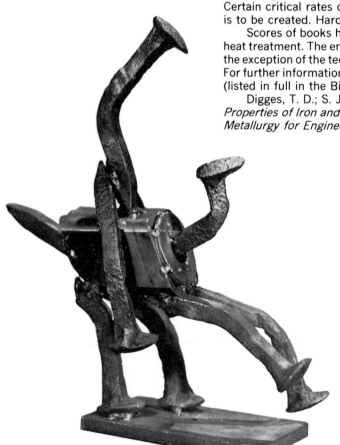

DON QUIXOTE. Jack Plovsky. Used railroad spikes and scrap steel forged and welded. 14" high, 12" wide, 6" deep.

Courtesy, artist

Heat treating consists of a series of thermal steps which subject the metal to a definite temperature/time process. The steel is hardened, tempered, and annealed in varying degrees depending upon the results desired. For example, heat treatment of a high carbon steel may involve quenching to harden the steel followed by tempering to toughen the steel. Certain critical rates of cooling must be achieved if optimum hardness is to be created. Hardened steel may be softened by annealing.

Scores of books have been written about the theory and practice of heat treatment. The entire subject is too vast to treat in this volume (with the exception of the technique described for bladesmithing, Chapter 10). For further information, the reader is encouraged to consult the following (listed in full in the Bibliography):

Digges, T. D.; S. J. Rosenberg; and G. W. Geil, *Heat Treatment and Properties of Iron and Steel* and Clark, D. S., and W. R. Varney, *Physical Metallurgy for Engineers,* and other texts on physical metallurgy.

IDENTIFICATION OF METALS

Courtesy, Hobart Bros.

metal / test	low carbon steel	medium carbon steel	high carbon steel	manganese steel	stainless steel	cast iron	wrought iron
appearance	DARK GREY	DARK GREY	DARK GREY	DULL CAST SURFACE	BRIGHT, SILVERY SMOOTH	DULL GREY EVIDENCE OF SAND MOLD	LIGHT GREY SMOOTH
magnetic	STRONGLY MAGNETIC	STRONGLY MAGNETIC	STRONGLY MAGNETIC	NON MAGNETIC	DEPENDS ON EXACT ANALYSIS	STRONGLY MAGNETIC	STRONGLY MAGNETIC
chisel	CONTINUOUS CHIP SMOOTH EDGES CHIPS EASILY	CONTINUOUS CHIP SMOOTH EDGES CHIPS EASILY	HARD TO CHIP CAN BE CONTINUOUS	EXTREMELY HARD TO CHISEL	CONTINUOUS CHIP SMOOTH BRIGHT COLOR	SMALL CHIPS ABOUT 1/8 in. NOT EASY TO CHIP, BRITTLE	CONTINUOUS CHIP SMOOTH EDGES SOFT AND EASILY CUT AND CHIPPED
fracture	BRIGHT GREY	VERY LIGHT GREY	VERY LIGHT GREY	COARSE GRAINED	DEPENDS ON TYPE BRIGHT	BRITTLE	BRIGHT GREY FIBROUS APPEARANCE
flame	MELTS FAST BECOMES BRIGHT RED BEFORE MELTING	MELTS FAST BECOMES BRIGHT RED BEFORE MELTING	MELTS FAST BECOMES BRIGHT RED BEFORE MELTING	MELTS FAST BECOMES BRIGHT RED BEFORE MELTING	MELTS FAST BECOMES BRIGHT RED BEFORE MELTING	MELTS SLOWLY BECOMES DULL RED BEFORE MELTING	MELTS FAST BECOMES BRIGHT RED BEFORE MELTING
Spark*	Long Yellow Carrier Lines (Approx. .20% carbon or below)	Yellow Lines Sprigs Very Plain Now (Approx. .20% to .45% carbon)	Yellow Lines Bright Burst Very Clear Numerous Star Burst (Approx. .45% carbon and above)	Bright White Fan-Shaped Burst	1. Nickel-Black Shape close to wheel. 2. Moly-Short Arrow Shape Tongue (only). 3. Vanadium-Long Spearpoint Tongue (only).	Red Carrier Lines (Very little carbon exists)	Long Straw Color Lines (Practically free of bursts or sprigs)

*For best results, use at least 5,000 surface feet per minute on grinding equipment. (Cir. x R.P.M.) S.F. per Min.) 12

FIREPLACE. Jim Wallace. Forged steel and fabricated. Isinglass on doors with copper piercing. 38" high.

Courtesy, artist

ALLOY STEELS

To overcome some of the limitation of plain carbon steel, alloying ingredients are added. These ingredients alter the solid state reactions which occur in the cooling of steel; they produce particular precipitates or solid phases which confer desirable properties on the alloy. For example, the addition of 18 percent chromium and 8 percent nickel to a very clean steel of 0.08 percent carbon results in an austenitic stainless steel termed the 300 series. If the smith is seeking a stainless steel for cutlery blades, this 300 series would *not* be suitable because austenite is a phase which does not harden by heat treatment. His preferred choice would be a martensitic stainless containing 13 percent carbon such as the low-cost general purpose 410 or the cutlery grade 440B. These can be forged and subsequently heat-treated to the hardness needed for a cutting edge. The selection and treatment of alloy steels is a specialized field requiring some investigation into the science of physical metallurgy equipment and considerable practical skill.

Briefly, the alloy steels are:

Nickel Steel

Nickel added to steel results in a strength and toughness that enable it to stand vibrations, shocks, jolts, and wear. It also retards rusting. Nickel steel is used for wire cables, steel rails, automobile and railroad car axles, and armor plate.

Chromium Steel

Chromium added to steel gives the steel a hardness, toughness, and a bluish cast. Chromium steel is a fine grain steel that resists rust, stains, shocks, and scratches; it is used for safes, rock crushers, and ball bearings.

Chromium is also the basis for stainless steels that contain from 11 to 18 percent chromium. They have a lasting bright, silvery gloss. One type is used for sinks, tabletops, tableware, pots, pans, and so on. Another type can be hardened for cutlery, medical instruments, and similar objects. Corrosion resistance is somewhat less than that of the nickel-chrome stainless steels.

Nickel-Chrome Steel

Nickel-chrome steel, containing 1 or 2 percent of these alloys, is hard and strong and used for armor plate and automobile parts such as gears, springs, axles, and shafts.

Manganese Steel

Manganese steel with about 12 percent manganese is a hard, brittle, grayish white metal. It purifies steel and adds strength and toughness to it. It is usually cast into shape. One peculiar property of manganese steel is that it hardens rapidly under blows, yet is soft enough to file. It is used for jaws of rock and ore crushers, steam shovels, chains, railway switches and crossings, and safes.

Molybdenum Steel

Molybdenum, a silvery-white metal which is harder than silver, is added in fractions of a percent to promote toughness and heat resistance. Molybdenum steel is used for automobile parts, high-grade machinery, wire as fine as 0.0004" in diameter, ball bearings and roller bearings.

Tungsten Steel

Tungsten, in amounts of 1 to 2 percent, is added together with chromium, etc., to steels and used mainly for dies. Tungsten is a heavy white metal that has a higher melting point than any other metal. It adds hardness to steel, makes a fine grain, and improves heat resistance. Some magnet steel contains from 4 to 5 percent tungsten. It holds magnetism well and is used in electrical measuring instruments.

Vanadium Steel

Vanadium steel contains small amounts of vanadium, a pale, silvery gray metal. It is brittle and resists corrosion. Vanadium improves toughness and strength and makes a fine grain. Because vanadium steel can stand shocks, it is used for springs, dies, gears, and tools.

Chromium-vanadium steel is hard and has great tensile strength; it is ductile and easy to machine. Chromium-vanadium steel is used for automobile parts such as springs, gears, steering knuckles, frames, axles, connecting rods, and other parts which must be strong and tough but not brittle.

High-Speed Steel (HSS)

High-speed steel is also known as high-speed tool steel and requires a complex heat treatment. Typically, it contains 18 percent tungsten, 8 percent cobalt, 4 percent chromium, 1 percent molybdenum, and 2 percent vanadium with up to 1 percent carbon.

High-speed steel is used for such cutting tools as taps, small cold chisels, cutters, and drills. It is called high-speed steel because cutting tools made of high-speed steel hold their edge even when red hot and, therefore, can be used at much higher machining speed than cutting tools made of carbon tool steel. High-speed steel costs from five to ten times more than carbon tool steel.

NONFERROUS METALS

The range of nonferrous metals—those that do not contain iron—is traditionally outside the realm of the blacksmith. Most can be softened for forging by coal or gas heat sources. The combinations of metals in a finished piece often exist. In many examples throughout the book, the craftsman with previous experience in metalworking, such as a jeweler or sculptor, is already familiar with some metals so he seeks to contrast the finishes, colors, and textures. The rich shiny gray iron in a gate may incorporate brass or aluminum parts; raised pots of silver, brass, and copper are made by cold forging; bronze—an important metal in the history of sculpture—is continuing to find its niche in the blacksmith's artillery, for it can be hammered and forged into shapes, fused by brazing or welding, or cut by saws and shears, depending upon its thickness.

Chapter 12 deals with many objects made of metals other than iron and lends substance to the theory that the more mediums the artist is familiar with, the greater will be his ability to exploit them for his visual statements.

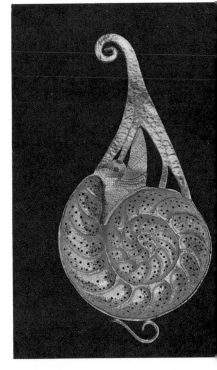

TEA STRAINER (inside view). By Dianne Porzel. Silver made by die forming and with a forged handle.

Courtesy, artist

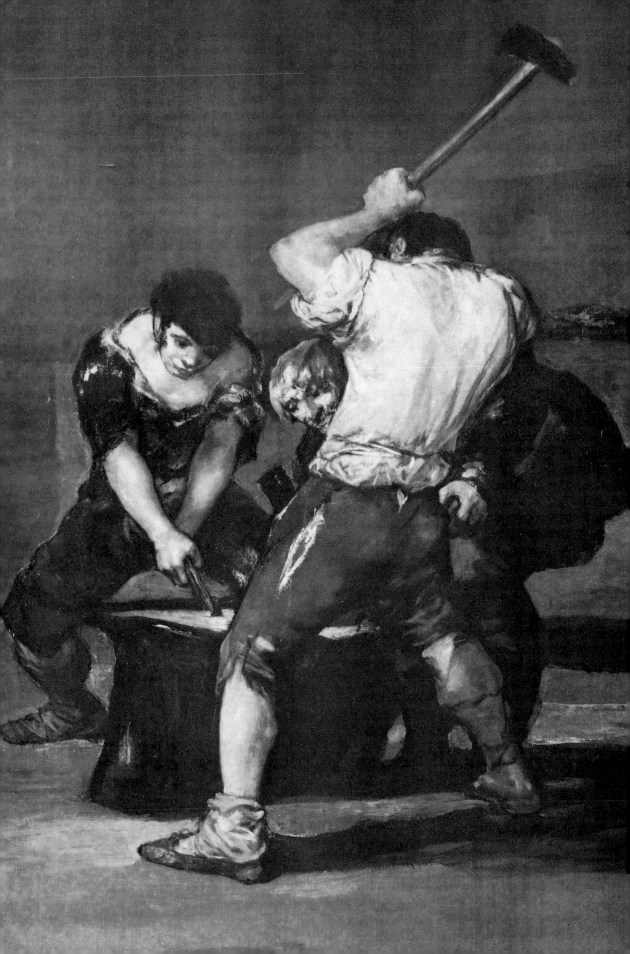

5

Basic Forging Procedures

DECORATIVE and functional ironwork with infinite variety, style, and design has been created for centuries and with essentially the same processes. How one handles these processes, what the artist's mind conjures and the hands fulfill, determines the essential differences between ironworkers as it does between painters and sculptors of excellence and mediocrity.

Christopher Ray's theory is pertinent. He says, "I find that of all the metals and methods, the forging of iron is the most expressive. There is a directness and an unmistakable relationship between the concept or purpose and the appropriateness of the end result. What is most delightful about the material is that the hand of the artisan shows, and the hand marks and peculiar traits in each unique piece are a reflection of the mental process of the originator. There is no hiding of one's weakness or strength. In this age of bland anonymity, it is a welcome relief to see the results of an individual who stands tall and naked and proclaims — I AM — without shame and regret."

The basic procedures offered in this chapter should be approached as exercises or learning problems. Once you learn to draw out, upset, flatten, split, punch, cut, twist, and perform the other techniques, you are ready to study the objects in chapter 6 and throughout the book with an analytical, educated eye. You should be able to emulate, then branch out and create your own design statement as you work.

In every subsequent chapter, you will be introduced to additional techniques that will enable you to gradually gather a total ironworking vocabulary. Creative metal forging as practiced today does not assign niches to its practitioners as was done in the past. The sculptor and gatemaker may delve into knifemaking or animal carving and employ a variety of surface treatments. The choice is yours . . . the more methodology you know, the greater will be your facility with the medium. Feel free to borrow any technique, any technology from other media so long as it serves your purpose.

THE FORGERS. Francisco Goya. A painting of the blacksmith and his strikers captures the energy and action of the nineteenth-century ironworker. *Courtesy, The Frick Collection, New York*

Begin with square bar, draw the end down to four sides, then finally to a round shape and a point. If you try to bring the piece to a point too rapidly, it may mushroom or crack on the edges.

DRAWING OUT

Drawing out means stretching or lengthening a piece of steel by the forging process. It is probably the technique most used. Begin with a piece of 3/8-inch or 1/2-inch square stock at least 12 inches long; you will work it down to a rounded point.

Heat the bar about 5 inches from the end to a bright yellow heat. Lay it on the anvil with the heated end away from you and begin to hammer about 4 inches from the end turning the bar over with each hammer blow and then turning it 90° so that you are hitting it on different sides alternately. The object is to work until the end is an elongated square and then eventually a point. Your initial attempt may require several "heats" until you get the feel of the hammer and the malleability of the steel. With practice, you may be able to draw down a bar up to 1/2 inch in one or two heats.

As you work, you will observe that bits of black residue flake off the iron. This is scale, the result of the air combining with an oxide film. Scale will either combine with the ash to form clinkers in the hearth or, under hammering, will accumulate on the anvil. The anvil should be wiped off regularly (between each heat) to prevent loose scale from being hammered into the metal surface and becoming an undesirable surface texture.

A square bar is being drawn out with the face of a ball peen hammer, maintaining its square shape at first.

The tip is drawn out further and rounded. The iron should be turned back and forth between each hammer blow. Let the hammer bounce back from the anvil to overcome the "lift" and minimize the energy required. A drawn-out bar such as this can be used to make a punch, fork tines, a poker, and so forth.

FLATTENING

A round or square bar can be flattened by heating the bar and delivering strong hammer blows first on one side, then turning the bar over and hitting the other side, gradually pulling the bar toward you as you work to the bottom. A flattened piece can be worked into a spoon bowl, the handle for an object, or, if high carbon steel is used, for a screwdriver or a chisel.

A round bar is tapered and then flattened by first drawing out, and turning the metal over from one side to the other as the blows are delivered with the flat face of the hammer.

The end is further drawn out, flattened, and the tip made thinner.

Another bar has been worked down to a wider and thicker edge than the one above. The action spreads the iron much as a bar of clay would be spread.

BENDING

Bending thin bars of iron may be done cold, but for thick bars and for making proper scrolls in thin bars, hot working is essential. Bends can be accomplished over the anvil edge or around the horn. The steel may be placed in a vise, in the hardy or pritchel hole and hit with a hammer or pulled with a wrench until the desired angle of the bend is made.

Wrought iron is composed of fibers running along the grain so the bend should be made in the direction of the grain. Mild steel can be bent in any direction. The outer side of the bend will stretch, the inner side will contract. To bend a long bar, place it in a vise or anvil hole, fit a length of pipe over the end for extra leverage where necessary.

Delicate-looking scrolls appear in many of the examples throughout the book. They are made by drawing out the bar, then hitting the end up from the tip and actually curling the steel in a rolling fashion while it is hot, as you would make a curl of paper.

A thick round bar has been tapered to a point and is heated and bent over the tip of the horn. The outer side stretches. When planning objects requiring specific dimension, the lengths to which a bar can be drawn out must be planned and allowances made for the extra steel needed for stretch when bending.

It can be further shaped by hitting on the side of the bend. Joe Nyiri will use this part in a piece of fabricated sculpture.

Michael Malpass has drawn out the steel to a very thin point; one bend is retained by placing it in the hardy hole. The scroll is then rolled up by hitting it with the hammer while the steel is hot.

A bend made over the edge of the anvil can be combined with a rounded portion made on the horn.

When the rolling action distorts the scroll sideways, it should be placed flat on the anvil and straightened with the face of a light hammer.
Courtesy, L. Brent Kington

Right: Frank Turley upsets the end of a bar. It is placed in the vise and given a hard hammer blow while it is hot.

Frying pan by Rick Cronin utilizes a handle that has an "upset" top end, a flattened half of the handle, and a beautifully free-form hammered pan shape.

Courtesy, artist

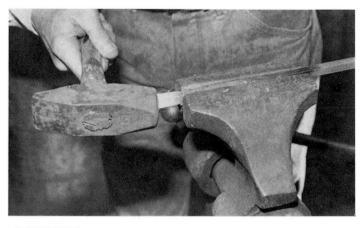

UPSETTING

Upsetting thickens or bulges a piece of metal. The head of a nail or bolt is an example of upsetting at the end of a bar or rod. When a thick portion is required in the center of a bar that portion must be heated, the adjacent portions cooled in water, and the bar hit with the hammer or rammed against the anvil. If upsetting is required within a portion of a bar that will also be bent, you must figure lengths carefully to allow for thickening and stretching while retaining the necessary circumference and length.

TWISTING

Twisting a bar is usually done for decorative purposes. Single, double, multiple, and reverse twists are evident in examples throughout the book. The hot bar is placed in a vise and the twisting accomplished with a wrench or other tool. The portions adjacent to the area to be twisted must be cooled with water. In some situations the portions to be twisted may be spot-heated with the torch. Some twisting can be accomplished with cold metal (see chapter 8).

A heated bar held in a blacksmith's vice is twisted with a wrench.
Photo, Ted Davidson

Spot-heating with a torch while twisting with vice-grip pliers.
Photographed at Virginia Commonwealth University, Richmond

SPLITTING

Splitting is a process of hot-cutting iron in its major dimension. Heat the iron to be split to a near welding heat and cut it with a hot chisel driven by hammer blows or by placing the end to be cut over the hardy and driving the steel down over the hardy edge. Splitting may also be accomplished with a hacksaw (see birdcage handle demonstration, chapter 6).

When you are splitting or cutting steel on an anvil, to avoid hitting and damaging the anvil face, reduce the force of the blow before you cut completely through. Make the final cut over a piece of plate between the work and anvil, or work on the pad of the anvil.

Michael Jerry drives a hot chisel with a sledgehammer to split the vice-supported iron bar.

Photo, Ted Davidson

A bar that was split, and the ends drawn out, is further split with a hand chisel driven by a hammer. Michael Malpass.

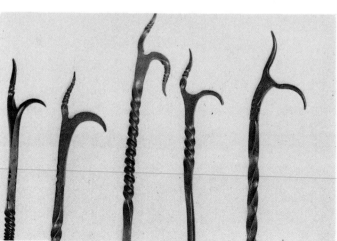

End details from five fireplace pokers by L. Brent Kington illustrate the combined uses of drawing out, flattening, bending, splitting, and twisting.

Courtesy, artist

A bar of iron heated to a bright yellow is placed on the anvil and held with the tongs. The smith places the set punch on it, and it is driven with hammer blows by the striker. When the hole is about halfway through, the iron can be turned over and the punch completed over the hardy hole.

PUNCHING AND DRIFTING

Punching, as the name implies, is the process of punching a hole in metal usually to receive a bolt, rivet, or other piece of metal for joining or sometimes for purely decorative reasons. Punches are both set and hand-held tools with tapered ends that spread the metal as they are driven through it. A plug of iron is *not* removed as when punching paper or drilling a peg in wood. The deeper the punch is driven, the wider the hole. The punch is placed on the metal, and the top is struck with a hammer or sledge by the smith or his striker. A drift is used to finish a hole that has been punched smaller than the required size.

To punch a hole, the iron should be brought to a near welding heat. If the hole is deep, the punch will become hot and need to be cooled frequently. After every three or four blows, the punch should be quenched in water. After punching deep holes, sprinkle a few grains of coal dust into the hole before replacing the punch to help prevent the punch from sticking.

The punch may be driven halfway or more through one side of the iron, then the iron turned over and punched from the other side over the hardy hole. Holes for some joining procedures are also made with a drill press. Sometimes the punch will tend to split the iron; in that event the bar must be contained in a die.

Wrought-iron railing (*detail*) by Sam Ogden, Jr. A punched horizontal bar receives the ends of the split uprights.
Courtesy, artist

HOT CUTTING ON A HARDY

The hardy, an indispensable anvil tool with a 60° cutting edge, is used for cutting hot metal. The square shank of the hardy is placed in the hardy hole, or in a vise, and the metal to be cut is placed on the cutting edge and struck with a hammer. The metal is nicked around the cutting line and then bent back and forth until it breaks or is knocked off with the hammer on the scored line. Round bars are rotated to produce a circular groove. A bright red heat is best 'for hot cutting. In some operations the hardy can be used for splitting.

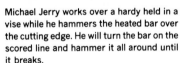

Michael Jerry works over a hardy held in a vise while he hammers the heated bar over the cutting edge. He will turn the bar on the scored line and hammer it all around until it breaks.

Photo, Ted Davidson

A bar drawn out to make a tenon for a mortise and tenon joint is ready for breaking off at the hardy edge.

JOINING TECHNIQUES

Collaring

A collar is a round or flat bar bent around two or more pieces of iron to join them. The collar must be measured accurately to allow for the stretch in the bend, and so it joins at the back by meeting—not overlapping or gaping. Various decorative treatments can be done with a collar: these can be observed in several of the details in chapter 14 and in examples throughout the book.

1. The bar of the width and thickness of the collar is brought to a near welding heat and bent by first placing it over the edge of the anvil to begin the bend and then hitting it with the hammer to complete the bend.

2. With another heat it is wrapped around a bar used as a mandrel that approximates the width of the final pieces to be wrapped.

3. The corners are squared by placing the U shape in the vise and hammering to shape.

4. The collar may be cut on a hardy or sawed off with a hacksaw.

5. The finished collar used to band together two pieces of iron can be further bent into shape with pliers, if necessary.

Demonstration, Jim Wallace

1

2

3

4

5

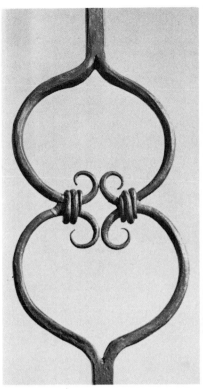

Entrance gate by Peter Happny of 5/8-inch-square iron bar bent and collared.
Courtesy, artist

Wrapping

Wrapping serves the same function as collaring but is made with two or more turns of the iron bar. The wrap is begun as with collaring, but once it is placed on the bars, it is difficult to achieve additional heats in the fire so that one must use spot heating with an oxyacetylene torch.

Wrapping two split and scrolled bars (detail from a candelabrum). By Barry Berman.

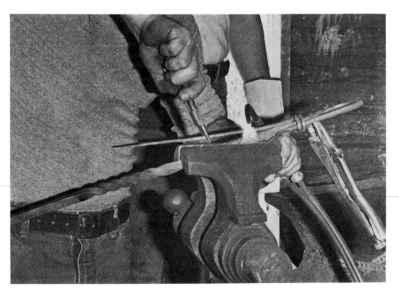

Wrapping is accomplished by placing the pieces to be wrapped in a vise. The round wrapping bar is forge-heated, bent around the bars, and held in place with vise-grip pliers. When it cools, it is spot-heated with a torch and brought around the bars with pliers or other gripping tool. Michael Jerry.
Photos, Ted Davidson

Mortise and Tenon

A mortise and tenon joint consists of a bar forged down to a narrow round or square bar called a tenon. This is pushed through a hole, called a mortise, which is drilled or punched in another member of the joint. Sufficient length is given to the tenon to allow it to protrude through and be hammered over the bottom of the mortised member to secure by riveting.

1   To make the tenon, draw down the end of the bar. Note the position of the bar over the anvil edge and the use of the flat hammer face.

2   Finish the tenon with the wedged end of the hammer . . . keeping the sides even by rotating it as you draw out.

3   Round the tenon, using the top and bottom swage.

4   Square off the shoulder of the tenon by means of a nail iron to which a piece of piping has been welded to protect the end of the bar.

5   Check the diameter of the tenon in the appropriate hole of a nail iron.

6

The tenon is cut off to the required length over the hardy.

7

An alternate way of squaring off the shoulder; place the nail iron over a swage block and hammer or bump the other end of the work. The tenon is hot during all these procedures.

8

The mortise (hole) has been drilled in the receiving member of the joint. The tenon is placed in the mortise.

9

The end is hammered to make a rivet-type closing.

Demonstration by Pedro Lopez Orozco and George Martin

Riveting

Riveting involves joining two or more pieces of iron together with a rivet shank placed in holes in the pieces to be joined. A protruding portion of the rivet shank is upset to make a head that locks the pieces together. To protect the original rivet head when securing the opposite end, it is placed on a heading tool containing a shallow indentation to fit the head. The other rivet end is formed either by peening or with a hammer-driven tool similar to the heading tool.

One heading tool, a rivet, and bars to be joined with punched or drilled holes. A hole should be slightly larger than the shank used for riveting. Rivets can be purchased ready-made to size or made by forging. A rivet should be about a diameter to a diameter and a half longer than the combined thickness of the steels to be joined.

The head tool, clamped in the vice, supports the rivet while the bars are slipped over the rivet.

Setting the rivet with the ball peen hammer to secure the joint.

The finished rivet head after hammer peening.

Demonstration by Daryl Meier

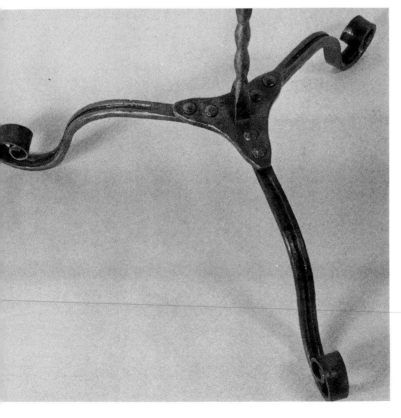

The use of rivets is dictated by the project. Details from the candelabrum (*following page*) by George Martin illustrate their placement as joining devices and decorative motifs. One can easily learn to read the basic methods used to create an object. Shown, in addition to the riveting, are bending, twisting, and splitting. The center square bar in the bottom photo is actually placed in a square hole as a mortise and tenon construction and riveted over on the bottom.

Courtesy, George Martin, Creative Metal Crafts, Los Angeles

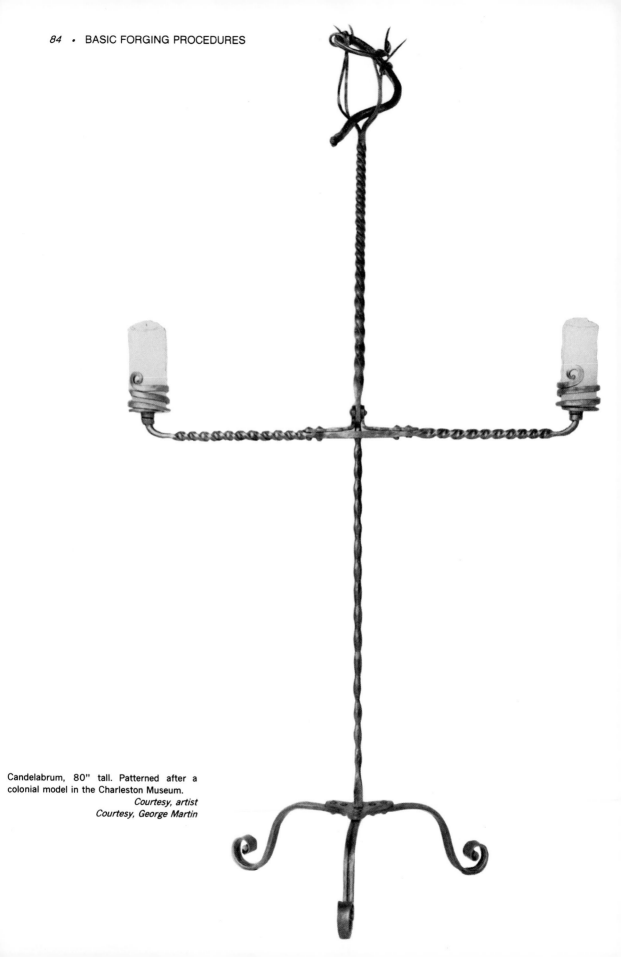

Candelabrum, 80" tall. Patterned after a
colonial model in the Charleston Museum.
Courtesy, artist
Courtesy, George Martin

FORGED IRON SCULPTURE. C. Carl Jennings. 42" high. The same ironworking-forging techniques used by the blacksmith for utilitarian items have been applied to sculpture; drawing out, upsetting, splitting, punching, riveting, bending.

Courtesy, artist

Forge Welding

Forge welding, a method of joining iron and steel to each other while in a plastic state, has been known since antiquity. Early applications include welding chains and shackles into homogeneous links and joining high carbon steel cutting edges into soft or tough backing material for weapons or tools.

Basically, the process is one of pressing together clean metal surfaces under the application of heat and the pressure of hammer blows. Cleanliness of the surfaces is achieved by a flux. Wrought iron is the material easiest to weld because it can be heated to a higher temperature than steels and is therefore softer at its working temperature. It contains slag in its structure which aids the flux. The higher the carbon content of steel, the more difficult it becomes to weld. Medium carbon steels can be joined to low carbon steels or wrought iron by using fluxes which introduce carbon into the joint. The most intricate welds, using a variety of steels of varying carbon content joined into one piece, are those produced by the Japanese swordmakers since the ninth century. Damascus steel, discussed in chapter 11, is also a process of forge welding different layers and types of steel.

A flux is usually required for forge welding; it is applied after the iron is brought to a red heat for the purpose of cleaning the surface. A flux will combine with the oxide skin layers and scale, to yield a low melting point compound which is easily squeezed out during hammering. Fluxes are usually sand or borax or a mixture of these for wrought iron and mild steel.

To make a forge weld, the parts to be joined are first hammered to upset and thicken the ends and produce closely fitting faces in a process called *scarfing*. The scarfs should be long enough to allow the two surfaces to "take" but not so long that the lips burn before the parts take a welding heat. The scarfed ends are placed in a clean fire with the lip sides upward and heated to a bright red heat, removed, and quickly sprinkled with the flux. By means of a long-handled spoon, flux can sometimes be applied to the parts in the fire without removing them. The parts are then allowed to heat *evenly* until they reach a welding, or near white, heat. With wrought iron, a welding heat has been reached when the surface of the hot iron appears to be covered by a liquid film.

Flux may be applied to the surfaces to be joined by sprinkling from a bottle or can or by dipping the red hot piece into the flux.

The scarf joint is hammer welded to obtain a butt joint.

When the parts are properly heated, the following actions must be done rapidly: the first piece is taken from the fire with the scarf face downward and tapped over the edge of the anvil to shake off any sand or other impurities clinging to it, then immediately turned over and laid face upward on the anvil.

The second piece is quickly removed, tapped on the anvil, then, with scarfed face downward, laid in position on top of the first piece so that the two semimolten surfaces stick to each other on contact.

The order of the hammer blows is important. The first blow is struck in the center of the top scarf so that air and dirt are driven out toward the end. The second blow is on the thick part of the top scarf so that it welds to the thin end of the under scarf, which is being cooled by the anvil face. The third blow is driven on the end of the top scarf before it cools.

If another heat is necessary, take it now, then remove and continue welding by turning the piece over and hammering both sides alternately, being careful not to reduce or expand the section differently from the original bars.

Quick, light hammer blows are recommended though some smiths prefer initial hard blows, but then reworking is rarely possible if the weld has not taken.

The finished weld should have the appearance in size and shape of the initial bars with no reduction of the section and with corners very slightly chamfered. It should be smooth.

In addition to the scarf joint, other possible joints are shown in the drawings, right. If the weld is done properly, the work is as strong as a single piece of iron. If it is done improperly, if air and scale are trapped between the parts, trying to correct the weld is usually impractical; it is usually advisable to take new stock and begin again. The unsuccessfully welded portion can be cut off, the remainder placed back in the stockpile and used for something else.

Making a forge weld takes experience and practice. It is essential to recognize when the iron is at the proper heat and then to work surely and rapidly, placing the pieces on the anvil correctly and delivering the hammer blows at the proper place and in the right order. It is also important to prepare the metal properly to suit the type of weld required and to have a clean, clinker-free fire with a good heart.

GEORGE MARTIN

Types of weld:

Scarfed—both joints

Butt

Single Fagot

Double Fagot

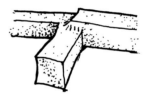

End of bar welded into corner

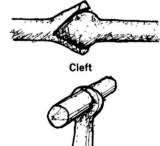

Cleft

Split

Drawing, Al Meilach

Two multilayered steel sections are placed on each other so they can be forge-welded on a trip-hammer.

FINISHING

The perfect finish for wrought iron is the natural iron itself. It has an alive look, a beautiful luster which is enhanced by a great variety of textural finishes from coarse hammer peening to a smooth polish. The color can range from a bright to dark gray depending upon the polishing accomplished. Wrought ironwork must be protected against corrosion, especially if it is to be placed out of doors. Rust, the product of oxidation on the natural patina, will change the color and, in time, may pit the surface. However, if the iron is waxed or oiled it will, under corrosive outdoor conditions such as being near the sea or swimming pools or in high moisture areas, develop a deep bronze patina which protects the metal literally for centuries. Mild steel, too, can be finished by oiling but may require repeated applications during its life. Under noncorrosive conditions, such as indoor use, the coating, if wiped occasionally, will preserve the metallic sheen.

Recommended finishing procedures are:

1. A mixture of 4 parts turpentine and 1 part beeswax applied with a rag and wiped.

2. An old smith's recipe:

Heat 1 chunk of beeswax on stove until melted. Turn off flame and add a little turpentine but be careful not to let it burn. (Keep a pot lid handy to douse a fire should it burst into flame.) Remove wax from stove and continue to add turpentine until you have about 1 part turpentine to 4 parts wax. Let it cool and solidify, then place in refrigerator until it is a waxlike paste. Apply the paste to the iron with your fingers, then rub with a very fine dust or dirt (must not be sandy or gritty). Wipe off with a soft cloth, nylon stocking, or piece from an old rug. This results in an antique finish with highlights of iron and is a fair rust inhibitor.

A darker but still metallic look will result with a linseed oil coating, and other oils, even used engine oil, give good results. There are varying methods of application:

1. Apply oil with a cloth, then heat the iron until the oil smokes but does not flame. Wipe off with a rag. The iron may be reheated several times for deeper tones. This is a good rust inhibitor.

2. Heat the iron to a black heat, then apply the oil, return the iron to the fire and burn it off gently. Don't overheat or the oil will burn off completely.

Coatings

1. Iron may be finished by coating with varnishes, lacquers, or clear acrylics. Steel should first be rubbed with a medium-grit emery paper to bring out the highlights and texture. These hard colorless materials may be used to protect a piece subjected to a great deal of handling. However, after some time lacquer may dull and is difficult to remove and replace.

2. Black paint, called "wrought iron" finish by many distributors, will tend to inhibit rust. Paints usually require reapplication frequently. One reason for much of the black paint coatings so liberally used in commercially made wrought iron pieces is to hide poor workmanship, weld spatters, and other errors.

When black paint finishes are used, the metal must be thoroughly cleaned by brushing or sandblasting to loosen any scale or oxides. Extensive commercial work, which does not aspire to a handwrought finish, should be given a primer coat and a finishing coat of alkyd, acrylic, or urethane base paint. High quality industrial grade enamels, in matte and gloss, are also available.

A number of local and federal government regulations apply to the seclection and application of these paints. Some of the older types of paints have solvents which are no longer permissible, and other paints may give rise to health problems unless appropriate precautions are taken.

Other coloring procedures such as bluing and browning, usually associated with weaponry and armor, may be used and these are discussed later. Industrial electroplating and other electrochemical coatings (not discussed) may be investigated.

Tempering, the heating process associated with carbon steels, may be applied judiciously to mild steel to achieve temper colors ranging from blues to yellows. Such coloring is effectively used in sculptures and many decorative objects.

GEORGE MARTIN

Scrolls within a right angle are used as part of a table base. By Erwin Gruen.
Courtesy, artist

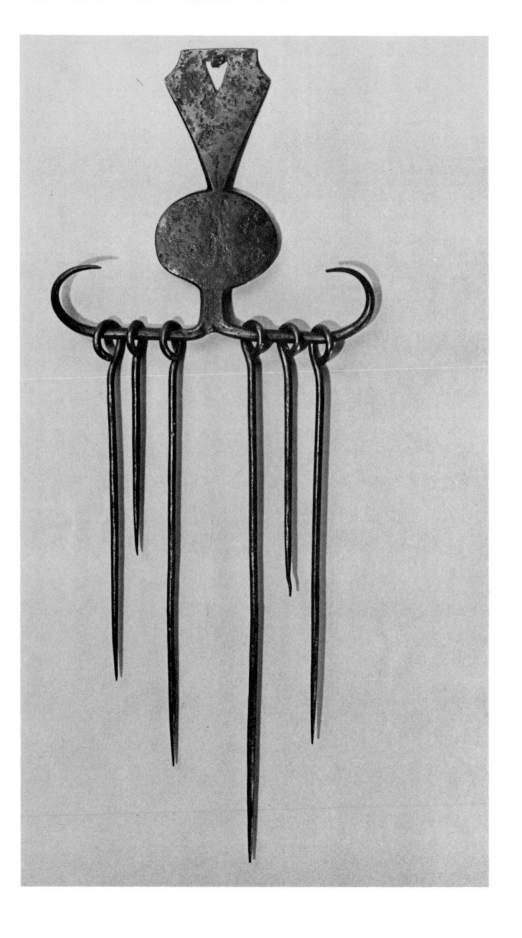

6

The Object-from Simple to Challenging

BLACKSMITHING has long been concerned with functional objects in addition to gates, tools, armor, and weapons with which, perhaps, it is most associated. A survey of ironwork history reveals an unending assortment of items which the contemporary craftsmen can study. They are loaded with ideas of what to make, how to combine basic techniques aesthetically and practically and offer a range of design concepts in metals.

The following examples are grouped by types of objects, where possible. They also progress from a simple-to-make item to those that are more complex. Even the simple object usually employs more than one of the techniques illustrated in chapter 5. Each object should be carefully analyzed for the methods used, drawing out, twisting, bending, upsetting, fabricating by collaring or riveting, and so forth, and then developed using your own approaches. They are not offered to be copied; rather they are shown so that you can use them to branch out and develop other original objects.

Additional methods for working the iron are offered and these can be applied to any of the items in other chapters.

In this renaissance of ironworking the examples illustrate a mood that seems to be permeating artistic consciousness. E. A. Chase describes it as "a mechanism operating within human society which struggles to prevent the loss of ancient skills. It is almost as if a deep running consciousness is aware of the survival value of maintaining the skills involved in the simplest relationship of humans and their earthy materials. It is fascinating to me," says Chase, "that artists have become the repository of these skills. If one meets, as I have, contemporary commercial ironworkers who know nothing of working their chosen materials except for what can be translated for them through modern machinery, it becomes obvious that the preservation of basic skills lies not with industry, but with the artist.

"Perhaps in this way, the artist transcends social directives, instinctively reaching for the most direct ways of dealing with materials on one hand and the elusive universal language on the other . . . or are they different facets of the same jewel?"

Skewer rack with skewers. By Forrest Morse. Wrought iron. Rack 5" high, 6" wide. With skewers, total length 15".
Photo, Mark Lindquist

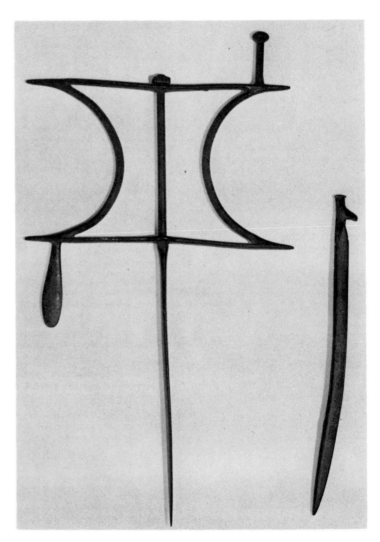

African money. Forged iron. Approximately 17" high, 2" wide at top, 1½-inch diameter with twist.

Early American surveyor's instrument. Riveting, welding, punching, drawing out.

Japanese horse bit. 18" high, 4" wide, each piece.

All objects this page, collection, Mr. & Mrs. Wayne Chapman, Solana Beach, Calif.

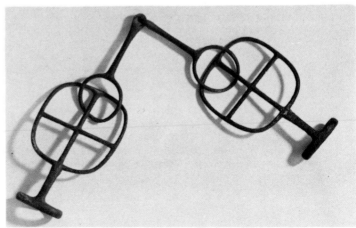

Contemporary jewelry—earrings, and pins —made by splitting, cutting, drawing out, and finishing with C-scroll endings. By Harriet Rawle Hemenway.

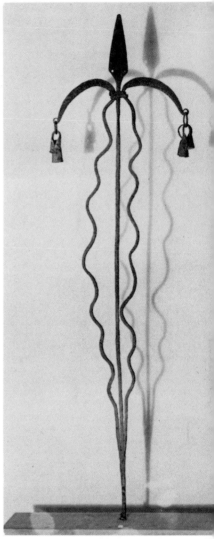

Dogon staff. The African blacksmith combines a versatile, vast technique repertory with individual expressiveness and native iconography.
Courtesy, Gallery II, Purdue University

French curling iron has a riveted center, carefully made ends, and tapering members.
Collection, Mr. & Mrs. Wayne Chapman, Solana Beach, Calif.

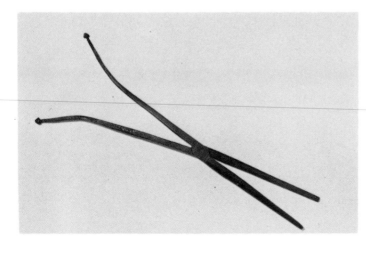

DIFFERENT WAYS TO MAKE A SCROLL

The evolution of a small hook made from a round iron spike. *Left to right;* the end is drawn out, the tip scrolled, the bend is made over the horn of the anvil, and the top cut off. The finished hook is about 3" long and 1¼" wide at the bottom bend. By Jim Fleming.

Photo, Bruce MacMillan

A scroll is formed by hitting the tip of the iron toward you with the hammer. Observe the position of the hand on the hammer as opposed to the grip used with a striking blow.

Photo, Ted Davidson

A bar that has been split has one end drawn out to begin a scroll; the same will be done on the other portion of the split. By Michael Malpass.

A scroll is made on a 2-inch-wide piece of iron by bringing the end to a bright yellow heat, flattening the end . . .

Above, left:
. . . then hammering the tip up to begin the scroll.

Above, right:
The bar is heated again, as necessary, and bent about 1½" up from the end over the edge of the anvil; this begins the bend.

The scroll is further rolled up with guiding hammer blows. The sides are squared against the anvil face. Scroll endings can be flared, tight, loose, split, and so forth. See additional examples in chapter 8.
Demonstration by J. Guadalupe Benitez, Muñoz Furniture Factory, Tijuana, Mexico

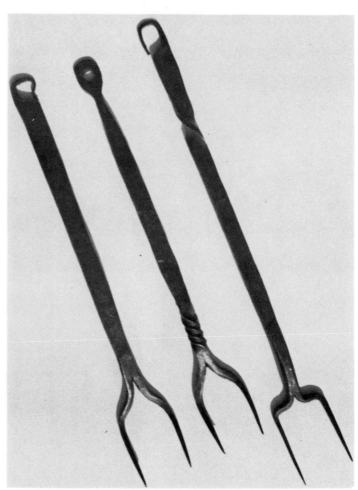

Spatula. By Keith Dean Farwell Rowland. An iron handle split, bent, twisted, and coiled is entwined with copper. The handle is forge welded to the blade which has a moon shape pierced with a jeweler's saw. The organic design has an Art Nouveau influence.

Courtesy, artist

Above, right:
Three simply designed forks by Barry Berman utilize several basic blacksmithing techniques: splitting, drawing out, twisting, and bending. A good exercise for a beginning project.

A triangle and a shutter hook and holder, of Early American design, offer the beginner several basic forging exercises. Once you are familiar with the rudimentary methods, you should be able to analyze a form and attempt to emulate it.

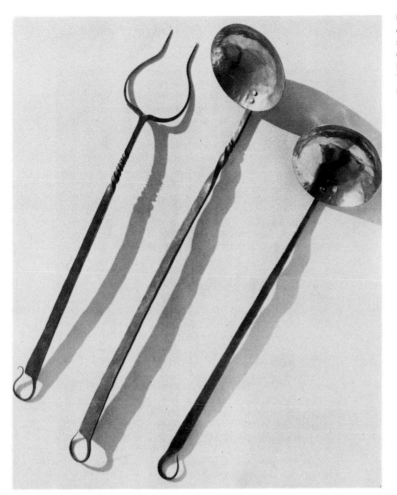

Utensils by Barry Berman. Iron handles are riveted to ladles with a brass and a copper bowl shaped by hammering the metal into a rounded-out portion of a wooden stump. The iron handles have very thin looped rattail endings. The center piece has a chiseled design. Pieces are 18" long.

Twisted and coiled hanging planter with copper bowl. By Donn Williams. 30" high.
Courtesy, artist

Pickaxe. Donn Williams. Carbon steel with a reverse twist. Hand-carved hickory handle.
Courtesy, artist

Plant hanger. By Jack Andrews. Blown glass by Gil Johnson.

Photo, Jack Andrews

Above, right:
Candle holder. By C. Carl Jennings. 30" high. Rust finish.

Photo, Stone and Steccati

Candle holder. By Sam Ogden, Jr. Wrought iron with serpentine. 15" high.

Courtesy, artist

Candle holders by Jack Andrews.
Courtesy, artist

Candle holder. By Sam Ogden, Jr. Hammer marks purposely give the wrought-iron finish some of its texture. 30" high.
Courtesy, artist

Hanging planter. By Thomas R. Markusen. Hot forged and pressed mild steel fabricated, coiled, and riveted. 75" high, 26" wide. 24" deep.
Courtesy, artist

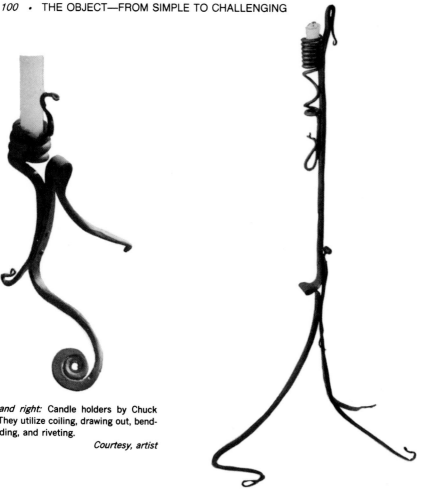

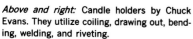

Above and right: Candle holders by Chuck Evans. They utilize coiling, drawing out, bending, welding, and riveting.

Courtesy, artist

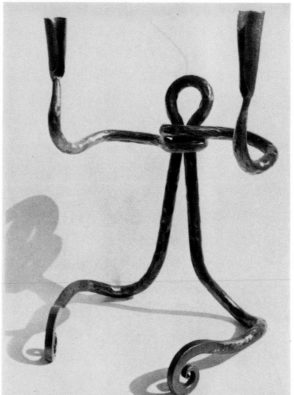

Candelabrum. By Pedro Lopez Orozco. 1/2-inch round wrought iron is hammered into square and scrolled endings for the feet and flattened and curved to receive tapered candles. 12" high, 8½" wide, 8" deep.

Photographed at Creative Metal Crafts, Los Angeles, Calif.

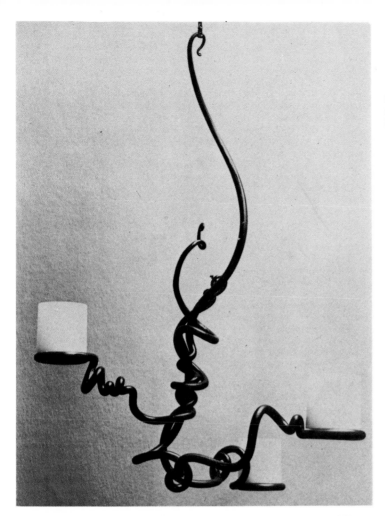

Chandelier. William E. Leth. Round iron bar hot-forged into sinuous curving designs. 32" high.

Below left and right: Candelabra by Dale Coughenour.

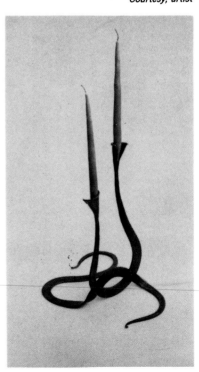

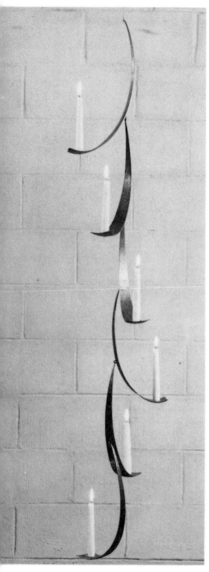

Hanging articulated candle holder. By Sam Ogden, Jr. Wrought iron about 6' high.
Courtesy, artist

Lily wall sconce. By Ranna Coddington. Mild steel and copper. 28" high, 18" wide.
Photo, Christopher Whitney

Chandelier. By Peter Happny. The sixteen
lights may be reassembled in any shape and
balance arrangement that works. 4' high.
Courtesy, artist

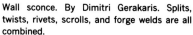

Wall sconce. By Dimitri Gerakaris. Splits, twists, rivets, scrolls, and forge welds are all combined.

Courtesy, artist

Above, right:
Candlestand. By Michael Spencer. Forged from bar and sheet steel. The dish is welded to a shank which is riveted to the base. 10" high.
Photo, Peter Barrs

Right:
Wall sconce. By Michael Spencer. Hot forged from one piece of 1/4-inch square mild steel. The heart shape was made over a jig; the helix formed around a mandrel. 15" high.
Photo, Peter Barrs

Far right:
Wall sconce. By Barry Berman. Forged iron back and arms with 18-gauge copper strip and 1-inch brass hammered candle cups.

Candle holder with detail. By Bruce LePage. A contemporary approach to the twists illustrates the manipulation possible with iron in a plastic state. Portions are fabricated using collaring and forge welding. 54" high, 12" wide.

THE BASKET MOTIF

The open multiple-twisted motif achieved by forge welding several rods at top and bottom and opening the unwelded members is referred to as the "basket," or "birdcage." The demonstration shown uses four 3/8-inch round rods. The birdcage motif may be used for handles of fireplace tools, bases for candles, bedposts, door handles, and anywhere the designer feels it will fit the mood of the overall job. Bruce LePage demonstrates the birdcage handle made with a reverse twist shank for a fire poker.

Four 3/8-inch round rods are used to form the basket handle.

The ends are heated and fluxed with borax and steel filings . . .

. . . then brought to a welding heat and forge welded.

The end is scarfed in preparation for welding to a shank of 3/4-inch square stock. Note that the rods are held together with a piece of iron wrapped around them.

The scarf weld is hammered so the basket handle is welded to the shank.

The ends flow into one another.

The finished weld.

Now the top of the handle with the basket is drawn out to a flat taper.

The end is placed over the anvil horn and bent . . .

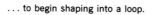

. . . to begin shaping into a loop.

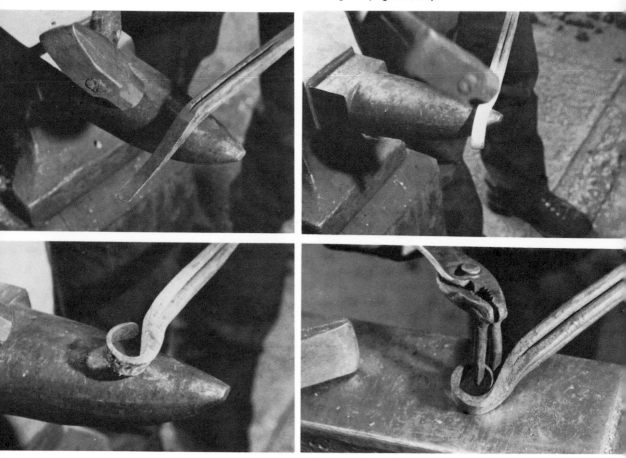

The loop is made . . .

. . . and a final bend made with a special tool Bruce has created for this bend . . . a pair of pliers with two extensions welded on.

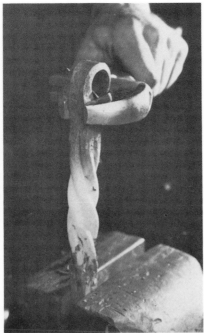

Now the basket handle will be upset. A heat is taken on the handle. The loop should be cooled in water to prevent deforming it. It is placed in a vise; the work must proceed rapidly while the heat is in the iron.

A wrench is used and the handle is given a three-quarters twist . . .

. . . and then quickly upset by hammering the looped end as shown. The four rods open up.

The finished basket (or birdcage) handle results. Now the shank will be given a reverse twist.

The midsection of the shank is heated, placed in a vise, and twisted with the vise grip.

A second heat is taken which bleeds into the first twist, then the shank is twisted in the opposite direction.

The finished twist. The piece is wire brushed to remove scale and straightened on a wooden block with a wooden mallet to avoid denting the ridges of the twist.

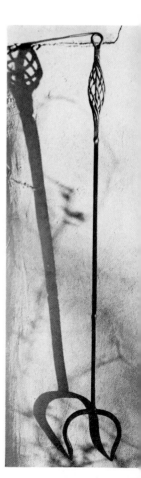

The end of the poker is pointed up in one heat.
Demonstration by Bruce LePage

The completed poker. By Bruce LePage

Kitchen utensils on a hanging rack. By Beau Hickory.

Photo, Larsen

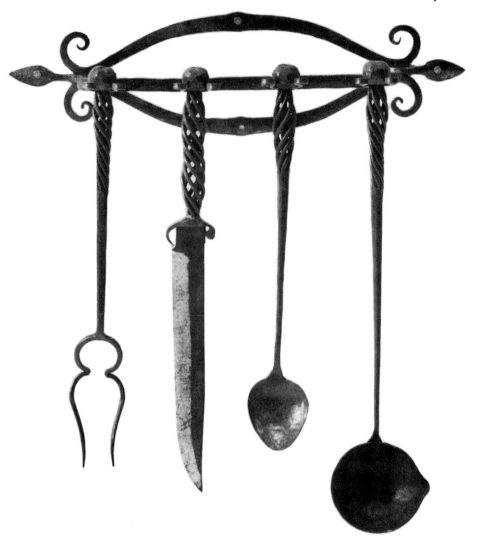

A fireplace poker with a basket top by Brian Anderson. The basket handle has six rods with a central straight rod.
Photographed at Southwest Spanish Craftsmen, Santa Fe, N. Mex.

Forged fire screen. By Larry Mann. Riveted and
arc welded. 24" high, 36" wide.
Photo, Sally Mann

Toaster, by Peter Ross, for use in a fireplace.
Forged from 3/4-inch round iron, 3/16-inch
square steel, and 12-gauge plate steel.
Courtesy, artist

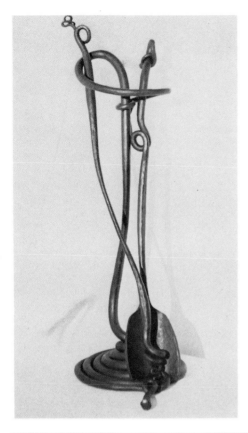

Fireplace stand, shovel, and poker using basket motif, coiling, scrolls, and collars. By George Martin.

Courtesy, artist

Above, left:
Fireplace tool set; poker, shovel, and stand. By Thomas R. Markusen. Forged, twisted, and coiled mild steel, 38" high.

Courtesy, artist

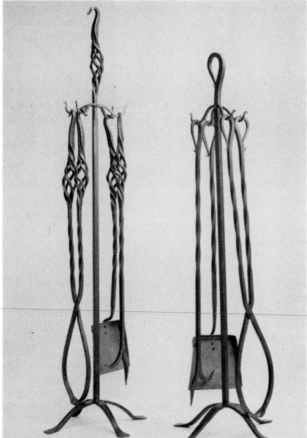

Fireplace sets by Dale Coughenour. The techniques can be easily determined; basket handle, twist, and so forth.

Courtesy, artist

Fire screen and fireplace set. By Nicolas Van
Horn. Wrought iron. Created for the study of
the K. Goodrich residence, Montecito, Calif.
Photo, Thomas J. Doty

Attached fire screen with opening doors, and fireplace set. By Nicolas Van Horn. Wrought iron. Created for the dining room of the K. Goodrich residence, Montecito, Calif.

Photo, Thomas J. Doty

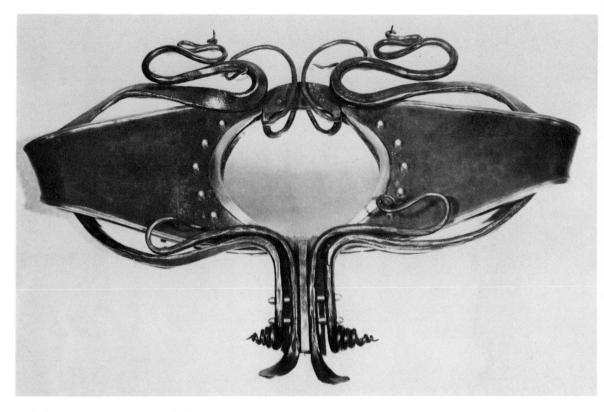

Mirror. By Joel A. Schwartz. Mild steel, Cor-Ten steel plate with upset edges, copper, and brass. 16" high, 18" wide.

Photo, Aaron Mascai

Mirror. By Robert Griffith. Mild steel forged with repoussé. 23" high.

Mirror. By William E. Leth. Brass and iron. 10-inch diameter.

Photo, Jean Levens

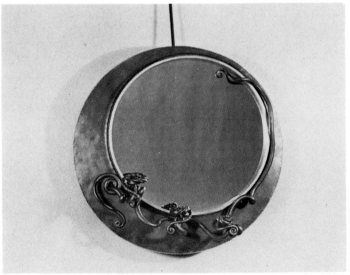

Mirror and coatrack. William E. Leth. Brass and iron. 30-inch diameter.

Photo, Jean Levens

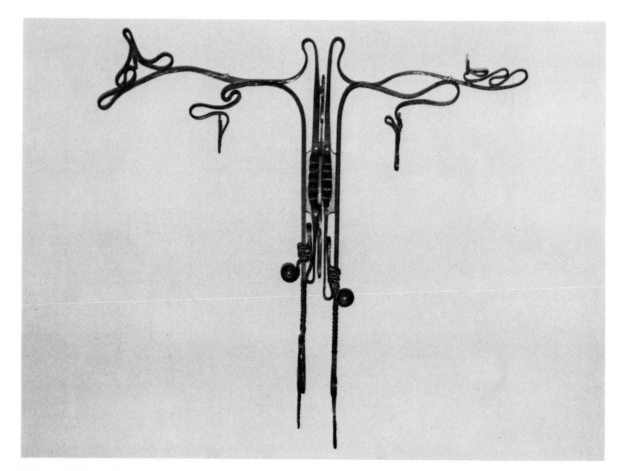

Wall tree. By Thomas R. Markusen. Mild steel and copper coiled, twisted, and upset. 48" high, 54" wide, 4" deep.

Courtesy, artist

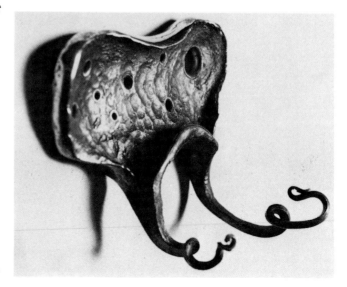

Small clothes rack. By Stephen Bondi. Mild steel with brass tubing inlay within the holes. 6" high, 4" wide.

Photo, John Jamiesen

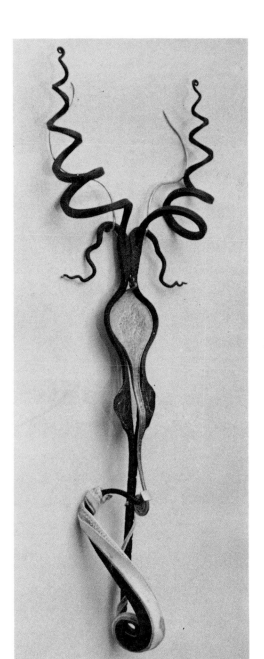

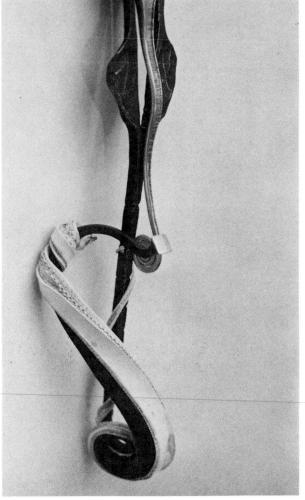

Wall-mounted clothes rack with detail. By Stephen Bondi. Mild steel, copper, and bronze with construction high-impact styrene.
Photo, artist

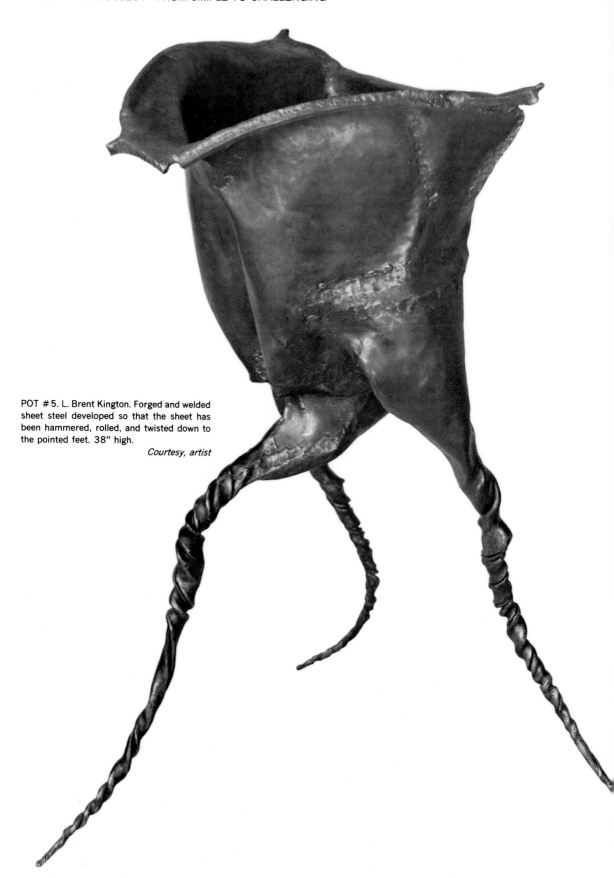

POT #5. L. Brent Kington. Forged and welded
sheet steel developed so that the sheet has
been hammered, rolled, and twisted down to
the pointed feet. 38" high.

Courtesy, artist

Architecture

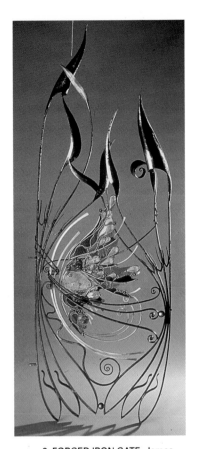

1. IL CANCELLO DEI GLADIOLI (GLADIOLA GATES). Alessandro Mazzucotelli (1865-1938). Forged iron gate (one of a pair) by a master ironworker of the Art Nouveau style who heralded a new direction in ironwork for the times and remains an inspiration for the modern ironworker. First shown at the 1906 International Exhibition of Decorative Arts in Milan, Italy. 1904-5. 14' high, 10' wide. *Collection: Il Museo di Arte Moderna Carlo Rizzarda in Feltre, Italy. Photo and courtesy, Stephen Bondi*

2. FORGED IRON GATE. James Hubbell. Forged iron, glass and brass. 7'6" high, 3' wide. 1985. *Courtesy, artist*

3. GATE OF THE CATS. E. A. Chase. Forged steel and stainless steel. 11' high, 18' wide. 1986. Los Gatos, California. *Courtesy, artist*

4. ENTRY GATE. Tom Joyce. Forged Iron. Private Residence. Santa Fe, New Mexico. 5' high, 18-1/4' wide, 1-1/3' deep. 1989. *Photo, Anthony Richardson*

5. ENTRY GATE (detail).

Opposite page:
6. PATTERSON GATE. Jim Wallace. Ironwork designed and fabricated by the artist. Memphis, Tennessee. 1992. *Photo, Hud Andrews*

Left:
7. IGUANA GATES. Jeffrey Funk. Forged of stainless steel, bronze, brass and copper. St. Thomas, V.I. 9' high, 9' wide. 1992. *Photo, Marshall Noice*

8. RAILING WITH NEWEL POST AND LAMP. Stephen Bondi. Forged mild steel with brass, copper and blown glass with electro-zinc plated, powder coated protective finish. Design inspired by works of Alessandro Mazzucotelli. Forging by Toby Hickman under the artist's supervision. Railing and landing 40' long; lamp post is 7' high. *Photo, Stephen Bondi*

9. NEWEL POST WITH FLOWER (detail). Mark C. Nichols. Forged 1ron. Used in the stairwell of a conservatory. 1987. *Courtesy, artist*

10. BALCONY (detail). Michael Bondi. Forged copper, bronze and monel. 1991. *Courtesy, artist*

11. SPIRAL STAIRWELL RAILING for Pat Kuleto's Houseboat. Toby Hickman. Forged mild steel with polychrome finish. Tuna-like fish are on the hunt swimming towards the ascending fleeing dolphins that form the balustrades. 36" to 48" high on a 30" radius. 1994. *Photo, Mario Parnell*

12. RAISED DINING RAILING. Toby Hickman. Forged mild steel with polychrome finish. Art nouveau design restaurant based on the style of Belgian architect Victor Horta (1861-1946). Railing inspired by one of Horta's bridges. Boulevard Restaurant, San Francisco, California. 36" to 42" high, 36' long. 1994. *Photo, Mario Parnell.*

13. STAIRCASE. Michael Bondi. Forged and fabricated steel stairs. Steel railing with a bronze cap rail and bronze perforated wirecloth. 1995. *Courtesy, artist*

14. TURICO RESIDENCE GATE (detail). Acanthus Leaf. Alice A. James. Forge welded steel. The full gate is 8' high, 8' wide. 1998. *Photo, Alice A. James*

15. ROOM DIVIDER. Tom Joyce. Forged iron. 5' high, 18-1/4' wide, 1-1/3' deep. *Photo, Nick Merrick, Hedrich-Blessing*

16. WITHERSPOON RAILS. Jim Wallace. Memphis, Tennessee. Forged iron. Designed and fabricated by the artist. 1992. *Photo, Murray Riss*

Large Sculptures

Left:
17. PROGRESS. Simon Benetton. Forged iron. 26' high, 8' wide, 8' deep. 1980. *Courtesy, artist*

18. HECTOR. Albert Paley. Forged and fabricated steel, monochromed. 95' high, 10' circumference. 1990. Private Collection. *Photo, Bruce Miller*

Left:
19. IMMENSE. Simon Benetton. Steel. Installed in the Arena of Rome. Padua, Italy. 15' high, 26' wide, 10-1/2' deep. 1993. *Courtesy, artist*

20. GENESEE PASSAGE. Albert Paley. Formed and fabricated weathering steel. 60' high, 13' diameter. 1996 Bausch & Lomb Headquarters, Rochester, New York. *Photo, Bruce Miller*

21. JIMMY'S SONG. Jeffrey Funk. Aeolian Harp: a wind actuated stringed instrument of forged and fabricated stainless steel and aluminum with iron used for the weights. 30' high, 4' wide, 4' deep. 1997. *Photo, Jeffrey Funk.*

22. METAMORPHOSIS. Simon Benetton. Forged steel. City hall outdoor stairs. Padua, Italy. 10' high, 3-1/3' wide, 5' deep. 1997. *Courtesy, artist*

Small Sculptures

23. TRACE. Fred Borcherdt. Forged steel and stone. 77" high, 28" wide, 93" deep. 1992. *Courtesy, artist*

24. XTAPOS-THE SOLE EATER. Virgil England. Sculptural handle of a ceremonial hand axe; one of a five piece presentation titled, "Artifacts of Atlantis." Forged and carved from one very large billet. 1993. *Photo, Virgil England*

25. SHALL WE GATHER AT THE RIVER. Christina Shmigel. Forged and fabricated steel, rust, pigment and gold leaf. The church is 24" high, 15" wide, 15" deep. 1993. *Photo, Tom Mills*

26. SPUR MARKER. Fred Borcherdt. Forged steel and stone. 12" high, 27" wide, 13" deep. 1996. *Courtesy, artist*

27. ANCESTOR FIGURE WITH BASKET
WEAVES. Brad Silberberg. Forged steel. 14"
high, 4 3/4" wide, 3" deep. *Photo, Greg Staley*

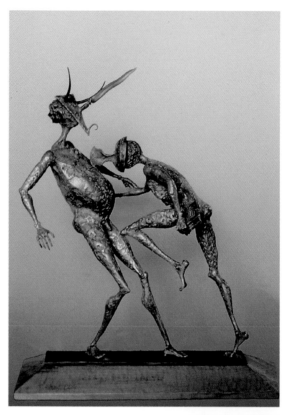

29. CONFLICT.
Christopher Ray.
Forged and
welded iron. A
work from the
Quadreverz
Series. 14" high.
1995. *Courtesy,
artist*

28. ANGLE RAISED SEAMLESS HOLLOW
FORM. C. Carl Jennings. 11" high, 7" wide, 7"
deep. *Photo, Hugo Steccati*

30. DREAMER OF THE DEER. Nana
Schowalter. Forged steel, with
copper and brass for color elements.
Spirit House Series. 28" high, 11"
wide, 12" deep. *Courtesy, artist*

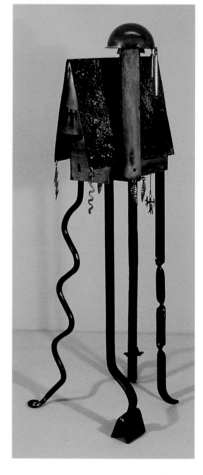

33. CORN MEDALLION FROM "AGRICULTURE IDEALIZED." John Medwedeff. One of ten forged steel agricultural motifs suspended in the 8-foot diameter inner rings of a roof truss system. John Deere Exhibit Pavilion. Moline, Illinois. 1997. *Courtesy, artist*

31. SIRENE. Corky Storer. Hot forged from 1/4-inch plate steel. 31" high, 24" wide, 8" deep. *Photo, Ben Van Houten*

34. NEW SPRING HAT AND FLOWERS WITH HAT BAND RIBBON. Elizabeth Brim. The hat is steel, inflated, forged and fabricated. Flowers and ribbon are forge welded. 7" high, 12" wide. 1998. *Courtesy, artist*

32. JUNGLE SCENE WITH CAPRICIOUS MONKEYS. E. A. Chase. Forged steel and copper. 42" high, 36" wide. 1996. *Courtesy, artist*

37. NINE PART WRAPPED WALL PIECE. Tom Joyce. Forged iron. 48" high, 48" wide, 1" deep. *Photo, Nick Merrick, Hedrich-Blessing*

35. CONTRA BASS. Kohgoro Kurata. Forged iron. 70" high, 28" wide, 28" deep. 1998. *Photo, Yoji Hatanaka*

38. RING. Jerry Hoffman. Forged steel. Five elements (the ring and four segments) combine to magnify the complexity of the piece to form a Celtic-like design. Made for the 1998 ABANA Conference ring project. 10" diameter. *Courtesy, artist*

36. PILLOW. Elizabeth Brim. Inflated and forged steel. 10" high, 12" wide. *Courtesy, artist*

Furnishings

39. LARGE DEMILUNE (presentation table). Albert Paley. Forged and fabricated mild steel, yellow zinc and Honduras mahogany. 34" high, 112" wide, 29" deep. 1992. *Photo, Bruce Miller*

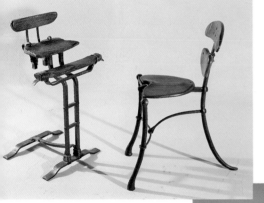

40. *Left:* CHAIR. Kohgoro Kurata. Forged iron and solid wood. 32" high, 17" wide, 15" deep. 1998. *Right:* CHAIR. Teppei Tsuitsui. Forged iron and wood. 33" high, 14" wide, 20" deep. 1998. *Photo, Yoji Hatanaka*

41. KELP BED. Russell Jaqua. Forged, repoussé, fabricated mild steel, wax finish. 78" high, 84" wide x queen size bed length. Center kelp leaf: 60"high, 48" wide. 1980. Collection: Richard Berger, Museum Associates, Seattle, Washington. 1980. *Photo, Paul Boyer*

42. BAPTISMAL FONT. Tom Joyce. Forged iron, bronze, granite. The wide ledge surrounding the font was forged from objects donated by parishioners of the community that commissioned the work. Each object represents an important memory from each person's past. 42" high, 72" wide, 40" deep. *Photo, Nick Merrick, Hedrich-Blessing*

43. BAPTISMAL FONT (detail).

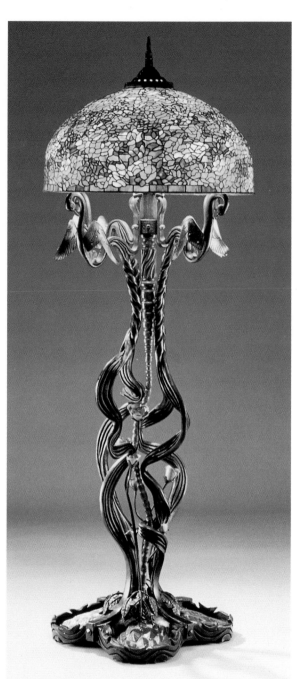

44. YELLOW ROSES WITH PREENING SWANS Floor Lamp. E.A. Chase. Forged steel, copper, brass and bronze. Stained glass shade by Douglas Kinklehahn. Number eight in a series of eight one-of-a-kind floor lamps. 6 1/2' high. 1995. *Courtesy, artist*

45. ENTRY TOWER HALL SCONCE. John Medwedeff. Forged steel and mica. 1998. 24"high, 18" wide, 5" deep. *Courtesy, artist*

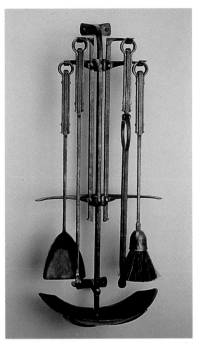

47. WALL-HUNG FIRE TOOLS. Tom Joyce. Forged iron. 36" high, 10" wide, 10" deep. *Photo, Michael Tincher*

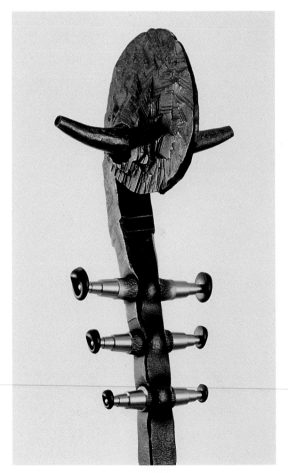

46. FUSION: L3-S1 (Coat Rack Detail). Stephen Bondi. Forged steel and bronze. The full rack curves like a spine and was inspired by the artist's need for a spinal fusion of vertebrae L3-S1. Assisted by Renato Ferrari. Detail: 22" high, 12" square; full stand is 7' high. *Courtesy, artist*

48. ETERNAL STRUGGLE FIREPLACE SET (detail of dragon base). Ward Grossman. Base is a dragon. Forged, carved and coiled using 4- x 4-inch. bar steel. Browned with nitric acid and hydrochloric solution. 1998. *Courtesy, artist.*

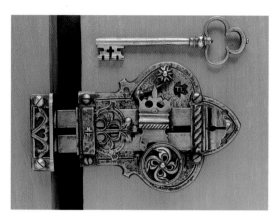

51. LOCK AND KEY. Tom Latané. All parts, including bolts and screws, were hand made of mild steel with a spring steel spring. Constructed for the interior door to a room housing a display of antique weapons. The key, used from the outside only, lifts a double tumbler and draws two bolts. 7" high, 4" wide. 1994. *Photos. Catherine Latané*

52. POMEGRANATE DOOR HINGE. Eric Clausen. Hand chased 1/4-inch steel plate. One of twenty hinges with matching hardware using the pomegranate fruit at the ends of the 1/8-inch diameter barrel. 12" long, 10" wide. 1998. *Courtesy, artist*

49. Door knocker, ELEMENTS. John Medwedeff. Forged steel created for the exhibition "FE, an Exploration of Iron Through the Senses." 26" high, 17" wide, 3" deep. 1995-96. *Courtesy, artist*

50. MOKUME GANE DOOR HARDWARE. Richard Schrader. Brass and copper forged, machined , sanded and polished. Mokume Gane is a Japanese finishing technique that results in wood-grained metal. 1998. *Courtesy, artist*

SUNDIAL #1. Joel A. Schwartz. Mild steel with a dial of brass inlay. 39" high, 14-inch diameter.

Photo, Aaron Mascai

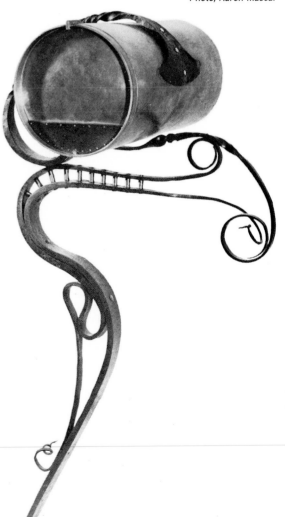

MAILBOX. Joel A. Schwartz. Mild steel with seamless brass tubes for decoration and a copper mail box. 39" high, 18" deep.

Photo, Aaron Mascai

PIERCING, PUNCHING, and CHASING

Piercing and chasing techniques are advantageously combined with ironwork. Piercing is the process of removing interior pieces of metal to create a negative within the design. The metal is removed by piercing a hole, then sawing or chiseling away the part to be removed. For sawing, a center punch, jeweler's saw, and a piercing hammer are used.

Punching involves essentially the same process. Holes and a variety of shapes may be punched out of the metal with punching tools which are usually made of rod steel and have different-shaped cutting edges.

Chasing involves cutting a design or a texture into the surface only (as opposed to punching all the way through), using various pointed chasing tools driven with a hammer.

The design is drawn on a piece of 18-gauge steel covered with gesso. The demonstration is by Liza Littlefield.

All photos: Aaron Mascai

LION PRINCE PUPPET. Liza Littlefield. Steel, plexiglass, brass, wood, and hair. 30" high. The steel has been pierced and chased.

A center punch is used to make an indentation in the sheet metal that will accept the drill bit and prevent it from slipping.

The drill bit is placed in the steel, and the hole is started that will be used to accept the jeweler's saw blade.

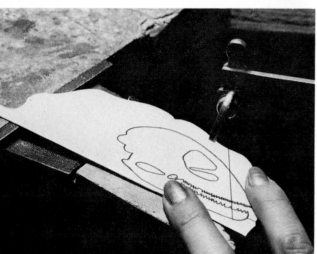 

The saw is in position, the blade attached to the saw, and the shape is developed.

A design is created on the surface of the steel with a chasing tool driven by a chasing hammer. The steel is held on a wooden blank with masking tape.

Demonstration by Liza Littlefield

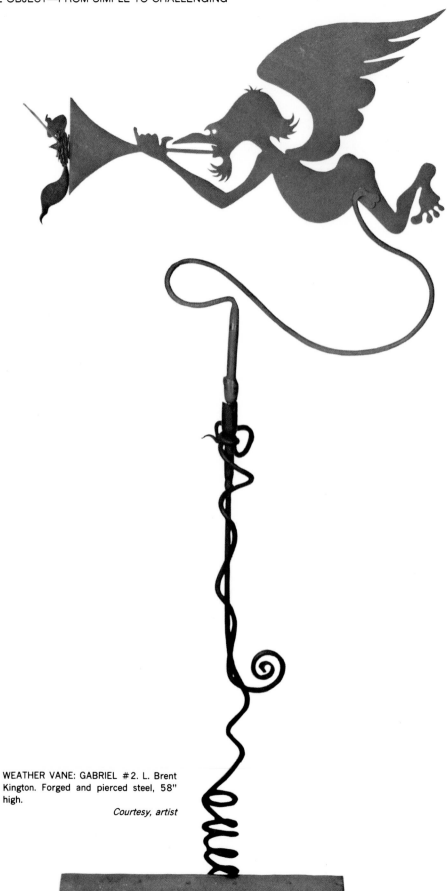

WEATHER VANE: GABRIEL #2. L. Brent Kington. Forged and pierced steel, 58" high.

Courtesy, artist

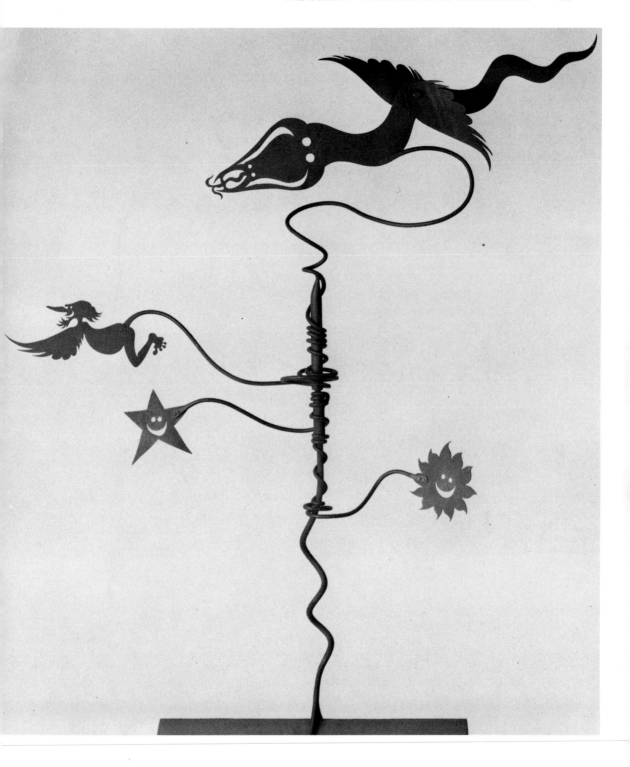

WEATHER VANE: ICARUS #3. L. Brent
Kington. Forged and pierced steel. 48"
high.

Courtesy, artist

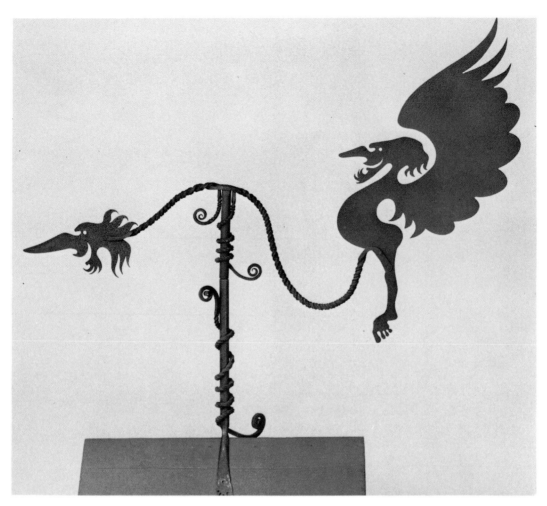

WEATHER VANE: ICARUS #1. L. Brent Kington. Forged and pierced steel. 36" long.
Courtesy, artist

Whirligig. By Robert A. Griffith. Mild steel,
pierced and chamfered. A browning finish has
been used. 11½" high 14" wide, 3½" deep.

Weather vane. By L. Brent Kington. Forged Cor-ten steel. 49" long.

Courtesy, artist

Weather vane. By Glen Gardner. Forged mild steel bar; stainless steel from an old stove top found in a junkyard has been pierced with a cold chisel. All sections are riveted. Vane part: 11" high, 44½" wide.

Courtesy, artist

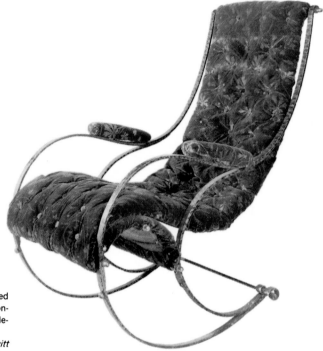

Iron rocking chair. Late 1700s. Associated with Peter Cooper. It is an example of functionalism and a forerunner of contemporary designs.
Courtesy and collection, Cooper-Hewitt Museum of Design, Smithsonian Institution

Headboard. By Erwin Gruen. A design exquisitely executed using the basket handle motif.
Courtesy, artist

Chair. By Max Segal. 45" high, 24-inch diameter. Made from 3/4-inch and 3/16-inch flat bars and 1/4-inch square bars.

Above, left:
Table. By Bruce LePage. Forged iron with hand-carved walnut wood top. The carved design in the wood repeats the design of the iron. 39" high, 22-inch diameter.

Wrought-iron table base with butternut top. By Sam Ogden, Jr. Approximately 48" long.
Photo, William G. Sargent

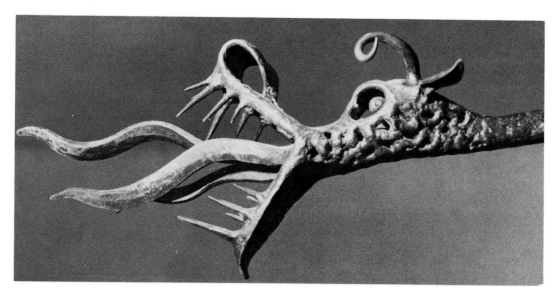

Dragon head (detail from a sculpture). By Christopher Ray. Carved and forged, then textured by dropping on weld metal with oxyacetylene. Detail shown, approximately 10" long.

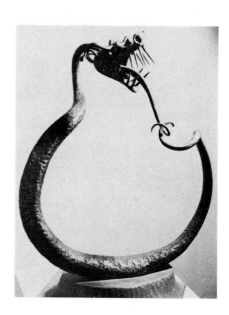

Sculpture with carved dragon head, elongated fabricated tongue. By Christopher Ray. Approximately 12" high.

Monster head, front view and profile. By Samuel Yellin. Detail shown approximately 15" long; head about 5-inch diameter.
Photographed at the Samuel Yellin Museum, Philadelphia

7

Carving Animals and Other Fantastic Forms

CREATING animals at the end of a bar of iron has piqued the fancy of artists in iron for centuries. Monsters, dragons, and other fantastic beings made by the smiths of the past are providing exciting stimuli. Contemporary smithies respect and emulate the inventiveness and imagination of their predecessors. First, they study the historic forms, perhaps try to copy them, then they strike out on their own. They apply what they have observed and learn by trial and error. There is little or no literature that shows how a smith created such forms: old blacksmithing books are geared to more practical aspects of the trade.

During the research and interviews for this book, it was fascinating to observe how many of the artists have achieved unusual imagery in the animal heads, dragons, insects, and so forth that they have carved. Only a few appear to have carried the technique as far as Samuel Yellin and the people of his workshop in the 1920s. The pieces in his museum could be studied for days to determine how they were accomplished; many are illustrated here for the first time. In addition to the Yellin Museum collection, scores of delightful figures were found in the ironwork at the Washington Cathedral, Washington, D.C., and many of these are attributed to the Yellin workshop.

Max Segal, who once worked in the Yellin shop but learned to carve as a young boy in Europe, showed several of the pieces he had created in copper based on his work in iron. One is illustrated on page 141.

Christopher Ray's work approaches the expertise of these past masters, and he adds the individualistic touch generated by his fertile imagination. More of his impressive figures and carvings can be observed and studied in his "Mansect" figures, chapter 13.

Eric Moebius and Michael Malpass provided the demonstrations illustrated in this chapter. Their work, reminiscent of the past, is peppered with their own imagination. They use the carved beings on lamps, sculptures, and door knockers, while our ancestors used them on grille endings, door hardware, fireplace screens, for example.

Usually, a carved form appears at the end of an iron member and is created by heating the bar and carving it—much as one would work a piece of clay. The metal is worked at bright red and yellow heats, then split, chiseled, punched, sawed, filed, and twisted. Portions may be fabricated such as long tongues and horns. The head can be given a variety

of surface decorations by engraving, chiseling, adding welding-rod drippings, and by using power and hand tools. Color can be achieved by colorants or by tempering the steel. Eric Moebius sums up the feeling he has for such work:

"Hand-forging steel represents the direct contact with materials I have always sought. When heated to a yellow color, the steel moves with the plasticity of clay and returns to a tenacious state upon cooling. The work period is short, so you must think quickly and act surely. The workability, color, and surface decoration possibilities make steel the most beautiful of the non-precious metals. The current re-birth of the blacksmith's art is producing work which follows no traditional forms. The past shows us many varied designs and techniques, yet places no restrictions. There is space for the totally new creation. The next few years, with the rise of the public's consciousness, will show the establishment of blacksmithing as an art and not merely a craft. Ironwork in the past has been an intregal aspect of society and should once again become a part of daily living."

Various animal forms by Samuel Yellin. The snake head, made from an upset and drawn-out bar, is chiseled to simulate the scales of the real reptile. For the ram, the bar is bent back to make the head, twisted and turned for the horns and ears.

Photographed at the Samuel Yellin Museum, Philadelphia

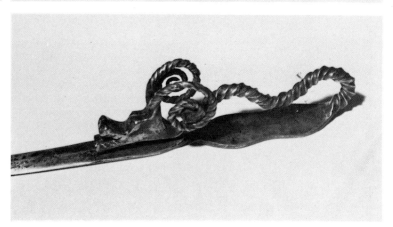

Fantastic flower forms with animal heads emerging from the centers. By Samuel Yellin. Each animal head is different in expression and detailing. (*Below,* detail)

Photographed at the Samuel Yellin Museum, Philadelphia

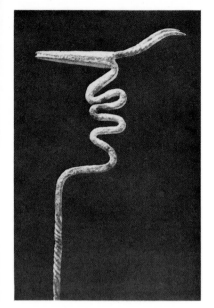

Dogon, Africa. Iron finial in the form of an antelope head with a curving neck. 8" high.
From the Wunderman Collection, New York
Photo, Lester Wunderman

Right:
Bakuba, Africa. Ox with drawn-out, upset, and forge-welded parts.
Courtesy, Linden-Museum, Stuttgart, Germany

Below:
Dogon, Africa. *Nommo* figure caught at the instant of metamorphosis into a crocodile. 3½" high.
From the Wunderman Collection, New York
Photo, Lester Wunderman

THE AFRICAN BLACKSMITH

It is always an extraordinary experience to be confronted by the work of African blacksmiths. Their attitude toward their material, what they create and why, results in a form stripped to its barest essentials, yet the statements are powerful in their simplicity. They can offer the modern smith a basis from which to carry on his own work. Analysis of the essential gesture of an animal or another form is created in iron almost as a line drawing with pencil on paper. Pieces are carved, chiseled, and fabricated. Simple bends and splits utilize the nature of the material to advantage. Once you are familiar with the vagaries of iron and how it reacts, you can begin to embellish any simplified form with features, surface engraving, and additional ''fleshing out'' as you like.

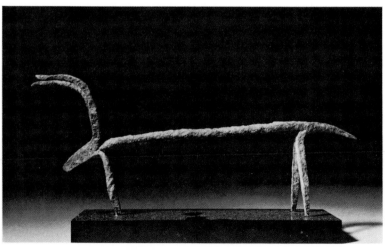

Right:
Dogon, Africa. Simply designed animal figures were placed on family altars and probably indicated the family's specific totem. 2 3/4" high.
From the Wunderman Collection, New York
Photo, Lester Wunderman

Drawing above, and crab (in progress). By Michael Spencer. 21" wide, 16" deep. Legs, claws, eyes, and nose are hot-forged from 1/4-inch mild steel bar. The carapace is from 1/4-inch deckplate scrap. The finished crab will be assembled to the center frame of a gate by riveting and collaring.

Photo, Peter Barrs

Animal. By Larry Jones. Forged from sheet steel.

Courtesy, artist

Animal head in progress and a finished head. By Tom Bredlow.

CARVING IN HOT STEEL

Eric Moebius demonstrates the step-by-step procedures for making the dog head (finished picture, page 138) from a piece of 1-inch X 3/4-inch steel bar. The entire procedure took about three-quarters of an hour including extra time while we photographed each step. Most of the work was done with the iron at a yellow or bright red heat. He worked fast and sure; his decisions for each step were made while the iron was heating. Once the bar was on the anvil, he knew exactly how he would proceed.

The end of the heated steel bar is forged over the edge of the anvil to form a shoulder . . .

. . . and when turned over it creates a head that is ready to be punched for eyes and nose.

The eyes are punched with the bar at the cherry red heat.

The nostrils are punched with a center punch. Note that the punching causes the area around the holes to spread creating the bulging eyes and nostrils.

The mouth is sawed with a high temperature molybdenum hacksaw blade . . . easy to do with the metal hot.

The mouth is pried open with a chisel.

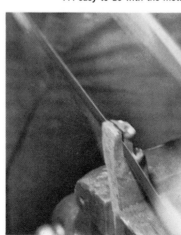

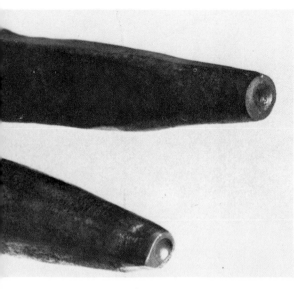

Chisels used to punch the eyes and nose can be made by the smith for any size and shape he wants: the top one is round; the bottom one has a round interior and square exterior.

Hot rasping can be efficiently accomplished with old, worn files.

The ear area is sawed into with the hacksaw.

A chisel is used to pry up the cut ear area.

The ears are split with the saw . . .

. . . and spread with the chisel.

Final shaping and filing are accomplished with a worn rattail file.

The teeth are cut in cold on the anvil with a fine chisel. . . .

. . . . and bent to look like fangs.

The finished dog head . . . by Eric Moebius.

Demonstration by Eric Moebius

Lizard with claws and chiseled back (detail of lamp, *right*). By Eric Moebius.

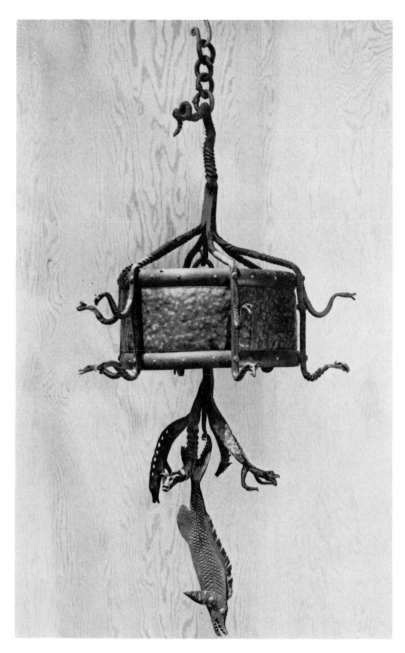

Hanging lamp with carved animals. By Eric Moebius. In addition to the carved heads, techniques include fabricating, punching, engraving, twisting, and riveting.

Snake, forged and carved. Seventeenth century.
Courtesy, Victoria and Albert Museum, London
Photo, Stephen Bondi

ENGRAVING, CHISELING

Engraving, or chiseling, is the process of incising lines, figures, letters, or other forms upon the metal to give it a surface decoration. Any sharp cutting tool such as a chisel, or engraver's burins, awls, or other pointed and shaped instruments, can be used. Other tools serve to texture areas. Florentining, a pattern of parallel lines, is done with a serrated chisel or a tool with multiple small teeth cut from a file. Fine details are engraved cold, but large areas, or deep-cut details, might be worked into the hot iron. A good source for material to make your own hot-working tools are the aerospace surplus high-speed reamers, which must be forged and ground to the desired shape.

Modern hand power tools such as a Dremel hand drill or a Fordham flexible shaft with a variety of drill bits are applicable. Combinations of hand and power tools offer infinite exploration. Chasing and punching tools already shown in chapter 6 can be used.

Engraving in steel can be accomplished with a variety of sharp chisels usually made by the smith of tool steel that can be sharpened frequently. The cutting edges can be flat, round, square, pointed, beveled, and so forth. They are driven with a hammer or by the palm of the hand. Engraver's tools with wooden handles can be used also.

Jim Wallace uses a beveled tool to create a relief design of letters. The metal being engraved should be held firmly in a vise. Large pieces can be clamped to a workbench. The design can be drawn directly on the metal surface, then scratched in with an awl to preserve the outline. Round objects to be engraved that cannot be clamped or held in a vise can be rested against a leather pad or a sandbag.

Eric Moebius lubricates the engraving chisel by dipping 1/4 inch of the chisel edge into cutting

oil, then turning the tool tip upside down and blowing on it to spread the oil up the shaft and provide an automatic oil feed.

Carved fish with riveted fins and an engraved body. By Eric Moebius.

Dragon clothes rack. By Jim Wallace. Carved head with curving horns and etched lines on feet and tail.

Dragon with etched details and twisted horns. By Max Segal. Copper. Some texturing was done with an awl. 5¼" long. The piece was drawn out of one piece of copper 4" by 3/4".

ANOTHER APPROACH TO CARVING AN ANIMAL HEAD

Michael Malpass carves an animal head using a different approach from that in the demonstration on page 136. He begins by drawing out the bar and shaping it on the anvil, but leaving the head larger than the bar.

The mouth is cut with a sharp chisel and then opened with a wider blade chisel. All work is done while the iron is bright red. The bar is held in a vise for this operation.

A punch is used to create the nostrils . . .

. . . and the eyes.

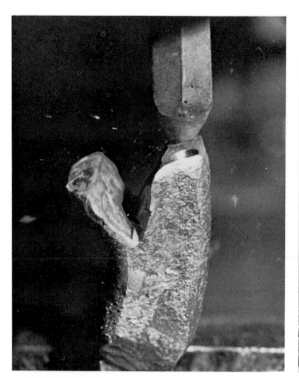

After the next heat, the mouth only is cooled so that the bottom doesn't distort while the ears are being chiseled.

Then the ears are quickly cut while the top of the iron is hot.

The teeth are cut with a chisel. The animal will be used as part of a door knocker.

Some finishing can be done with a rasp.
Demonstration by Michael Malpass

Iron door knocker with animal head. By Michael Malpass.

Courtesy, artist

Above right:
Door knocker wth carved animal head and forged body. The wings are welded to the body. By Anita Riley. 18" high, 5" wide.

Courtesy, artist

Right:
Gate detail. Washington Cathedral, Washington, D.C. By Samuel Yellin. 1928.

Door knocker. Sam Ogden, Jr. 12" high.
Photo, William G. Sargent

Forged-iron decorative motif attached to a wooden door. Washington Cathedral, Washington, D.C. By Jacob Schmidt, mid-1950s.

Handle for a doorstop at the Washington Cathedral, Washington, D.C. By Jacob Schmidt—mid-1950s. The animal's whiskers are curved to fit the finger for lifting.

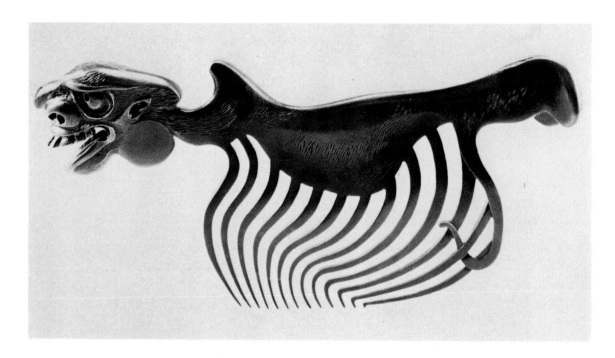

Two combs of forged and chiseled mild steel.
By Michael B. Riegel. Surface decoration was
done with a flexible-shaft drill and burrs.
Courtesy, artist

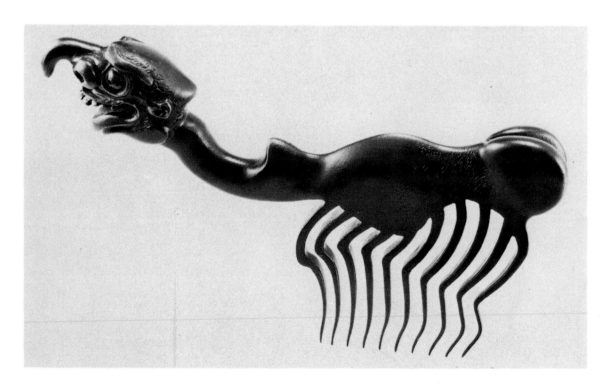

Detail of "Rocking Horse" on page 18. By L. Brent Kington. 44" long. Surface decoration was chiseled and chased.

Courtesy, artist

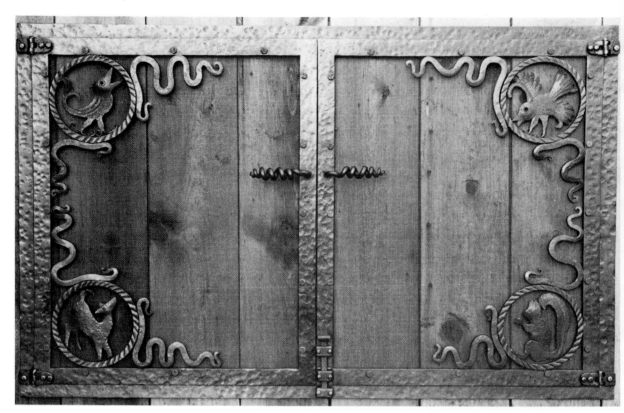

Fireplace screen with carved animals (*detail below*). By Eric Moebius. The surface texture is made with the peen head of a hammer.

Courtesy, artist

Design within a gate section converges in the center with six different animal heads. By Samuel Yellin.

Photographed at the Yellin Museum, Philadelphia

Two-toed gargoyle. By Michael Spencer. 7" high. Made from a 1-inch round bolt found in the scrap pile.

Photo, Peter Barrs

Heads of royalty. By Samuel Yellin.
Photographed at the Yellin Museum, Philadelphia

Andiron. By Sam Ogden, Jr. 24" high. Stylized wing forms are riveted to the animal body; head is carved.

Photo, William G. Sargent

Devil figure. By Samuel Yellin.

Whimsical animal forged from one piece of round bar . . . back part hammered flat and legs split off. By Samuel Yellin.

Photographed at the Yellin Museum, Philadelphia

Rooster. Circa seventeenth century. The
total animal forged and fabricated of iron
illustrates the virtuosity of the ironworker
in history.
*Collection of the Victoria and Albert
Museum, London
Photo, Stephen Bondi*

Gates, Grilles, Railings

IN the history of ironwork, gates, grilles, and railings have been basic to the craft because of their functional and architectural importance. They were integrated with the churches, mansions, palaces, and designed to fit the style of the times. Smaller objects were important to the lives of the people, but gates, balustrades, grilles were the items that concerned the historians. Therefore, we know more about them, have more documentation of them, and are able to study them in great depth.

Ironwork used for gates and grilles was most often referred to as wrought ironwork, possibly because the iron used was wrought iron and because the definition of "wrought" is "fashioned, formed." Much of the bending and shaping could be accomplished without heat forging, hence the term "wrought iron" is generic. Today, the definition would more likely be "ornamental metalwork," which is the way it appears in many contemporary books.

Large projects such as those shown must be carefully designed and developed using drawings and plans resembling those of the architect. Samuel Yellin, a master gate maker of the 1920s to 1940, whose magnificent structures may still be seen in buildings in New York and Philadelphia, lamented the use of iron where it was only for show and not for function, where the practical potential of the iron was ignored. He wrote, "A window may have a delicate grille or ornamental gate, neither of which has any practical use whatsoever. It is conspicuously placed to attract the attention of the passer-by; the ironwork does not play into its architectures and is not in harmony with its surroundings."

He suggested that an architectural sketch on paper could not do full justice to the ironworker's ability; often it was necessary to make pieces in the actual material before it could be illustrated on paper. He lamented the worker who slurred over areas which did not seem important or did not show. Instead, he said, "the craftsman should simplify the designs to meet the allowance given, in order to make the work in the best possible manner."

The change in twentieth-century architectural styles from traditional to contemporary can be seen in many of the illustrations shown. Some artists rely heavily on Art Nouveau linear plant forms, others work from images that are suggestive of sculpture and painting. Anything can be a design stimulus if the resulting object is executed with the greatest care

DELAWARE RIVER GATE. By Christopher Ray. Forged iron. 80" high, 72" wide. Installed at Penn's Landing Square. Second and Spruce Sts., Society Hill, Philadelphia, Pa. 1972.
Courtesy, artist

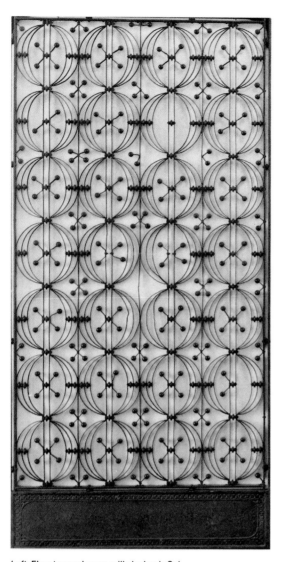

Left: Elevator enclosure grille by Louis Sullivan. 1892. Cast and wrought iron.
Courtesy, The Art Institute of Chicago. Gift of Kenneth Newberger

Right: Wrought-iron door for the southeast transept of the Washington Cathedral, Washington, D.C. By Howard Keyser. 1930s.
Courtesy, artist

and with a convincing respect for the material and techniques.

Says George Martin, "Craftsmanship is the ability to achieve a desired design, function or statement in a selected medium. Iron, more than any other medium, demands from the crafts smith a facility for making rapid decisions, a steady hand on the hammer and an accurate eye for its temperature. Its rewards are richness of color and texture, a variety of possible shapes and a long lasting life in combinations not achievable in any other medium."

Finishes for outdoor ironwork must be carefully considered, the metal must be rustproofed or otherwise protected from the elements while still retaining the nature of the iron. See chapter 5 for finishes.

Gate by the Benetton Studios, Italy. A radical departure from the traditional gate concept. 1970s.

Courtesy, Simon Benetton

The McCauley Gate, Washington Cathedral, Washington, D.C. By Thomas G. Bredlow. 1973. The gate is Mr. Bredlow's original design. Detail of handle: the leaf motif of the gate is repeated within the lock area.

Photos: H. Byron Chambers for the Washington Cathedral

Gate in progress. By Thomas G. Bredlow. A large drawing of the gate is mounted at left for easy reference to size and design. Detail of lock, *below* (in progress), with a carved lion face.

Interior of Tom Bredlow's work area with details of scroll and leaf designs from various jobs; some are "sketches in iron" of motifs with which he experimented.

MAKING SCROLLS BY COLD AND HOT BENDING

Lightweight stock up to about 1/4 inch thick may be bent cold with little effort and with the aid of a vise for securing ends. A bar can be twisted by placing one end of the bar in the vise, placing a wrench near the top and turning. The length of the metal decreases when it is twisted so that an allowance should be made when figuring the length required. Bends utilize length also, so generally an allowance of one half the thickness of the bar must be figured onto the length for each bend. When bending, an allowance must also be made for the natural springback in the metal.

Twists, scrolls, and bends can yield infinite variety to ironwork. The parts can be fabricated by welding, joining with collars, rivets, and other types of joints as illustrated in the examples throughout the book. Collars, wrappings, and joining members can be chiseled for more decorative effects; traditional accompaniments such as leaves, fruits, and other carved items can be added. A more contemporary look is the use of pieces of other metals turned on a lathe as in the examples by Thomas Markusen and Albert Paley.

Twists and scrolls can be designed combining cold bending and hot forging technqiues; ends of scrolls can be splayed, fluted, made wider like a fishtail, snubbed, or made like a ribbon. The forged end should be accomplished before placing the metal in a scroll jig. Sometimes you will have to create a scroll jig to fit, or you may be able to bend the tip around with hammer or pliers and position the tip so that the remainder of the curve can be created in the jig.

A wide variety of twist and scroll combinations may be studied in the historical surveys of ironwork listed in the bibliography. Additional procedures for fashioning them can be found in books dealing with wrought ironwork such as Gerald K. Geerling's *Wrought Iron in Architecture* and the three books published by The Council for Small Industries in Rural Areas, England.

A bend can be started by hitting the steel over the anvil edge.

The steel can be placed in a vise and close to the jaws to begin the bend.

Obtuse angles, more than 90°, may be made with a hand wrench.

Ninety-degree angles for squares may be made by placing the metal in the vise parallel to the jaws. To avoid grip marks, use vise jaw protectors or a vise with well-worn jaws.

Acute angles, those less than 90°, are made in the vise after the initial bend has been started. Some springback will occur in all these bends.

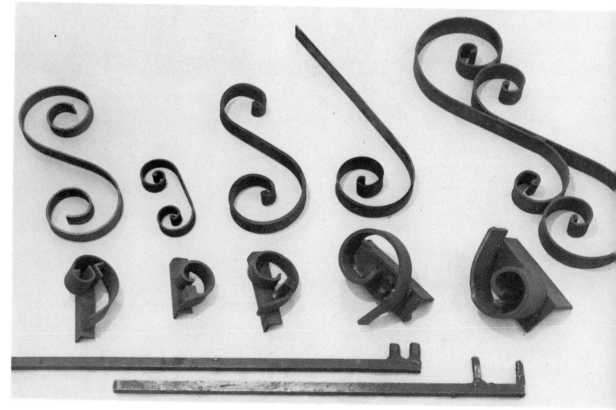

Scroll irons (or bending jigs) are used to make a variety of repeat, identical scroll shapes. The scroll iron is secured in the vise. Thin metal can be bent with the hands or a wrench. Heavier strips may require the bending fork (also called a scroll fork) which enables the worker to get the necessary leverage. The tip of the scroll may be flared or drawn out by hot forging before making the scroll, depending upon the effect desired. Scroll tools can be fashioned by the smith or bought ready-made.

The bar is placed within the jig held in the vise and the first part of the bend is manipulated with the hand.

A bending fork is applied for additional leverage.

Depending upon the design and the shape of the jig, the steel strip is moved down.

When both ends are to be bent to make a reverse scroll, the bending procedure is repeated at each end. One curve blends smoothly into the other.

George Martin

A special jig, built by the craftsman, fashions large circles. It consists of a square post and a piece of wood bolted to the base of the jig. The metal is placed between the post and the wood and bent all the way around for a perfect circle.

Tools and demonstration by
J. Guadalupe Benitez

A homemade bending jig held in the hardy hole is used with a split-ended bending fork and special leverage tool by E. A. Chase. He creates twists in long pieces of flat 2 X 1/4-inch bar.

The tip is placed between the posts and pulled around with the aid of the bending fork.

A slotted twisting tool is placed in the end opposite to the one held in the vise and pipes are placed over the handles for additional leverage. The tools is turned . . .

. . . resulting in a twisted bar bent without heat, using lots of muscle. This is good for wide twists.

Twists can also be made cold by improvised mechanical means. A regular twist is accomplished along a twenty-foot bar in about half an hour, using the transmission of an old truck at one end with the opposite end clamped in a vise. The slow turning by the geared-down motor results in a gentle, even twist. The longer the bar turns, the closer the twists.

By J. Guadalupe Benitez

Scrolls and other shapes can also be formed on various industrial bending machines that have interchangeable jigs for altering the radii of the scroll. They are versatile for narrow strips and rounds of metal (*left*) or for wide pieces (*right*). The metal strip is placed between the posts which can be put in any of the holes for different settings. An interchangeable center jig alters the size of the bend.

MAKING A SCROLL WITH HOT METAL

Blunt end scrolls are easy to form cold in a jig as shown in the previous demonstrations. But more decorative and inventive shapes are made by forging the ends hot and then shaping the bar around the jig either hot or cold. George Martin demonstrates the procedure for fashioning a fishtail scroll.

The end is flattened and drawn out.

A split is begun by hammering the end on a hot chisel mounted in the hardy hole.

The split is cut up further.

The end is held off the anvil edge and curled up with the hammer.

The scroll ends are further curled.

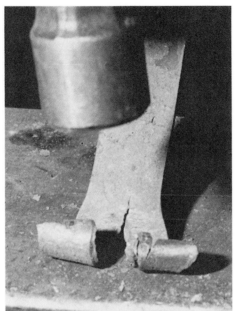

The fishtail scroll is placed on a jig designed for the purpose, and the end is held against the form with pliers as the bar is bent around the jig for further shaping.

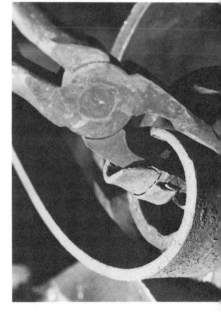

A double scroll with a fishtail at each end.
Demonstration, George Martin

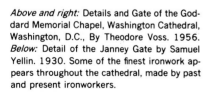

Above and right: Details and Gate of the Goddard Memorial Chapel, Washington Cathedral, Washington, D.C., By Theodore Voss. 1956. *Below:* Detail of the Janney Gate by Samuel Yellin. 1930. Some of the finest ironwork appears throughout the cathedral, made by past and present ironworkers.

EARTH GATE (*left*) and AERIAL GATE (*right*), by Christopher Ray, illustrate the contemporary departure from the traditional designs of those at left. These were installed at Penn's Landing Square, Society Hill, Philadelphia, Pa., in 1972.

Courtesy, artist

Entrance to the Solarium restaurant, Tucson, Ariz., by E. A. Chase. Forged and wrought-iron work done on site using an oxyacetylene heat source.

Detail of the cut areas with the scrolls worked from iron remaining in the cutaway portions.

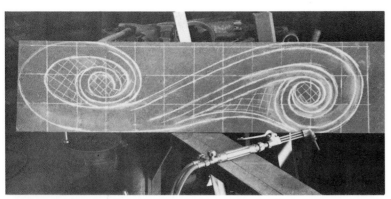

E. A. Chase photographed a demonstration as he worked, showing cutting with oxyacetylene and placement of a colored geode within the ironwork for a decorative detail.

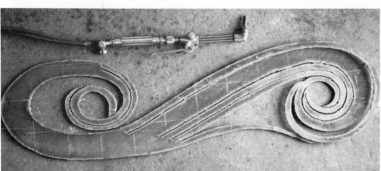

1. The pattern is enlarged from a graph and drawn directly on the iron. Cutting will be done with the torch tip. Cross-hatching indicates the area to be removed.

2. The pattern is cut and ready for forming and grinding.

3. Areas have been bent up and twisted by both hot and cold working.

4. Bezels are welded within the smaller scroll.

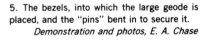

5. The bezels, into which the large geode is placed, and the "pins" bent in to secure it.
Demonstration and photos, E. A. Chase

Gate for Stuart Resor, Architects, Encinitas,
Calif. By E. A. Chase.

Photo, Jan Stewart

Gate. By Dieter Müller-Stach. For a residence
in Newport Beach, Calif.

Courtesy, artist

Above and below: Gates. By Benetton Studios, Italy.

Courtesy, Simon Benetton

Grille for the Downstate Medical Center, Brooklyn. N.Y. By Sidney Simon. 9' high, 45' wide. Bronze forged. Max O. Urbaun, architect.
Courtesy, artist

Detail of above.

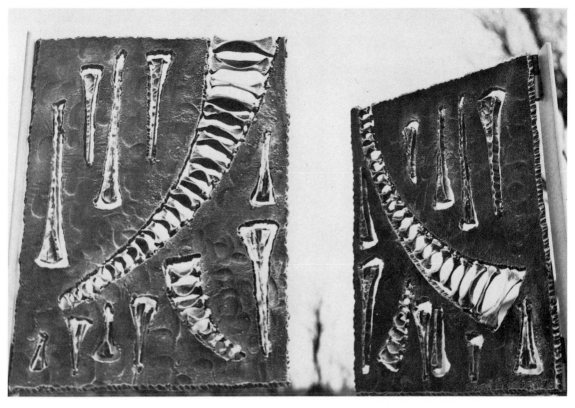

Exterior gate of forged and torch-cut iron. By Benetton Studios.

Courtesy, Simon Benetton

Interior grilles of forged iron. By Benetton Studios.

Courtesy, Simon Benetton

Stair railings and detail. By Benetton Studios. The railing, *opposite,* converges at the bottom in a sculptural newel that repeats the motif in the railing.

Courtesy, Simon Benetton

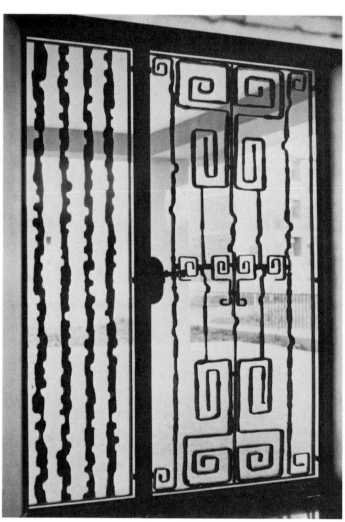

Two doors by the Benetton Studios.
Courtesy, Simon Benetton

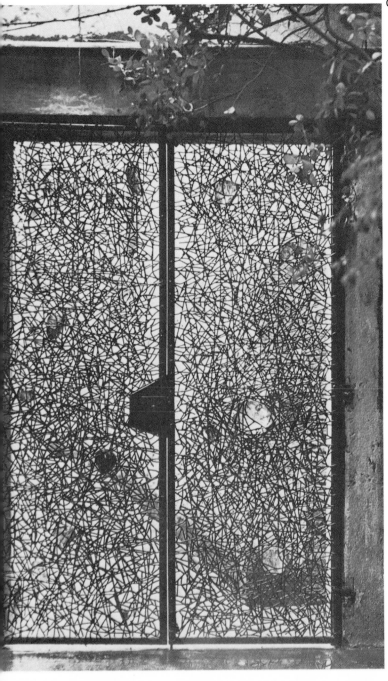

Bent and welded iron gate for the Guggenheim
Museum for Contemporary Art, Venice, Italy.
1961. By Claire Falkenstein.
Detail showing the use of colored rocks and
glass cradled in the iron members.

Courtesy, artist

Opposite: Architectural screen. By Thomas R. Markusen. Forged mild steel with lathe-turned brass elements. 64" high, 46" wide, 4" deep. 1974.

Photo, R. Armord

This page: Details of gate by Thomas R. Markusen.

Photos, D. Meilach

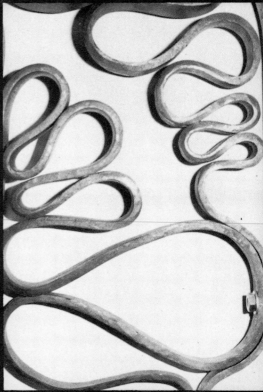

Gate. By Albert Paley. One complete section of a three section unit used to enclose a sculpture court at the Hunter Museum of Art, Chattanooga, Tenn. Total length 85'; height, 6' 4". Weight, 13,000 pounds. Photo shows a 32-foot long section. Sandblasted and painted finish.

Courtesy, artist

Two gates by James Hubbell for his residence in Santa Ysabel, Calif. Designs are derived from Art Nouveau motifs with inspiration from Antonio Gaudí.

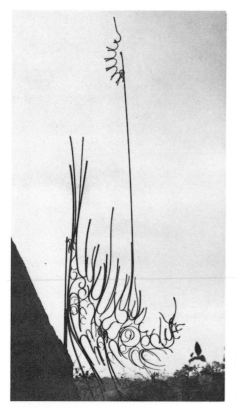

Portal Gates for the Renwick Gallery of the
Smithsonian Institution, Washington, D.C. By
Albert Paley. Mild steel, brass, and copper with
a sandblasted and chemically treated surface.
90" high, 72" wide. Weight 1,200 pounds.

Albert Paley and assistant during the fabrication of the Portal Gates for the Renwick Gallery (*previous page*).
Right: Bending a scroll on the anvil.
Below: Assembling the bent forms.
Opposite above: Assembling.
Opposite below: Mating a hot element to a metal form and clamping in place until cooled in shape. Forming was accomplished by hand hammering and by using a trip-hammer.
Courtesy, artist

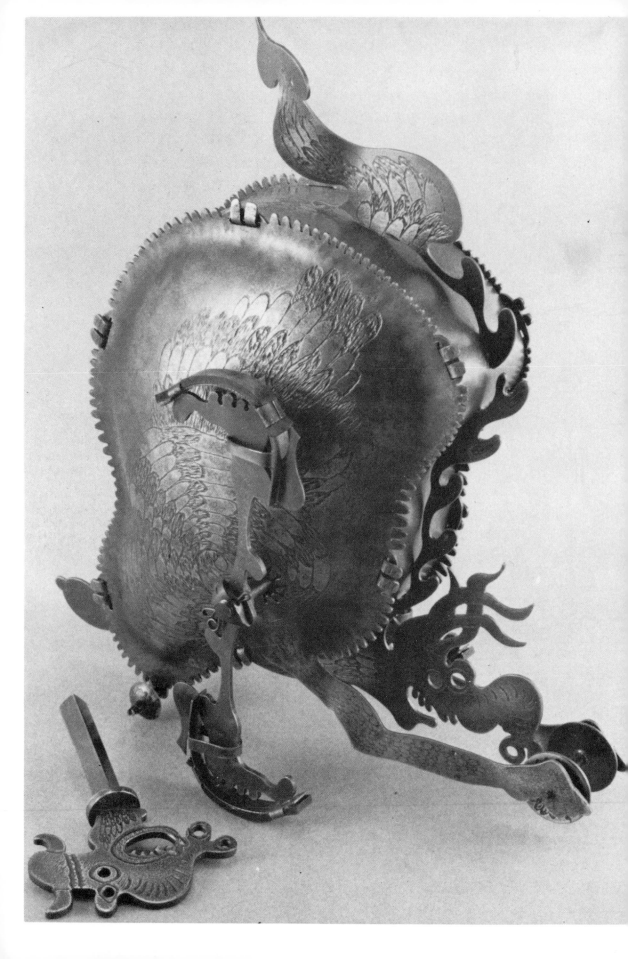

Locks, Knockers, and Other Hardware

DOOR knockers, locks, hardware, and mechanical devices have always offered a special challenge to the design concepts of smiths. Until the advent of cast iron, all decorative door hardware was individually made by the blacksmith or locksmith. A stroll down the side streets of any European country where old work still adorns gates and large wooden doorways is like a walk through an ironwork museum. (We were chased away when we tried to photograph a door knocker on a house in Florence, Italy. Perhaps they were afraid of pilferers with screwdrivers?)

While antique hardware offers scores of ideas to the contemporary blacksmith, often it is not in keeping with the architectural requirements of a contemporary building. The artist must develop a modern design idiom. The examples in this chapter attest to his ability to do so.

Hinge hasps, knobs, knockers, and doorplates are forged with a new linear concept. They utilize many metalworking techniques including chamfering, die stamping, etching, and coloring by methods frequently associated with gunsmithing. In some cases, the demonstrations are offered to suggest an approach that may require additional research for your particular purposes. For example, the introduction of bluing on metal can be further researched in books on firearms listed in the bibliography. It is offered to increase your awareness of the possibilities applicable to ironwork.

Techniques introduced in earlier and later chapters may also apply to your individual vision and interpretation of hardware; you might want to combine metals using methods in chapter 12 for additional shaping and embellishment. Punching, chasing, piercing, engraving, and carved animal forms are also used extensively for door hardware.

Exterior hardware must be finished to make it weatherproof; all hardware must be carefully finished so that when it is touched it will be smooth and inviting. It should be designed so that it is functional, in scale with the location, and compatible with the accompanying materials. The design of the metal can be repeated in the carving of wood, or the design of stained glass so that a motif can be carried throughout. E. A. Chase and Jim Hubbell accomplish this phenomenon beautifully in buildings they have completed in California and Arizona. They agree that commissions and architects that allow the artist a free rein to develop a total concept in various media are extremely satisfying but hard to come by.

Toy dragon with high heels. By Michael B. Riegel. Mild steel. Fabricated with tab and slot construction, surface drawing, wind-up motor. 8" high.
Courtesy, artist

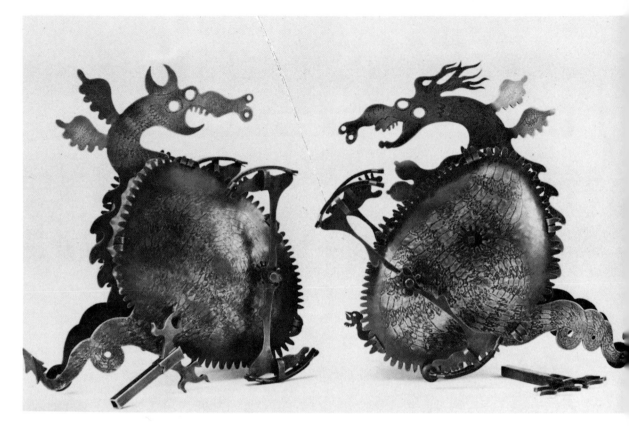

Two toy dragons by Michael B. Riegel. Mild steel fabricated with tab and slot construction and surface drawing with flexible-shaft tools. Left toy is 5½" high; the right one is 5" high.

Courtesy, artist

LOCK OF GIN. By Michael B. Riegel. Mild steel and carbon steel forged, fabricated and drawn upon. The facial features were made with dies: a technique illustrated on page 188.

Courtesy, artist

Doorknobs. By Michael B. Riegel. Mild steel carved with surface drawing. 2-inch diameter.

Courtesy, artist

Lock. By Michael B. Riegel. Brass, mild steel, and carbon steel forged, fabricated, tempered, with surface drawing. 4-inch diameter.

Courtesy, artist

THE DIE AND STAMPING PROCESS

Die stamping is widely used in ironwork as well as with other metal techniques. An original die is carved taking care to avoid undercuts. Carving may be accomplished by punching, filing, and chiseling with hand and power tools. A negative imprint in steel is made from the original die and cooled. Hot metal pressed into the resulting negative re-creates the design of the original die. In this manner one can make several imprints from the same die.

Demonstration by William Leth: Photos, Jean Levens

1. The end of a 5/8-inch round rod of tool steel is upset, and a face carved with a carbide die grinder. This will be the die used to stamp into another piece of hot steel. It is attached to a twisted wire handle while working.

1

2

2. The negative die blank (*top*) and the carved die are ready for stamping.

3

3. The negative die blank is heated to a yellow heat and placed on the bottom of the trip-hammer with the die on top. It is given a few hard hits with the 50-pound trip-hammer. A multiple-slot bottom swage is used in the hammer.

4

4. The blank now has the imprint of the die. The die can be used several times.

5. A railroad spike is heated and hammered parallel to the shank of the spike.

6

6. Now the negative die is placed on the hammer with the heated spike head on top to result in the positive die stamp (as in the original die) on the spike end.

5

7

7. The negative die and the resulting positive on the spike.

8. The spike shank is heated for drawing out into a tapered end.

8

9

9. Drawing out the end . . .

10

10. . . . and tapering and rounding.

11. Bill Leth, *left,* planishes the taper as apprentice Warren Spindler watches.

12. The finished door knocker using the stamped head.

Demonstration, William Leth
Photos, Jean Levens

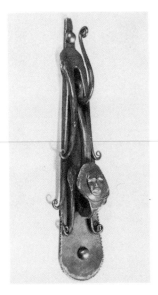

11   **12**

CHAMFERING

Chamfering is the process of beveling and finishing the edges of a metal object. In the following demonstration by Robert Griffith, the tools used are those already shown for chiseling, piercing, and punching, plus assorted files. The door latches at far right are finished by the chamfering procedure. Observe the use of vises to support the pieces. A comfortable working position gives optimum control over the tool and eliminates postural stress.

Tools used for chamfering are a jeweler's saw, flat, round, and three-cornered files, and hand chisels.

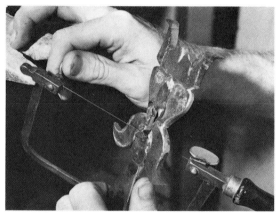

The saw blade is placed through the hole and attached to the frame. The teeth point toward the handle.

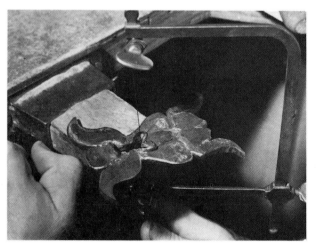

The iron plate is held against a block, and the saw blade pulled down to clean up the edge made by punching.

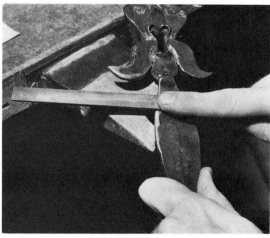

A flat file is used to bevel the edges.

A drill press vise can be converted into a horizontal vise by clamping it into a bench vise . . .

three-cornered file is perfect for hard-to-get-angles.

The finished door latch plates. By Robert Griffith

. and placing the flat plate within the jaws to old it securely on a horizontal plane while iseling or carving.

Demonstration by Robert Griffith

1

1. Brush resist ground on the plate avoiding brush marks. Dry.

ETCHING AND COLORING

Etching has been used since antiquity for decorative effects on armor, weapons, and jewelry. Basically, etching is a "resist" process; the metal is covered with a ground that protects it from the action of an acid. A design is scratched into the ground exposing the metal in certain areas. When the metal is dipped into the acid solution, the exposed areas are eaten away by the acid resulting in a sunken etched portion while the area with the ground has resisted the acid and remains the same.

Iron and steel can be etched by a variety of acid solutions. Typical mixes are:

    a. 5 percent sulfuric acid.
    b. 1 part nitric acid in 4–8 parts water.
    c. 1 part hydrochloric acid in 2–3 parts water.

Before etching, the back of the metal must be covered with the ground. Following the acid bath, the metal should be neutralized and washed thoroughly in water. Most cities prohibit dumping spent acid into the sewer without neutralizing it first.

In addition to acid, metal may be colored by processes used on firearms such as bluing and browning. Before using these solutions, all traces of acid must be removed; the ground can be cleaned off with acetone. Prepared bluing and browning finishes are available and should be used according to manufacturer's directions. In addition, the following recipes are offered:

2

2. The ground will resist the acid: scratch with a scriber the areas you want to become inscribed with the design.

3. Place the plate in a piece of stainless steel wire folded around so it can be dipped into the acid and lifted without handling with the fingers.

4. Mix acid and water in a glass beaker large enough to accept plate. ALWAYS pour the acid into the water; never the opposite. The solution will bubble. Leave in acid 15–25 minutes depending on the depth of the etch desired. Take out and check it frequently. Then remove the acid from plate by cleaning in water.

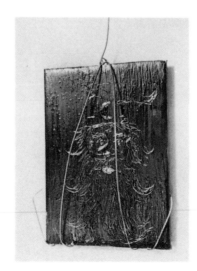

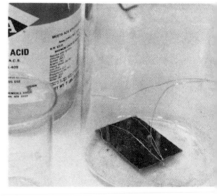

4

3

1 • For a tucker bronze:

Grease the polished iron and expose it for 2 to 5 minutes to the vapors of a bath of concentrated hydrochloric acid. Coat the iron with Vaseline and heat until the Vaseline decomposes.

2 • For a blue finish:

Boil a solution of 8 ounces sodium thiasulfate and 2 ounces lead acetate per gallon of water. Dip the steel into it.

3 • Blacking steel; two solutions for dipping.

a Caustic soda, 8 pounds.
sodium nitrate, 1 1/2 ounces.
sodium dichromate, 1 1/2 ounces to one gallon of water used boiling

b Caustic soda, 80 ounces per gallon.
potassium nitrate, 30 ounces per gallon.
potassium nitrate, 20 ounces per gallon of water used boiling.

5. Prepared finishes for coloring steel can be purchased where firearms are sold or through mail order suppliers. Use rubber gloves. Use acetone to clean the metal and a rag to spread and wipe.

6. The finished etched and colored plate by Robert Griffith.
Demonstration by Robert Griffith

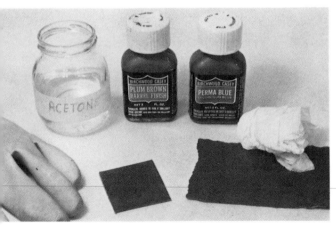

5

6

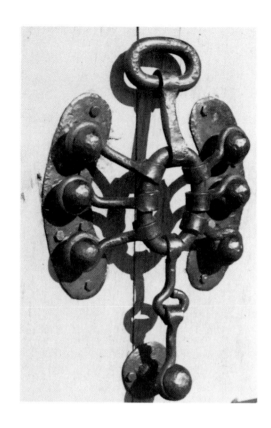

Two door knockers by James A. Davies II. These are forged iron that have been developed by first creating them in a wax model using the process described below.

Photos, artist

PLANNING AN OBJECT IN CAST WAX

A wax three-dimensional model of a proposed iron knocker or other object is more descriptive than a two-dimensional drawing, believes Jim Davies. It also enables you to determine, in advance, how much metal to use and the exact proportions of the parts.

Jim makes his model of micro-crystalline casting wax available at sculpture supply houses. Its dark color closely resembles the color of forged steel. It is malleable, yet stiff enough to hold its shape and to be shaped by hand or with a hammer.

Jim simulates iron rods by pouring "models" of wax rods in a two-part plaster piece mold using the following procedure:

1. Make a two-piece sprue mold using No. 1 modeling plaster and various sizes of wooden dowel rods from 1/4 to 1 inch in diameter. Put a separating medium on the dowels (Vaseline or other) to prevent sticking to plaster.
2. After mold is made and plaster dries, separate halves and remove the dowels. Reassemble the mold and secure with strips of old tires or other binding. Pour melted hot wax into the mold, fill, and cool. Separate the mold and remove the wax "rods."

The result is a stock of round wax rods of different diameters that can be worked with the same forging techniques as iron and used in models. They can be tapered, punched, riveted, upset, and so forth. If square rod is desired, hammer the round ones square. For simulating flat sheet, pour wax into a flat damp surface such as a tray, until the desired thickness is reached.

Courtesy, Jim Davies

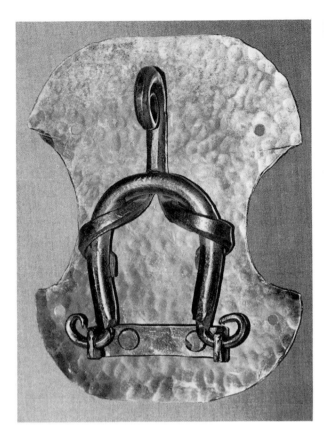

Right:

Door latch and knocker by Samuel Yellin, 1938, photographed at the Washington Cathedral, Washington, D.C. Forging, punching, and chiseling.

Left:

Door knocker by Larry Mann. Mild steel. Background plate has a peened texture; the knocker portion is riveted to the backplate. Wrapping was done by heating the iron with a torch.

Photo, Sally Mann

Handles and latch for a gate. By Erwin Gruen. He utilized the nature of the material beautifully and draws the scroll out sideways.

Courtesy, artist

Below left:

Door knocker by William Leth. 1/8-inch iron plate and 1/2-inch round bar.

Courtesy, artist

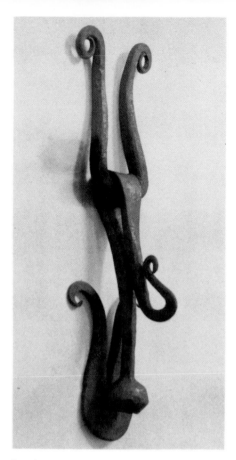

Door knocker. By Chuck Evans.
Courtesy, artist

Door hardware. By C. Fletcher Coddington.
The hinges are forged; the knob is a six-
strand terminal knot tied in nine feet of
1/2-inch mild steel bar stock.
Photo, Christopher Whitney
Courtesy, Kevin Cunningham

Door pull. By Stephen Bondi. Forged steel
and styrene plastic.

Photo, John Jamiesen

Door hardware. By Beau Hickory. Carving, punching, hammering into and stretching, and chiseling illustrate an accomplished repertoire of ironworking techniques.

Photo, Larsen

Door hardware. By James Hubbell.

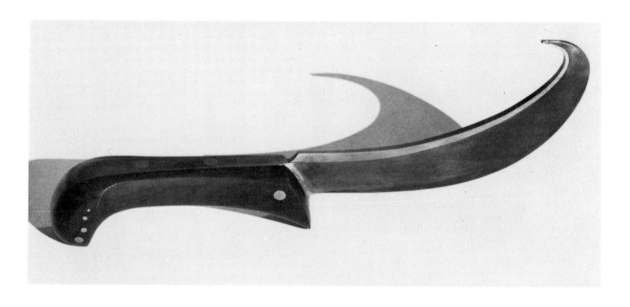

Knife. By C. James Meyer. Brass and steel with wood handle.
Above: Blade assembled and finished.
Below: The parts, showing the construction.

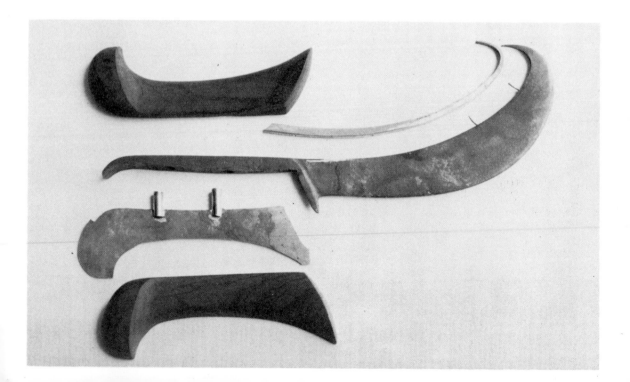

10

Bladesmithing for Knives, Choppers, and Scissors

FUNCTIONAL and decorative cutting tools are among the many items being created by the contemporary blacksmith. Often, he learns the processes of forging a piece of tool steel to a sharp edge and tempering it for chisels and other forge-oriented cutting procedures. After he becomes proficient with the techniques involved in working with tool steels (those with a high carbon content as opposed to mild steel), hardening and tempering, he can attempt to make a simple knife and then move on to more complex forms.

Knife techniques vary considerably from one blade to another; the function of the finished knife dictates the technique. Among the most popular knives is a general purpose camping or hunting knife with a normal 6-inch single-edge blade. C. R. Hudson of McDaniel, Maryland, offers the following discussion of bladesmithing, the procedures and drawings for making such a knife.

Steel

Steel tools are usually limited in purpose and are made accordingly with certain qualities paramount. For example, a wood-cutting chisel and a metal-cutting cold chisel are not interchangeable. A knife, however, is one of the few steel tools that is crafted to accomplish a great variety of tasks, for it is often a one-piece tool kit to a camper, hunter, or soldier. Consequently, the steel blade must have its properties modified for many extremes. A blade that will hold a fine cutting edge almost indefinitely must be tempered very hard, and thus it loses the ability to chop, pry, dig, hammer, open tin cans, and so on, without chipping or breaking. A blade tempered soft enough to accomplish these ends would not hold an edge long enough to be properly termed a knife; therefore, the dilemma of the bladesmith: a happy medium.

Before consistent cast steel first became available to the smith, the happy medium was achieved in the logical—yet difficult—and time-consuming method of smelting true Damascus (see chapter 11) ingots or forge-welding the imitation Damascus bars of iron and steel. The resulting blades could be as flexible as iron and yet as hard and resilient as steel. There is still controversy regarding the relative merits of true Damascus blades versus tempered carbon steel cutlery.

Iron blended with approximately one percent carbon was the traditional medium for knife blades, and only in the last fifty years or so has it been improved upon. Additions of vanadium, tungsten, molybdenum, manganese, chromium, and silicon create qualities far surpassing those of plain carbon steel. These elements also increase the smith's problems and can contribute to disastrous results if the steel is not properly treated. The smiths of old could simply fish through their scrap pile for a piece of carbon steel. Now it is hard to approach a rusty pile of metal with confidence unless you have an advanced degree in metallurgy.

The "perfect" blade would have to include the right proportions of alloy and be forged, hardened, and tempered within exact temperature specifications for this particular blend. Unfortunately, this would involve equipment which even a professional blacksmith seldom has; so a compromise with economics results in "rule of thumb" techniques. These are usually sufficient to create a blade with qualities still superior to commercially available knives. Commercial blades are heat-treated in large batches and tempered to a single temperature; the back edge, point, tang, and cutting edge are all the same degree of hardness. Handmade blades can be individually treated so that the back edge is springy, the point somewhat softer than the cutting edge, the tang fairly soft, and the cutting edge hardest of all. Thus the ideal, all-purpose blade can only be crafted by hand and eye.

The steel chosen by the novice bladesmith could be of several kinds and from many sources. The easiest and most reliable source is a steel supply house where you know exactly what you are buying and can readily determine how to handle it. But many craftsmen successfully discover their raw material in the junkyards and metal scrap bins. Leaf springs from an automobile or carriage are medium to high in carbon; the more vintage ones have little or no additives in the steel, which makes them an excellent first choice. Coil springs are equally good, but additional forging is necessary to change the shape from round to flat. Old files with *all the teeth ground off* can result in a good, hard blade if springiness is not too important. Sections of old two-man crosscut saws or circular saws are good if a means of cutting out a piece for the size knife you want to make is available; modern saws have too much tungsten for ease of forging.

When purchasing tool steel, a piece of "0–1" or "W–2" is the best choice for it has an excellent blend of alloys, yet handles much like pure carbon steel. Since it is easily available, most smiths have 0–1 tool steel on hand for toolmaking: therefore, it is used in the following example.

Forging

After selecting a piece of tool steel, you should check it for carbon content on a grinding wheel. The tang end of a file held to the wheel should show approximately the same type and amount of sparks. The piece can then be cut or forged to a rectangular shape 6 inches by 1 inch by 1/4 inch (for a knife which, when completed, will have a 6-inch blade and 4 1/2-inch handle).

Build a deep fire with a cave, using charred coal. Green coal will release too much sulfur, which is absorbed by the hot steel, making it weak. Keep a layer of coal several inches deep over the tuyere and use the least amount of air possible. This will minimize oxidation and scaling of the steel. Holding the piece with flat tongs, heat to a cherry red color and forge a square-shouldered tang from the end 2 inches of the bar. Care must be taken to stop hitting when the color of the steel drops to a blood red, at which time reheating is necessary.

Just how much to curve the blade depends on the final shape desired because the blade will curve upwards naturally as the hammer bevels the cutting edge in the next step.

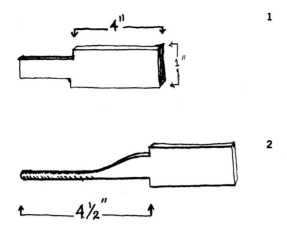

1

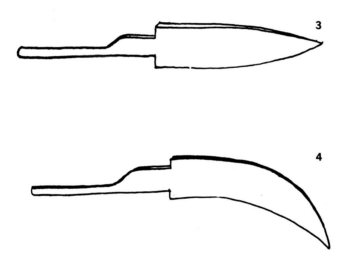

2

3

4

1. The first step is to forge a square-shouldered tang from the end two inches of the bar.

2. The tang should be drawn out to about 1/2 inch wide and to the original thickness of the bar where it meets the blade. From this width, it can be drawn out to a 1/4-inch round rod for the handle.

3. Reverse the bar and hold the tang in round tongs. (Do not quench the steel at any point in forging as this might harden it.) Draw the blade end out to a tapered point 6" long.

4. The next step is strictly hit or miss until experience is gained. Curve the blade down toward the planned cutting edge over the horn of the anvil until it assumes a similar shape.

The cutting edge is held on the edge of the anvil, and outward glancing blows of the hammer reduce the thickness by half. The blade is flipped over, and the procedure is repeated on the other face until the bevels meet to form a wedge-shaped cutting edge. *Each side should receive the same kind and number of blows* or the blade will warp during hardening. The blade can now be hammered lightly to straighten it or remove any hammer marks. *Do not, however, hit either edge vertically.* Not only will this dull or bend the cutting edge, but also the tightly packed crystalline structure will be destroyed that has been imparted to the steel by the hammer blows on the flat.

The final forging step, "packing," is done now by heating the blade evenly to a *dull red as seen in the dark* and hammering lightly from the cutting edge toward the middle all along the blade on both sides. Do not let the blade cool down to black while hammering, or cracks and uneven strains in the steel will develop. Reheating several times will be necessary to complete the packing.

Heat Treating

(1) ANNEALING.   Holding the tang with the cutting edge up, heat the blade to cherry red, or "critical heat." This temperature can be determined easily by touching a magnet to the steel occasionally as it is nearing cherry red. When the magnet no longer sticks to the steel, critical heat has been reached. Remove the knife from the fire and quickly thrust it deep into a box of wood ashes. Leave it in the ashes until cool (approximately five hours). The steel will be fully "annealed," or soft, at this stage. The shoulders of the tang can be filed perfectly square now and the flats and edges of the blade trued up. By drawing a somewhat worn file perpendicularly up and down the blade, a smooth surface can be obtained. Besides softening the steel for filing, the annealing step releases strains in the steel which could cause it to fracture on hardening.

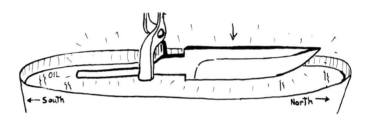

(2) HARDENING.   Heat the blade slowly to critical heat again; and, holding the tang at a right angle with the tongs, *quickly* lower the knife with *the edge down and parallel to* the surface of a container of oil (motor oil, vegetable oil, or linseed oil if commercial quenching oil is not available).

Move the knife around in the oil until cold enough to handle with bare hands. The entire knife is very hard and brittle at this point.

(3) TEMPERING.   The entire knife should be brought to a shiny metal finish with sandpaper or emery cloth in order to clearly see the oxidation colors which will appear during tempering. Two firebricks are placed parallel to each other on top of the fire and separated to form a channel about 1/2 inch wide. This will concentrate the heat along the back edge of the knife. Holding the knife by the tang *with the cutting edge up,* gently blow the fire to heat up the back edge first. A light yellow color will appear on the metal first which will travel upward to the cutting edge. If this step is done carefully, the yellow color will reach the cutting edge at the same time a blue color forms on the back edge with the other colors of the spectrum in between the two. The point of the blade should be a purple color; and the tang, where it joins the blade, should be blue. These colors travel very fast, and constant attention is necessary to avoid overheating. When all the colors are in the right sequence, the knife is plunged in the oil (or water) to stop the tempering. Often the tempering step is repeated one or more times for insurance. If the tempering was carried too far at any point on the edge (e.g., blue color on the edge), the whole process of annealing, hardening, and tempering must be done over. The final step is to heat the last inch of the round tang to cherry red and stick it in the ashes for an hour. This will soften it for threading or peening over the butt of the handle.

TEMPERED STEEL HEAT COLORS (0°F)

As high carbon steel is tempered, it will display these approximate colors at the temperatures indicated.

No Color	200°
Pale Yellow	390°
Bright Yellow	430°
Straw Yellow	450°
Dark Yellow	470°
Brownish Yellow	500°
Purple	520°
Violet	540°
Dark Blue	550°
Cornflower Blue	570°
Bright Blue	600°
Bluish Green-Gray	630°

Finishing the Knife

(1) To achieve a mirror finish on the blade, sand it with progressively higher numbered grades of sandpaper. Start with #150, then use #220, #340, #400, and, finally, #600. At each change of grit number, sand in a perpendicular direction to the previous direction. This will ensure that all the coarser lines are removed. Buff to a high gloss on a cotton wheel impregnated with buffing compound.

(2) A piece of brass, nickel silver, or steel will be needed for the guard and butt cap. (A separate book could be written on this subject, so I won't go into any detail here.) The guard piece must be drilled and filed to fit the tang where it meets the blade. A tight fit is essential. It is then silver-soldered to the steel, and care must be taken to avoid heating the steel to a point past its original temper (570°F).

(3) The handle can be crafted from a piece of hardwood, bone, horn, or ivory by drilling a 1/2-inch-diameter hole through its length. This hole

Knifemaker William F. Moran, Jr., uses a heavy spring attached to the anvil base to serve as a third hand as he cuts a knife tang. It prevents the steel from jumping up.

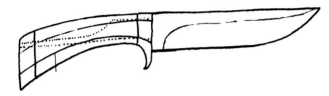
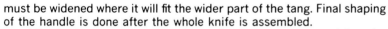

must be widened where it will fit the wider part of the tang. Final shaping of the handle is done after the whole knife is assembled.

(4) The butt cap, or pommel, usually of the same material as the guard, is also drilled with a 1/4-inch bit and countersunk slightly on the outside face. Or it may be tapped to take the threaded end of the tang if this method is preferred.

(5) Final assembly consists of filling the handle hole with epoxy and slowly sliding it onto the tang. The butt cap follows; and the knife is placed vertically point down, in a vise or on a block of hardwood, and the tang end is peened until it fills the countersunk portion of the butt cap hole. This will lock the whole thing together, and the epoxy will set hard in about twelve hours.

(6) The complete handle is filed and sanded to shape and buffed on the cotton wheel. Approximate time from start to finish for the entire knife—three days.

Most Common Mistakes Made

(1) Overheating the steel in the fire. Once carbon steel reaches white heat, the carbon burns out of it, and it is rendered useless. A very easy mistake to make, especially when the edge is thin.

(2) Hitting the blade when it is below a blood-red heat.

(3) Ignoring the annealing step prior to hardening.

(4) Working with a fire which is too small, causing uneven penetration of heat and subsequent fracture of the steel.

(5) Too many heats used in forging the knife. The least number of heats possible should be aimed for.

C. R. HUDSON

Knife by C. R. Hudson. Made by the procedures demonstrated. Also, refer to the color section.

Courtesy, artist
All drawings by C. R. Hudson

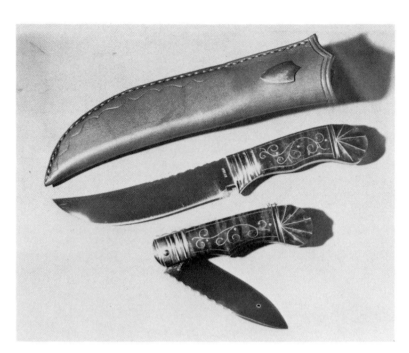

Two knives with leather sheath. By William F. Moran, Jr. Tool steel with silver inlay in the handles. Top knife is 11" long, bottom knife, 10" long.

Persian scissors of forged tool steel. 6" long.

Collection, Mr. & Mrs. Wayne Chapman, Solana Beach, Calif.

KNIVES IN HISTORY

Actually, the knife is probably one of man's first weapons. Early knives were made of shaped stones. With the Copper Age, pure metal was used for cutting instruments in Egypt, Mesopotamia, India, and the Great Lakes regions of the United States. But pure copper is relatively soft and brittle; it is hardened considerably by hammering it cold. The ancient smiths sharpened and hardened the edges of their daggers by careful hammering after they had shaped the pieces. Such dagger blades, dating from about 6000 B.C., were usually a short broad triangular shape as the blade had to be thick and wide to prevent it from crumbling and breaking while in use. As designs advanced in time and with technology, some had a raised ridge down the blade center to provide greater strength and rigidity. All had handles usually made of bone, wood, or ivory.

Tin added to copper ore was developed to produce the alloy bronze. Knives made from bronze were harder and stronger than those made from pure copper. By 2500 B.C, the Sumerians at Ur in Mesopotamia were creating fine daggers of both bronze and copper with ribbed blades and strong tangs. During the next thousand years, bronze knives were developed in Europe beginning in Greece shortly after 3000 B.C., advancing as far as Great Britain by 2000 B.C. and, finally, to Scandinavia after 1500 B.C. Each area developed its own special knife and dagger designs, and a study of knives makes identity by country and time period a relatively easy endeavor based on the shape, size, and decoration of the blade.

When iron was discovered in the Near East, knife design had developed to the point where the new material could be efficiently exploited. By 1500 B.C., the process called "steeling" was developed by smiths living in the mountains of Armenia. Steeling, or hardening, as it later became known, was a process carefully guarded by the rulers of the Hittite Empire. Only when the empire was invaded was the secret of hardening iron revealed, and it quickly spread. Fine iron weapons gave the Philistines their advantage over the Hebrews. It is believed that the

Tomahawk. By Michael Jerry. Handle twisted and wrapped.

Photo, Ted Davidson

giant Goliath carried an iron dagger or short sword and an iron-headed spear when he fought David. The defeat of the Philistines by the Hebrews initiated the beginning of the Iron Age for the Jews between 1025 and 975 B.C. In another hundred years, the Iron Age had spread as far as Britain and even to India, where skilled native craftsmen soon developed true crucible steel.

Throughout the centuries, man developed a huge assortment of specialized knives, swords, and daggers. Essentially, the tool was designed for its required job. Piercing knives have slender blades with sharp points. Chopping knives need heavy blades to give weight to their blows. Knives for precision cutting have short, sharp blades that can be guided accurately. The shape of the point, length, weight, and design of the blade and handle all contribute to a knife's effectiveness. And the blade may be only one-third the work put into making the knife because of handle design and decorative effects.

The scissors maker establishes additional problems from the knife maker. If scissors are to cut well, the blades should touch in two places only: at the joint, and at a single spot along the blades, wherever the cutting is taking place. The blades are made to twist or curve toward one another and, when completely closed, the points of the blades should touch. Both blades must be accurately tempered to equal hardness.

Today, one can walk into shops devoted entirely to cutlery tools, and the assortment is mind boggling. Most, of course, are machine made as the handmade knife is almost an anachronism in our industrialized society. Yet the intrepid craftsman, making one-of-a-kind cutting instruments for himself or for fine collections, still exists as one can discover in the following examples.

Persian scissors with drawn-out and bent handles.

Collection, Mr. & Mrs. Wayne Chapman, Solana Beach, Calif.

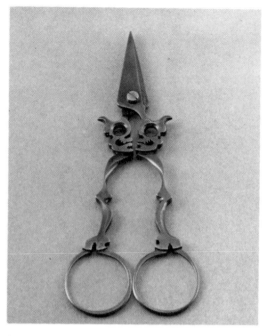

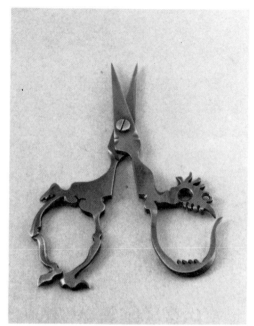

Sewing scissors #1 (*left*) 4" long. And #2
(*right*) 3¾" long. By Michael B. Riegel. Carbon
steel forged and chamfered.

Courtesy, artist

Pig chopper. By Michael B. Riegel. Carbon steel
and brass. Chamfered and tempered. 5½"
long.

Courtesy, artist

Food chopper. By Martin Kascewicz. Tempered iron with carved animal and chiseled design.
Courtesy, Art Independent Gallery,
Lake Geneva, Wisc.

Vegetable chopper. By Keith Dean Farwell Rowland.

Courtesy, artist

Food chopper. By Donn Williams. High carbon
steel with a hand-carved hickory handle. 6-inch
diameter.

Courtesy, artist

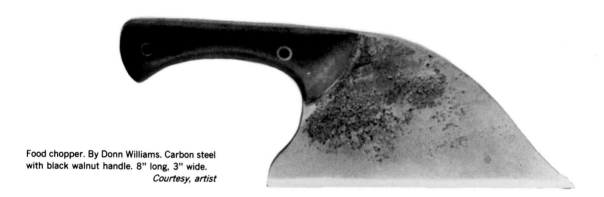

Food chopper. By Donn Williams. Carbon steel
with black walnut handle. 8" long, 3" wide.

Courtesy, artist

Winged sickle. By Donn Williams. Made from a
high carbon steel file. Copper wings added.
14" long, 10" wide.

Courtesy, artist

Four choppers by Barry Berman with different handle arrangements. Made from 3/8-inch-high carbon steel springs from junkyard, cut with torch and hammered.

Details of two blades above showing the textures achieved by hitting with the hammer peen and against the anvil.

Kindling hatchet. By L. Brent Kington. Tempered carbon steel blade with twisted handle.

Courtesy, artist

Walking cane with concealed dagger (*top detail*). By Rick Cronin. Mild steel, carbon steel, sterling silver, and maple.

Photo, Alida Fish Cronin

Kitchen knife. By Glen Gardner. Forged from a truck coil spring found in junkyard. 10" long. Serrated top edge done with cold filing.

Courtesy, artist

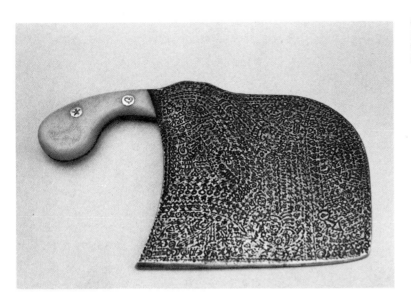

Chopping knife with bone handle. By Gary Noffke. Blade made from an old hoe forged, machined, carved, and etched. Sterling silver insets in bone handle.

Courtesy, artist

Food chopper. By Donn Williams. High carbon steel blade with pierced areas. Handle is vegetable wood with sterling silver decorations. 9" long, 3" wide.

Courtesy, artist

Forged utensils. By Donn Williams.
Courtesy, artist

Chopping knife. By Glen Gardner. Forged from
a truck leaf spring. 3½" high, 2½" wide.
Courtesy, artist

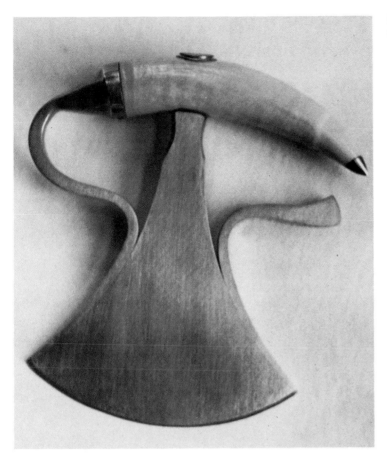

Chopper. By C. James Meyer. Steel blade with a horn handle.

Courtesy, artist

Sausage knife. By Rick Cronin. Steel blade with bone handle and sterling silver rivets.

Photo, Alida Fish Cronin

.35 CALIBER MATCHLOCK TOY CAN-
NON. Robert Griffith. (Fires .34 caliber
lead ball with black powder load.)
Damascus twist barrel of sixteen layers
wrapped and welded to a mild steel
core. Curly maple carriage with brass
trim, hand-forged lock.

Courtesy, artist

Damascus Steel

The following material and demonstrations have been prepared by Robert Griffith, Daryl Meier, and Jim Wallace, Southern Illinois University at Carbondale. The author acknowledges and deeply appreciates their valuable contribution. Photos by Aaron Mascai unless otherwise credited.

THE term "Damascus steel" often conjures images of magic metal. Most people equate it with steel manufactured in Damascus, like "Sheffield steel" in Sheffield or "Swedish steel" in Sweden, but beyond that, all knowledge of the material ceases. Damascus steel is not even made in Damascus; Europeans titled the material "Damascus" because that is where they first encountered it during the Crusades.

There were two basic methods by which true Damascus was made, both involved molten and semimolten metal. The first method is referred to as *wootz,* and was first produced in India. By melting a high carbon steel (1.5 percent to 2.0 percent C) in a crucible and allowing the material to cool slowly, some structural segregation occurs in concentric rings, roughly corresponding to the shape of the crucible. By carefully forging at a very low heat, the segregated structure became more aligned to the axis of the object. Selective incising or grinding was used to further develop pattern. After polishing, a light etch would bring the "damask" or "water" out of the steel in the form of light and dark areas.

Although research is lacking, a reasonable hypothesis as to a second method of manufacture also involved a molten material. Certain nineteenth-century Persian blades indicate that the material consisted of a stack of very thin iron sheets stacked together and "quenched" in molten high carbon cast iron. Capillary action would then draw the cast iron between the iron sheet and "weld" them into a single mass. This material was most likely forged very little since it would be extremely brittle at a red heat. Shaping was primarily a process of stock removal.

The true Damascus steel procedures described depend on the structures developed during a melting and cooling process that few smithies are equipped to undertake. For this reason this chapter will deal exclusively with pattern-welded material often referred to today as "Damascus steel," but this is not actually true Damascus.

Twisted knife pattern handle. By William F. Moran, Jr.

Photo, D. Meilach

PATTERN WELDING

Pattern-welded steel depends on the structure of the material for visible surface pattern as does true Damascus. The structure of pattern-welded steel is not developed by a melting and cooling process, but rather by a series of forge techniques. By forge-welding alternating layers of at least two materials which have different amounts of carbon, phosphorus, or nickel, a laminated material is made. Extensive pattern can be introduced into the material by further manipulation.

In the process of manufacturing any object, the smith soon learns about grain or structure in his material. This is especially true in the case of wrought iron, and to a lesser degree in modern steels.

In the early history of iron manufacturing, sufficiently high temperatures were not obtainable to reduce the amount of iron silicate (slag) by direct melting to produce a fine-grained material. For the production of most utilitarian noncutting implements, this material was satisfactory; however, for an object which required a finished or polished surface, the material had to be refined by the smith. This was done by fagot-welding the material and drawing it out a number of times. The result was a more dense material with finer particle and fiber size with the structures aligned parallel to the axis of the bar.

Old wagon wheel rims closely approximate what the early smith received as raw material. The fiber structure was quite gross as well as usually being red-short. An application of nitric acid (one part) and water (three parts) would reveal a gross natural damasklike pattern in wrought-iron wagon wheel rims.

By forge-welding refined iron in conjunction with a higher carbon steel in a series of layers, a definite laminated structure became visible. Early smiths developed this visible pattern and its appearance became the consumer's insurance of the proper forging of a blade.

The earliest known pattern-welded objects are swords and spear points of the Merovingian Franks and Vikings, the earliest being from a Roman site in Britain dating from the second century A.D. The principal location of manufacture is uncertain. Dr. Cyril Stanley Smith postulates that they were made on the Rhine, while A. Liestøl argues for Scandinavian and J. Piakowski in his article "The Manufacture of Medieval Damaskeened Knives" cites the possibility of their manufacture in Poland. Merovingian pattern-welded products are generally characterized by the decorative "damask" center section while the actual cutting edge of the blade is a single piece of higher carbon (.15 percent carbon) steel. A high phosphorus content also contributed to increased hardenability. Two pieces of wrought iron often sandwiched the steel edge. The methods of assemblage differ from region to region.

For some reason, pattern-welded blades disappeared from west of the Baltic around the tenth century. However, Piakowski has analyzed three knives, ranging from the eleventh to the fourteenth century, found in Poland. By the end of the fourteenth century, pattern welding was out of vogue in Europe and knowledge of the technique waned and eventually died. It was 450 years before interest was again rekindled with the experiments of J. J. Perret in Paris around 1779.

Metallurgy was a young science in eighteenth-century Europe and there were many attempts to reproduce the Damascus steel that originated in India. Experiments and research by the Frenchman J. J. Perret and later the German C. R. Herrman dealt almost exclusively along the pattern-welded line of investigation. Herrman kept extensive notes and some of the most important were his logs of material consumption and loss in the pattern-welding processes.

Perhaps some of the most elaborate pattern welding was done in 1817 by Degrande-Gurgey of Marseilles when he crafted a presentation sword which read *Premier Essai d'un Art Nouveau D.N.G. 1819* as an

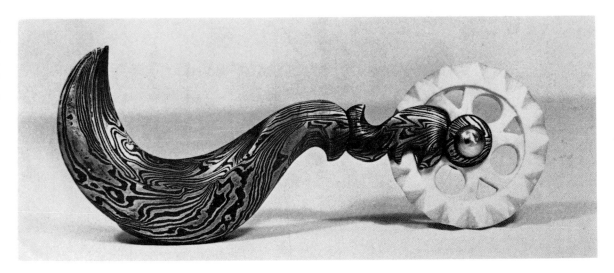

PASTRY TOOL. Robert Griffith. Damascus steel handle with ivory cutter and brass axle.

Courtesy, artist

Damascus-bladed ivory-handled knife (*detail*) by Daryl Meier. Knife is 8½" overall, the blade is 1½" wide.

Photo, D. Meilach

Table knives with pattern welded blade. By Jim Wallace. Each 8½" long. *Top:* Rosewood with brass. *Bottom:* Rosewood.

Photo, D. Meilach

By Jim Wallace. A composite blade made of nickel 200 and wrought iron with a high carbon inserted edge. Approximately 250 layers. Made by incision and reforging.

Photo, artist

integral part of the blade. A few years earlier, another Frenchman, named Clouet, manufactured a bar of steel which, when sectioned perpendicular to the axis anywhere, revealed the word *Liberté*. Pattern-welded material was produced commercially in Europe until the start of World War II. Damascus twist shotgun barrels were manufactured until about 1900 and some knives were produced in Germany for some time after that.

The Kris

The European world did not hold a monopoly on pattern-welded steel. Two other cultures which employed extensive use of the technique were the Malayan and Japanese. In the Malaya Archipelago, the Malay and Indonesian people have developed a unique and extremely exquisite blade known as the "kris," which can be dated as far back as A.D. 1342 and most likely much earlier. By the end of the fifteenth century, the kris was adopted all over Malay and some parts of the Philippines. Essentially, the kris is a short pattern-welded-edged weapon, usually with a wavy blade. Krises are noted for their sinuous, graceful curves, and it is interesting that the curves are always counted alternately and are always an odd number; the greater the number of curves, the higher the rank of the owner. The most common number was seven.

The material used in the manufacture of the blades sometimes appears to contain some layering with meteoric iron. During the late nineteenth century, nickel steels were popularly used in making the kris. Some twentieth-century authorities note that a European "stainless steel" was used, whatever that was.

The Japanese Sword

One of the most advanced achievements in pattern-welded steel is

Ladder pattern blade dagger. By William F. Moran, Jr. High carbon vanadium steel. Leather sheath with silver.
Photo, D. Meilach

evident in the Japanese sword which involved extremely sophisticated forge practices in control of composition, heat treatment, and in a very refined finish which reflected the structure of the blade.

As with many other things, the method of making swords was imported from China and then developed beyond recognition. By repeated welding and forging, a very fine grained, layered material was developed, and as early as A.D. 650 Japanese swords showed a definite lamellar structure which almost certainly indicated intentional incorporation of at least two different metals. By the thirteenth century the blades were so finely and intricately developed that they were being polished to bring out the wood-grained damask in the metal and the intricate interface between the hardened steel edge and the softer iron body.

The heat treatment was a sophisticated process involving the application of a refractory layer over the body of the blade. Thus, when quenched, the exposed part (edge) became hardened while the covered parts (body) stayed soft and flexible. By selective application and shaping of the refractory, a decorative watermark could be developed.

The complexity of the Japanese sword is not within the scope of this work. It would be difficult to do justice to even the furniture of the sword, let alone the entire piece.

Thus, the scope of pattern-welded steel becomes a little better defined. Historically, different cultures produced the material, all apparently to develop first a structurally superior product, and secondly to develop aesthetic ideals. Pattern-welded steel is not necessarily superior to modern alloy steels and may indeed be inferior to some of them in its properties. The inherent beauty of pattern steels has remained relatively untouched by contemporary craftsmen: perhaps this chapter will give some craftsmen an introduction to the basic working knowledge that may lead to more individual experimentation.

PASTRY TOOL. Robert Griffith. Sixteen layers of ASTM A203E and wrought iron.
Photo, Aaron Mascai

MATERIALS

The first consideration when choosing materials should be the function of the end product. A knife blade used for skinning or whittling must hold a fine edge and at the same time be flexible to some degree. Therefore, a high carbon content steel should be considered with wrought iron being an excellent companion laminate choice. The carbon steel, when hardened properly, will allow the blade to hold its edge; the wrought iron will provide flexibility.

A pattern-welded piece of jewelry does not need to have the characteristics of a knife blade, but must be decorative with a clearly defined pattern. Any combination of materials which will "etch" and "color" to a high contrast will serve, such as ASTM A203E nickel alloy steel and 1020 mild steel.

The material analysis chart, below, indicates several possible laminate choices for pattern welding. Experimentation will be the key to discovering the proper materials for a particular purpose while the chart Possible Laminate Choices, opposite, provides information on possible laminating combinations and characteristics of various materials.

METHODS OF ASSEMBLING VARIOUS MEROVINGIAN BLADES

Pattern Welded Blades

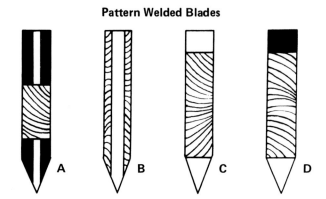

■ Soft iron

□ Steel

▨ Pattern welded section

A. Sixth century, Lorrain
B. As described by Herrman and Perrett
C. Eleventh century, Poland
D. Same as C.

MATERIAL ANALYSIS CHART

Material	Carbon %	Phosphorus	Nickel %
Wrought iron	.02–.06	.15–.37	—
1010	.08–.13	.04	—
1040	.37–.44	.04	—
1095	.92–.97	.04	—
W1	1.00	.04	—
Astma 203–D	.20	.035	3.5
Nickel 200	—	Trace	100

LAMINATION

The next factor one must consider prior to lamination is how many layers—i.e., how fine the pattern—will be necessary for the end product. For example, the knife blade may require 500 or more laminations to hold its edge and provide flexibility while the decorative ring may require only 8 layers to display a high contrast pattern. However, a ring of 200 layers may be as beautiful as one with 8 if properly polished, etched, and colored. The knife may not serve as a superior tool or weapon with as few layers as 8. A general rule to remember is, the greater the number of layers, the more difficult etching and coloring will be.

Preparation

The first preparation in lamination is to cut the materials to a size which will be convenient to handle in the fire and can be welded with as few heats as possible. For this reason, a recommended size would be 3/16 inch or 1/4 inch thick by 1 inch to 1 1/2 inches wide and about 6 inches long.

Four layers of material are convenient to begin with, although more layers could be used. Cut with a hacksaw or cutting torch (torch cuts must be ground) and stack the layers alternately, tacked at one end with a gas or electric weld. The pieces also could be wired together until forge welded. If tacked by gas or arc welding, this end (1/2 inch) should be cut off after all laminating is complete. Welding with gas or electricity at any time will introduce a foreign material (filler) and will "scramble" the pattern. It will also change the crystalline structure of the material. For easy handling one can weld on or leave an extension on a low carbon piece to serve as a handle during welding. This will be cut off later and makes welding far easier than trying to handle the "billet" in a pair of tongs. Mill scale may be ground off prior to stacking, but this is not always necessary.

Care in building and maintaining a "tight" welding fire of a fuel that must pack and coke well is imperative. The billet should be placed on edge deep in the fire and the air blast should be slow and steady. It is very important that each layer of material be brought to welding temperature

POSSIBLE LAMINATE CHOICES FOR PATTERN WELDING

MATERIALS	WORKABILITY	COLORABILITY	USES
1 WROUGHT IRON plus 1095 or W1	Difficult to weld due to high carbon content of 1095 or W1. Red short.	Colorability based on carbon differences only. Medium color contrast.	Hardenable in water, can be used for cutting tools.
2 ASTMA 203 D or E plus 1095 or W1	Same as above.	Colorability based on nickel and carbon differences. Very sensitive to acid; good color contrast.	As above, and any decorative application.
3 PURE NICKEL plus 1095 or W1	Most difficult to weld due to high carbon in 1095 or W1 and rapid oxidation of the nickel.	Same as above. Most brilliant color contrast.	As above.
4 ASTMA 203 D or E plus WROUGHT IRON	Broad range of welding temperatures. Will not be more red short than the wrought iron used.	Colorability based on nickel difference. Sensitive to acid; good color contrast.	Nonhardenable. Decorative applications only.
5 ASTMA 203 D or E plus 1020	Broad range of weldable temperature. Will red short.	As above.	As above.
6 1020 plus 1095 or W1 or old files	Same as 1.	Same as 1.	Same as 1.

WELDING PROGRESSIONS

No. of Layers at Start	Weld No.: 1	2	3	4	5	6	7	8	Seg*
2	2	4	8	16	32	64	128	256	Two
4	4	8	16	32	64	128	256	512	Two
6	6	12	24	48	96	192	384	768	Two
2	2	6	18	54	162	486	1458	4374	Three
4	4	12	36	108	324	972	2916	8748	Three
6	6	18	54	162	486	1458	4374	13122	Three
2	2	8	32	128	512	2048	8192	32768	Four
4	4	16	64	256	1024	4096	16384	65536	Four
6	6	24	96	384	1536	6144	24576	98304	Four

L = Total number of layers $L = N(C^{n-1})$
n = Number of welds
C = Number of segments*
N = Number of layers at start

*Segments denotes number of pieces the bar is cut between welds.

at the same time, so heat slowly. If the outside layers are consistently hotter than the inner ones, the air blast is too strong and heating is too quick. The inner layers will not weld if this condition persists.

Fluxing also requires some experimentation. Straight borax is excellent, especially anhydrous borax, obtainable from ceramic suppliers. Commercial forge-welding fluxes containing iron filings do not make welding any easier and introduce a "foreign" matter to the material with each weld.

Welding

The first welding procedure for the beginner involves welding the layers at one end or directly in the middle. To accomplish this properly, use light, rapid hammer blows rather than heavy ones. After this preliminary welding, another heat should be taken and welding should continue from the previously welded spot out toward the end, forcing the flux and slag out. Experience will allow the first welding of four layers to be done in two heats, but the beginner may take more.

After welding the four layers, check to see that welds are sound. You may wish to grind one or both edges to examine the welds. It also may be desirable to draw the billet out slightly at this point before cutting and going on to the next welding operation. If this is the case, the edge should be ground. During welding some of the layers will shift, leaving one layer extending out from the next. It is important to grind or hot rasp any such layers flush before hammering on that edge so that layers do not fold back on themselves.

Some attention should be paid to the condition of the layers being welded. They should be kept flat and even to minimize the problems of layers shifting and of slag inclusions caused by air pockets. Most likely

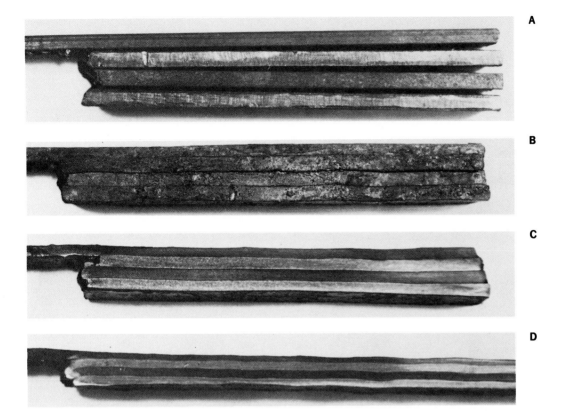

more than four layers will be desired and for this reason it is essential to draw the billet out and cut it in half or in thirds. After cutting these pieces, they should be stacked so the bottom layer of one piece will be welded to the top of another. This is important because a loss of one layer will occur at this point if like layers are welded together.

It is not always necessary to cut and stack to achieve laminating. The piece can instead be drawn and folded back (see chapter 5 section on forge welding); however, the fold will create a significantly different pattern. A layer of material will also be lost with each fold because the layer is welded to itself. This layer will then be wider than the others when finished.

The same basic laminating techniques described here can be repeated until the desired number of layers is achieved. It is helpful to draw out to a convenient size for welding between cutting and stacking operations. This will require forging primarily on the top and bottom of the piece. If it becomes necessary to forge the laminate on the sides or edges of the layers, remember to file or grind them flush prior to forging.

There will be a problem of material loss, possibly as much as 60 percent as a result of scaling (oxidation) and condensation of material. To cut down on this material loss it is desirable to keep the number of welding heats to a minimum and be careful not to overheat. This material loss will also depend on what materials are being used.

During welding operations, carbon will migrate from areas of higher concentration to those of lower concentration. This may adversely affect hardening, etching, and coloring procedures. Since carbon migration is a function of temperature and time, it is advisable to perform all welding operations at as low a heat as possible and in the shortest amount of time. For cutting tools, carbon migration may become a severe problem. Final forging should be done at around 800° C (bright red) or lower.

Initial welding sequence:
A. Two iron and two steel pieces stacked in alternating layers.
B. Same four pieces welded.
C. Same four pieces ground and etched to show layers.
D. Same four pieces drawn out, ground, and etched.

Second stage of welding sequence:
A. Two sections of four layers are forge welded together.
B. Eight pieces ground and etched to show pattern.

The four pieces are fluxed at a light red heat before welding.

Above right:
Welding with hammer blows.

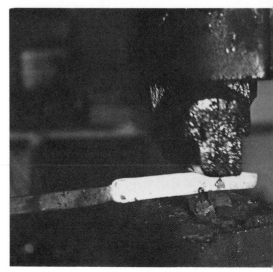

Drawing out at high heat on the trip-hammer.

PATTERN DEVELOPMENT

Creating a pattern can be achieved in a number of ways. Its development is limited only by the imagination of the craftsman. Three basic techniques for pattern development to be discussed are:

1. Material removal (grinding, incising) followed by forging.
2. Surface manipulation (punching, piercing) followed by material removal.
3. Twisting.

Within these three main categories many variations are possible.

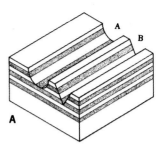

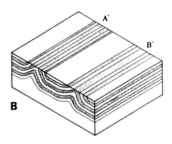

Material removal followed by forging.
A. Round bottom chisel cut
B. V bottom chisel cut

Material Removal

The material removal process makes it possible to develop a pattern by exposing subsurface layers of the laminate by grinding or by cutting away some material with chisels. This technique is most effective within a lamination of at least 32 layers, but can be used with as many as 500. Remember that the more layers of material, the more "lines" that will be exposed by an incision or pass with a grinding burr. Similarly the deeper the cut, the more layers will be exposed.

It is possible to develop lettering or to "draw" patterns into the material. The success of this type of pattern will depend on the craftsman's ability to control the tools he is using, and by some experimentation with etching and coloring solutions to bring the pattern out.

After grinding or chiseling to the desired pattern, it is then necessary to reforge the material flat so that subsurface layers are forged to the same plane as the surface. This should be done by using a polished flatter and a clean anvil surface. The material removal techniques of pattern development are most easily performed on flat pieces which can be later shaped, if necessary. Incising or grinding should be done when the product is as close to the finished form as possible to minimize pattern change during subsequent forging. The depth of the cut must be controlled to expose the desired number of layers with a minimum of flattening. This technique produces a pattern which is shallow and can be "erased" if final grinding is not performed carefully.

Surface Manipulation

A similar technique for pattern development can be achieved by stamping, peening, or forging. A pattern of concentric rings can be developed by using the ball end of a ball peen hammer over the surface. This can also be achieved by punching or stamping the surface with a round convex punch.

The depth of the punched or peened area again should be controlled so that ultimately the desired number of layers can be brought to the surface. The next step in this technique is to grind the surface flush with the bottom of the stamped or peened mark to expose the desired pattern. The deeper the mark, the more grinding must be performed consuming a great amount of material. Forging of the piece to achieve a uniform surface would in this case only flatten the manipulated areas into their original form.

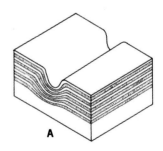

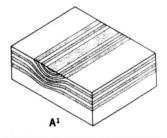

Surface manipulation followed by material removal.
A. Deforming multilayer materials by grooving with fuller.

A¹. Revealing multilayer pattern by cutting across parallel to the surface.

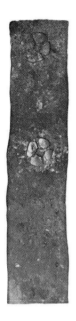

Twisting

A variety of patterns can be achieved by controlled twisting of the laminated material. This process, an integral part of the Merovingian blades, was extensively used in the manufacture of gun barrels as late as 1900. Before twisting, it is first necessary to laminate a suitable number of layers. This number (usually at least 16 layers and no more than 64) may vary. Some early knife blades with high numbers of laminations had a "slow twist" in them consisting of many layers; the more layers that were used, the finer was the line pattern. After completing the preliminary welding of the appropriate laminates, it is necessary to "draw" the billet to a rod approximately 1/4 or 5/16 inch square. This dimension can vary slightly depending on what the finished product will be. One very important point is that the rod of 1/4 or 5/16 inch must be consistent in its dimension from end to end and as close to square as possible. Before forging the billet into a rod, however, it will be necessary to grind or file (hot rasp) the edges of the laminates flush.

A laminated billet which measures 1 X 2 X 6 inches when drawn to a 1/4-inch rod may yield a piece 92 inches in length (depending on material loss during forging). While drawing out, welds should be checked and any "open" welds must be rewelded, being careful not to reduce the dimension of the rod. When drawing is complete, the rod can then be cut up into shorter pieces to make twisting easier. Another factor which must be considered prior to twisting is the number of twists per linear inch. A pattern developed by 13 twists per inch (counting edges of twist) will differ from a pattern developed by one of only 8 or 9 twists per inch. More than 13 twists per inch on a 1/4-inch rod is difficult to obtain while less than 8 will tend to "straighten out" during reforging and welding operations.

Pattern development by punching. Top shows a pattern made with a decorative punch; bottom shows the area after it was ground.

Stock removal by using a chisel. Note the layered blade held in vise jaws.

Before twisting the square rod, it is helpful to check for sharp edges and eliminate these by filing or hammering them slightly. This will help eliminate stress cracking during twisting.

Depending on what materials were used in laminating, some experimentation is necessary to determine at what heat to twist. In most cases, this should be done at a bright yellow heat, being careful not to burn the material. Too low a heat may cause the welds to come apart or shear. Heating must be uniform to prevent the rod from twisting more at a hotter area while resisting at colder spots.

The size of forge and tuyere will determine how much of the rod can be heated for twisting at a time. Six-inch heats are easily controlled. A vise should be as close to the fire as possible to prevent heat loss due to traveling time. An adjustable wrench with a handle welded on opposite the original one is handy for twisting.

During twisting, it is essential to watch and "feel" (resistance) very carefully for weld separations or shearing. Some separations can be left to be rewelded if reforging operations are to follow twisting. Fire scaling will be heavy and it is necessary to wire-brush frequently to "read" the twisting.

Straight laminations ground to knife edge.

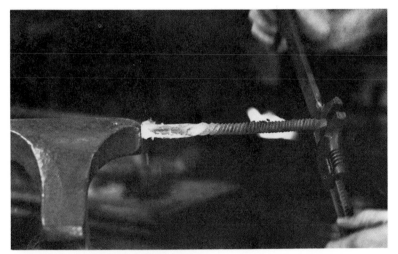

Twisting.

Removing scale from the twisted bar.

By localizing heats with the torch or in the fire, it is possible to even up the twisting if necessary. It is helpful to quench the twist by dipping it in water or pouring water from a can to cool down areas which have already been twisted completely. Remember that the rod will always twist at its hottest point. Quenching, however, may induce cracking in laminations consisting of high carbon.

The next factor which should be considered is the direction of the twist, i.e., clockwise or counterclockwise. This is especially important if two or more twisted rods are to be welded together. A "chevron" pattern can be created only by welding two pieces together of opposite twisted directions. In this case the twisted pieces (now welded) can be forged slightly and ground to expose the chevron pattern.

When twisting is complete and if two pieces are to be welded together, it may be desirable to "resquare" the twisted rods (now round from twisting) by reforging. It is possible to weld without resquaring; however, a thoroughly welded seam is more difficult. The disadvantage of resquaring is that the forging will cause the twists to "straighten" and distort slightly. This can be kept to a minimum by not forging excessively. In some cases it may be desirable to resquare only partially.

After welding two or more pieces of twisted rod together, it should be determined how far to grind to expose the desired pattern. The pattern will show significant change as the material is removed by stock removal. The center of a twisted rod will display a much different pattern from the surface. Many interesting patterns have been exposed by stock removal from a piece of twisted laminate which was seemingly uninteresting on the surface.

Two pieces of opposite twist before welding.

The same pieces after being welded, slightly ground, and etched.

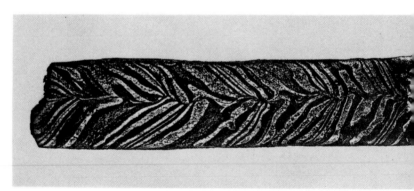

FORGING

Regardless of the method used for pattern development, any subsequent forging will change this pattern. In addition, one must also consider those changes in the size of the materials (laminates) reduced by forging. For example, if a bar of 200 layers per 1/2 inch in thickness is to be forged to an 1/8-inch taper on one edge, these layers will be compressed to 200 layers per 1/8 inch which is equivalent to 800 layers per 1/2-inch thickness.

HEAT TREATMENT

If a cutting tool is being made, the next step after final shaping will be heat treating. Normal blacksmith hardening and tempering techniques should be used for this operation (see chapter 10). Make the cutting edge the hardest part, with the body portion of the tool drawn for maximum strength. The quenching medium used should be the same as normally used for the high carbon component material. If sufficient carbon migration has occurred during the welding/forging operations, it will be necessary to utilize a faster quench. Only through experimentation and checking can it be determined what will be the proper quenching medium for any particular piece of pattern-welded steel. If there are any welding voids or pockets of slag contained in the pattern-welded piece, they will show up as blisters or breaks after the quenching operation.

If the object being made will not be used as a cutting tool, heat treatment may not be necessary.

FINISHING

To get the best visual effect from the various layers of material exposed at the surface of the object being made, it will be necessary to develop a topographical or color difference between them. This result can be achieved by subjecting the surface to an agent that will react to one of the layer materials differently from the other. Since a clean surface is necessary to facilitate such a reaction, the surface must be properly prepared. It will be generally found that abrasive techniques will be superior to pickles or descaling baths for this operation. Successively finer grades of abrasives should be used ending with no coarser than #400 grit paper. The finish can be carried on as far as a full mirror polish with buffing wheels, but this will not be advantageous if subsequent acid bath is used.

Topography can be developed on the surface of the pattern-welded piece by immersion in an acid bath which will attack one layer of material at a faster rate than the other. After the final sanding or polishing operation, wash the object with acetone, acetic acid, or other degreasing agent. Then subject it to an etching solution composed of water and HNO_3, H_2SO_4, HCl, or a combination of above. A commercially available ferrous pickling solution such as Sparex #1 also may be used.

The following general rules should be kept in mind:
1. The stronger the acid, the faster the reaction.
2. The higher the temperature, the faster the reaction.
3. The faster the reaction, the rougher the surfaces will be and the more likely pitting will occur. Very fast local reaction results in holes deep in the surface of the metal.
4. The crystalline form of the steel affects the rate and amount of reaction of the acid. (On a hardened knife, the reaction will be different on the hard edge from on the softer body.)
5. Unclean surfaces will have uneven action of the acid.
6. The action of one acid on the surface will affect the subsequent reaction to a second acid.
7. The finer the lines of the alternating layers, the more difficult it is to achieve a smooth differential etch.
8. Atmospheric conditions affect the reaction.

The proper acid to use will depend on the particular mix of materials used to make the pattern-welded object. Some acid treatments will impart a color difference to the various layers as well as develop topogra-

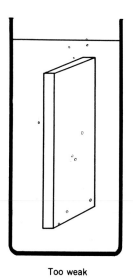

Wedding band. By Jim Wallace. Pattern welded steel with sterling silver. Eight layers of ASTM A203E and wrought iron twisted and ground near the surface. Etched with 15 percent nitric acid, 15 percent hydrochloric acid, and 70 percent water.

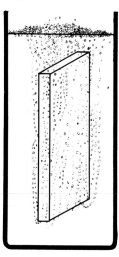 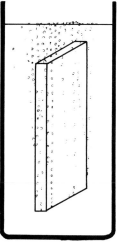

Too weak   Too strong   Good

Bubbling action caused by strength of etching solution.

phy. Again, experimentation will be necessary to determine the best solution to use on the particular pattern-welded piece being treated. A slower acting (weaker) solution will generally give a more permanent color reaction. The proper strength of the acid solution can be determined by judging the amount of bubbles being produced during etching. Other solutions can be used to develop color without etching (causing topography). Examples of these solutions are acetic acid, fruit juices, vinegar-salt-charcoal mixtures, and so on.

A method that has good results on cutting tool grade pattern-welded materials is:

1. Finish sanding with #400 grit paper
2. Wash with soap and water
3. Wash with acetone
4. Immerse in boiling Sparex #1 for 3–15 seconds
5. Rinse in running water
6. Immerse in 10 percent HCl, 20 percent HNO_3, 70 percent water solution for 2–6 minutes
7. Rinse in running water
8. Gently rub surface with wet cloth or paper towel to remove superficial dark film
9. Neutralize with baking soda
10. Rinse with running water
11. Dry with cloth or paper and immediately oil to prevent rust

The above process gives a slight topography with medium color differential.

A smooth deep etch with little coloration can be achieved on some iron and steel mixes by using hot diluted sulfuric acid with agitation. It is necessary to stir or wipe the surfaces with a feather or lightweight material edge during etching to prevent pitting and encourage uniform etching. After neutralizing, the piece can be buffed on a soft cloth wheel to polish the high spots. The surface should then be oiled or waxed for protection from rusting. This type finish is found on some antique gun barrels and on contemporary pattern-welded knives.

A completely different colorization system, controlled rusting, was used to show pattern in the gun barrels found on fowling pieces of the eighteenth and nineteenth centuries. In this process, a rusting agent (salt water or any cold browning solution) is applied to the work and is left to work for from 4 to 24 hours in the air. The superfluous red rust is then removed by abrasion (steel wool, wire brush, wire wheels, and so forth).

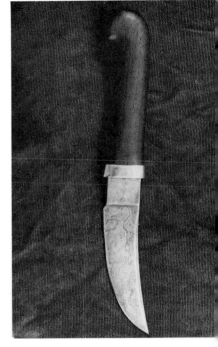

Knife. By Don Hastings. Blade contains 512 layers of ASTM A203E and high carbon steel forged to final shape.

Courtesy, artist

Detail of above blade pattern.

A second application of rust agent is given and more rusting time allowed before again removing loose surface rust. The process is repeated from 3 or 4 to 30 times until the desired result is achieved.

After any acid or rusting treatment is finished, the object should be neutralized to prevent further reaction or rusting. Baking soda will suffice as neutralizing agent for most acids and rusting agents.

An additional manner in which a color difference can be developed on pattern-welded material, is to use heat oxidation. If a pattern-welded piece is heated slowly, when it reaches 450° F the surface will start to form an oxide by combining with atmospheric oxygen. As the temperature is increased the oxide will change color until approximately 630° F is reached. The colors of oxide developed by heat alone will vary from yellow to brown to purple to blue to gray. This technique can be used after a topography has been developed to color the entire piece. By buffing lightly the color can be removed from the higher material leaving a distinct color difference. In the case of pattern-welded pieces made of pure nickel (nickel 200) mixed with any iron or steel, the heat oxidation will occur only on the ferrous material. The nickel remains bright at these temperatures, resulting therefore in a very noticeable color difference.

A final coating of the surface with oil or wax should be applied to any colored pattern-welded piece to prevent further action caused by atmospheric acids or mild abrasions by handling.

It is hoped this information will enable the craftsman to produce a quality pattern-welded steel without too much difficulty. Although the

Hand mirror. By Robert Griffith. Damascus steel with ivory. Sixteen layers. Pattern developed by twisting.

Photo, Jim Wallace

The "Damascus Steel Research Team" at Southern Illinois University at Carbondale: *Left to right,* Jim Wallace, Daryl Meier, Robert Griffith.

Courtesy, "Team"

technique appears difficult, anyone with forge-welding abilities will be able to manufacture it to some degree. The materials, techniques, and ideas presented here are not necessarily the only way to do things, and individual experimentation is encouraged.

ACKNOWLEDGMENTS

The Damascus steel researchers, Robert Griffith, Daryl Meier, and Jim Wallace, express their gratitude to the following people who have contributed significantly to this project:

Dr. Cyril S. Smith for his time through conversations and correspondence; Professor L. Brent Kington for his support and enthusiasm for this research; to United States Steel Corporation for providing essential information; to Huntington Alloys, Huntington, West Virginia, for their contribution of materials; to Turner Kirkland and Dixie Gun Works for taking time to discuss the manufacture of twist barrels; to the Southern Illinois University Graduate School and Dean Thomas O. Mitchell for supporting the project with two special research grants; to Aaron Mascai for doing a fine job of photographing; and to Carol Maguire for typing while deciphering manuscripts written by hands better suited to hammers than pens.

Classic quillon dagger by William F. Moran, Jr., with blade of pattern welded steel.
Courtesy, artist

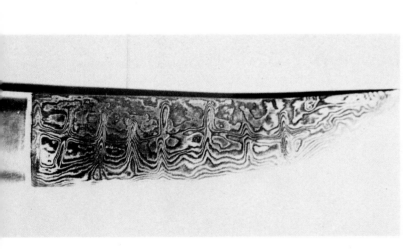

Blade from one of set of knives with different blade patterns. By Jim Wallace.
Photo, Jim Wallace

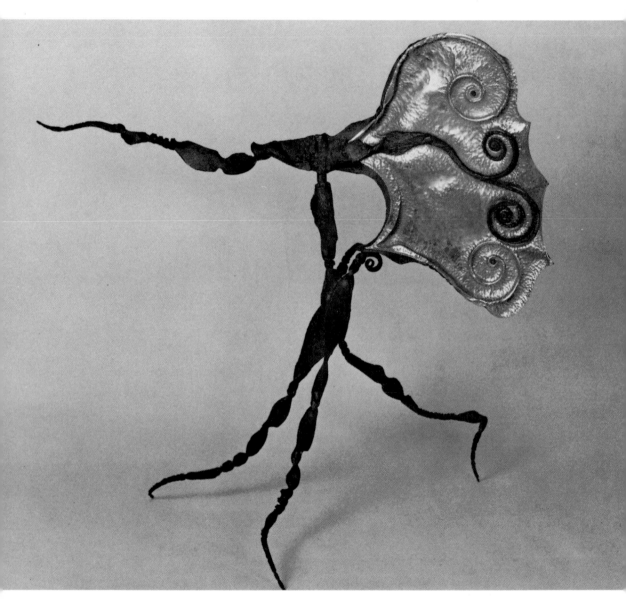

Weather vane # 3. By L. Brent Kington.
Forged steel and copper. 58" long.
Courtesy, artist

12

Mixed Metals - More Techniques

THE variety of available alloys and the treatments for exploiting them have never been greater. Considering the background of today's blacksmithing enthusiasts, it is only natural that they employ other metals in combination with or in addition to iron and steel. Many of them have had training in metalworking as jewelers, in shop classes, in sculpture. Their background is rarely that of the traditional smith who has had the anvil sound in his ears from father to son. Even those who have learned smithing from a previous generation of smiths inevitably explore the nature of other alloys. Material purists may denigrate combining the materials, while others strongly support the theory that media exist for the purpose of expression, that one should use whatever he can, whatever he knows how to use, to make his statement. The more familiar one is with the variety of metals, the better able he is to communicate his ideas.

With this mixed media philosophy permeating the metalworkers' consciousness, the examples and techniques in this chapter are presented. They may be used with the metals shown or adapted to other metals. Essentially they are illustrated to help you expand the potential of the art form. Many of the methods, many of the detailings shown in one metal can be transferred to another; some in brass, bronze, or silver can be adapted to steel. Conversely, some of the steel procedures can be advantageously developed in other metals.

A study of the composition of alloys, experimentation with them in cold and hot working stages are the best methods of coping with their characteristics. Most metals suitable for cold working have to be annealed to keep them in soft working states. Hot forging provides constant annealing because the metal is reheated during the working period.

Joining techniques vary with the types of metals being joined; soldering, brazing, and fusion welding may be required as opposed to forge welding. Riveting, collaring, bolting, slotting, or folding parts into one another, and so forth may be used with all metals. Often the joining member is made of another material so that it is decorative as well as functional. The colors of nonferrous metals lend themselves well to combinations with the bright and dark grays of steel.

Container. By C. James Meyer. Steel, 14K gold, sterling silver, whale's tooth. 5½" wide, 3-inch diameter.

Courtesy, artist

SOLDERING AND BRAZING

Soldering and brazing utilize a minimum of heat; the metals are joined with the addition of another metal to fill in the joined area. The filler flows onto the joined pieces, hardens and fuses them together. Two types of soldering processes are: 1) soft soldering, and 2) hard soldering, also called silver soldering. Brazing is also a form of hard soldering, and at high temperatures it is a process of joining dissimilar metals.

Soft soldering utilizes the heat of the electric soldering iron or the air-acetylene torch. A compatible flux and solder must be used in combination with the metals being joined; the solder must penetrate deeply into the joint.

Hard soldering requires about twice as much heat as soft soldering. A coil of silver solder is used as the joining agent along with a flux. It flows into small parts easily and is preferred where close tolerance soldering is required. An air-gas unit is a satisfactory heat source unless the metal is rather thick; then the oxyacetylene torch may be more efficient.

In both soldering techniques, it is important to heat the parts just enough so that the heat of the metal, not the flame, will cause the silver solder to melt and flow evenly and deeply into the joint. The solder will ball up if there is not enough heat or if the metal is not properly cleaned. It will burn up if the torch is applied directly to it.

Brazing is used both for fusing joints and for coating surfaces. For brazing, the fusing metal is bronze, copper, aluminum, or other alloy, depending on the metals being joined. The amount of heat necessary for any job is one of the determining factors in selecting the proper rod. All the hard solders (used in silver soldering) melt at temperatures below 2500°F. Silver melts between 1280° and 1500°. Bronze rod melts at about 1600°F; copper at about 1900°F, and all other rods used for brazing purposes will melt below 2500°F. Other factors that determine the type of rod to use are strength, color, and flow.

The air-acetylene torch can be used for any work ranging up to 2500° of heat. When the metals to be brazed are quite thick, oxyacetylene heat may be required.

Brazing rods for each metal are available in various diameters. The heavier the parent metal, the heavier the rod that should be used. Some rods can be purchased with a flux precoating, others are plain and must be dipped in flux before brazing.

A bronze rod is most often used for joining on steel, copper, brass, and cast iron, but not on aluminum. It is versatile and makes a very strong joint. Areas to be joined with the rod should be wire-brushed and cleaned to remove any greasy material or impurities. The pieces to be joined should be placed in a clamp device or propped to keep them from separating during the joining process.

Aluminum offers some problems since it doesn't show a change in color when heated and may suddenly collapse if it is overheated. It should be backed up, or supported, when brazing to prevent it from collapsing. The flux used with aluminum is a corrosive fluoride and must be washed from the joint after brazing. The flux is mixed with water until it forms a light paste; this is painted on the joint and the rod. Pure aluminum rod is used for all commercial aluminum alloys. The torch flame should have slight excess acetylene. To determine the amount of heat present, mark a piece of blue carpenter's chalk on the joint; when the chalk turns white, the aluminum is hot enough to weld.

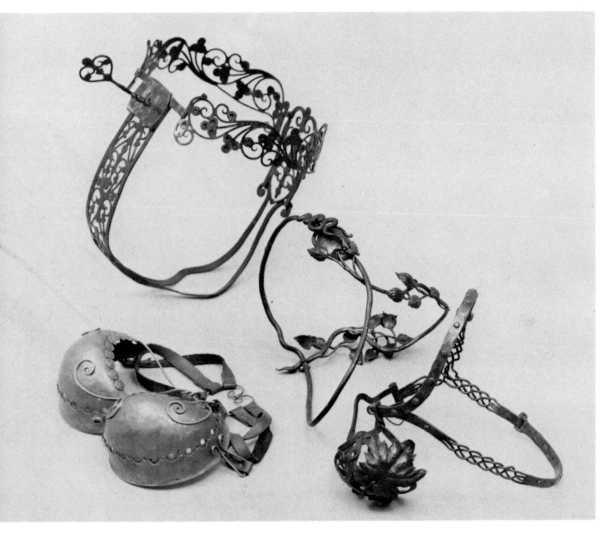

Chastity belts of iron; breast cups are copper and brass. By Beau Hickory.

Photo, Larsen

MAKING A FORGED BRACELET

A bronze rod, forged and welded, becomes
a bracelet in the hands of Kevin Hammond
of the Jack Boyd Studio. Similar methods
can be applied to steel and other alloys.

Below:
Observe the stake anvil in the hardy hole used
for finishing small work.

Right:
The stages involved in making the bracelet
from a bronze rod include wrapping, welding,
forging, polishing, cleaning, and buffing.

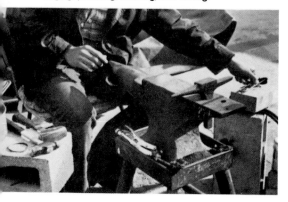

A 3-foot piece of 1/4-inch bronze rod is
wrapped around a piece of pipe held in a vise.
Oxyacetylene is the heat source.

Above, right:
A bolt cutter (one handle is secured in the vise)
is used to cut the rod and separate the coils.

Right:
The ring is welded using a 1/16-inch rod.

The bracelet is now forged over the anvil horn; the vise grip is used as a helping hand.

The bracelet is forged on the inside plane.

Finishing includes sanding with a metal-cutting 80-grit sandpaper disc followed by shaping on a Craytex wheel and polishing on a cloth buffing wheel with tripoli.

It is washed in hot water with a strong detergent to remove the tripoli compound, then final-finished by buffing with jeweler's rouge, rewashing, and rebuffing.

Demonstration, Kevin Hammond
Courtesy, Jack Boyd

Assorted jewelry: pendants, rings, necklaces, and a sculptural box lid cover using forged bronze rod. By Jack Boyd.

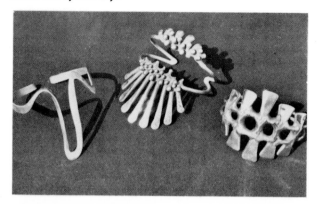

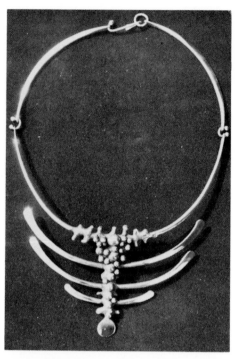

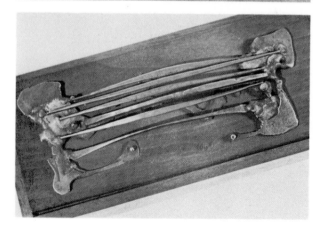

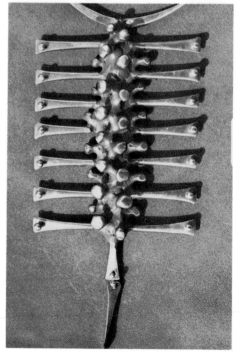

Assorted jewelry. By Beau Hickory. Buckles are iron with brass inlay.

Photo, Larsen

Neckpiece. By William E. Leth. Stainless steel. Twists and reverse twists yield an undulating linear flow. Oxyacetylene heat and wood mallet were used.

Bracelet. By L. Brent Kington. Forged steel and 18K gold.

Courtesy, artist

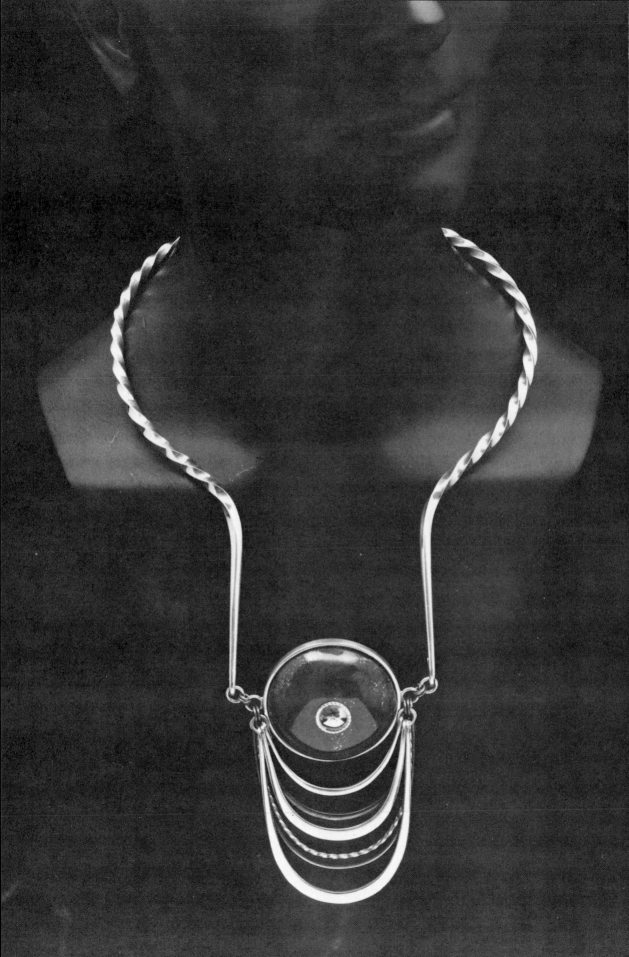

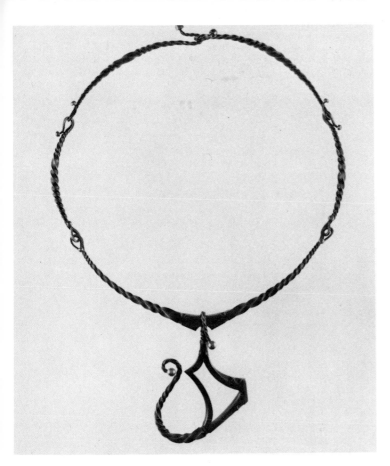

Necklace. By Joseph Snead Clift, Jr. Mild steel with brass accents.

Courtesy, artist

Fibula. By Joseph Snead Clift, Jr. Mild steel with brass accents.

Courtesy, artist

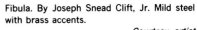

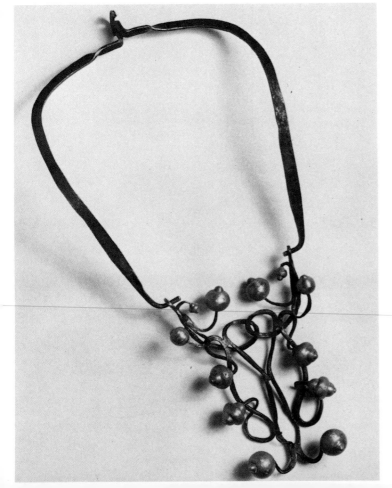

Necklace by Mark C. Ferrón. Scrap iron, brass, and gold. Cold and gas forged with jeweler's saw cut areas.

Courtesy, artist

MANIPULATING AND FORGING BRONZE

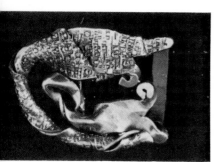

Forged bronze belt buckle by E. A. Chase. One example of an endless variety of possibilities.

E. A. Chase, sculptor-blacksmith, has applied traditional blacksmithing techniques to bronze forging. He uses the oxyacetylene torch as a heat source because of the rapid heat dissipation of the relatively small diameter rod. The hammers used are the same as those he uses to fashion his gates and sculptures of steel.

Some of the photos in the series show techniques that would be difficult to employ with steel such as drawing out by stretching, reverse molding, and intricate work with pliers. The evolution of these methods by Chase is based on the unique nature of the material as he has discovered and exploited it.

Detail of a forged bronze mirror frame by E. A. Chase. Leaf and flower motifs have been formed by the technique shown in the following demonstration.

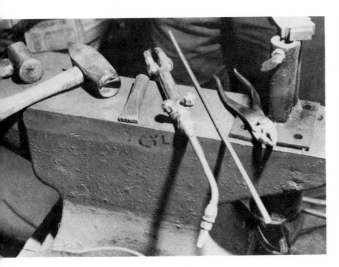

Tools used during the forming of a belt buckle "blank." *Left to right:* copper hammer, 3-pound cross peen hammer, name stamp, torch, rod to be formed, and pliers. The forming jig is used to "size" the buckle.

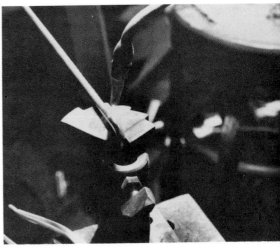

The bronze rod is heated to enable the blank to be bent and forged.

A stamp with the sculptor's name is impressed into the buckle bar. A soft copper hammer is used to prevent chipping the hardened stamp.

The formed blank is clamped into a specially constructed anvil/vise.

A bead is fusion welded to provide the mass for a leaf shape.

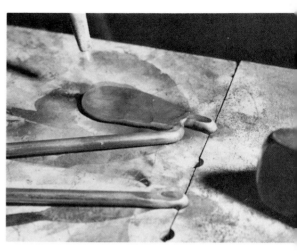

Continuous heat is applied as the metal is spread with the 3-pound hammer.

A hot chisel is used to apply the leaf's central vein.

A lighter hammer with a chisel edge is used with sharp, rapid blows to finish "veining" the leaf.

Another leaf takes shape as the rod is again doubled over and welded.

The cross peen is used to draw out the shape for a thinner leaf.

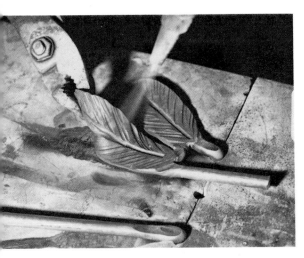

Specifically designed pliers are used to twist one of the leaves, while hot, into a single coil.

Smaller pliers are used to stretch the coiled shape into a flowing pattern.

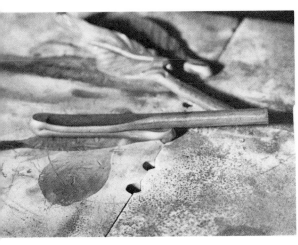

The rod is doubled over and the upper area selectively heated and flattened.

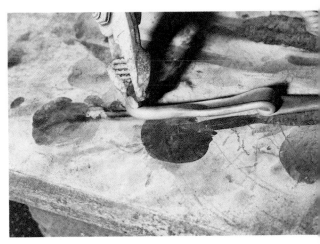

As the flattened rod is "peeled" back, the molding of its shape to the cooler round rod is exposed. Pliers are used to make another coil for forging a flower.

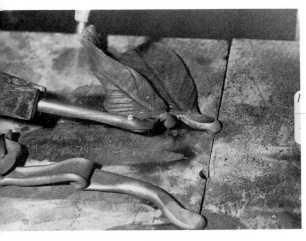

Heat is applied to stretch the 1/4-inch-diameter rod into a thinner flower stem.

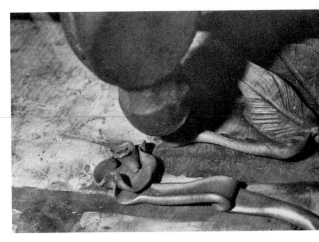

The upset end is shaped with a ball peen hammer.

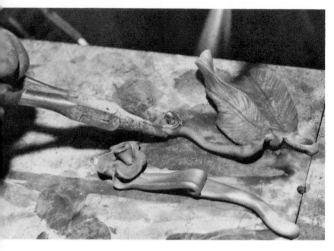

A small piece of bronze is welded into the cupped shape for a stamen.

Integration of the spontaneous design occurs as the elements are literally entwined.

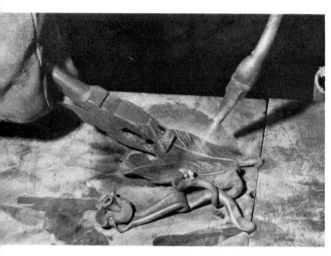

More stretching as the composition is formalized.

Forging complete. The buckle is removed from the anvil/clamp. All buckles are actually formed from one piece of rod.

The buckle-holding stem is welded onto the back. Flux is used for the first time.

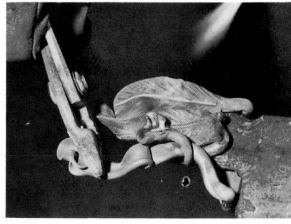

The last step involves shaping the buckle to fit human contours.

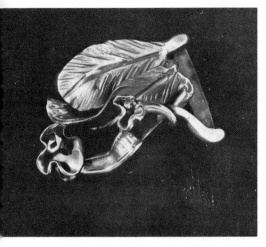

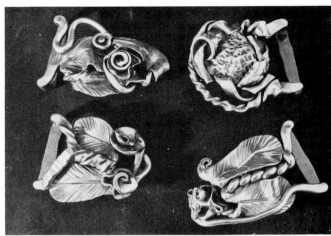

The finished buckle. After forging, it was cleaned in a nitric acid solution and flushed with clear water. Patination was next, using a metallic sulfate solution. Final buffing with white diamond compound draws out the luster.

Additional examples of belt buckles by E. A. Chase fashioned from one piece of bronze rod suggest the tremendous variety possible.

The mirror frame illustrates the possibilities for larger applications of bronze forging. The forged sections have been welded into a finished composition. 26" high, 30" wide.

Demonstration and finished examples by E. A. Chase

ANGLE RAISING COMBINED WITH FORGED ELEMENTS

Raising is the process of making a hollow form from a flat metal sheet by bringing the sides up gradually by hammering the metal on anvils, annealing, and finishing in a series of stages. Technique-wise, raising does not change the cross-section thickness of the metal as forging does, but rather changes the shape or flow of the metal from a flat disc to a hollow seamless vessel. Raising, more often associated with silversmithing for creating pots, bowls, and so forth, is frequently used in conjunction with many objects made by the blacksmith. He may use mild steel sheet, or alloys such as copper, brass, and silver as portions of utensils and for sculptural form. It is rapidly becoming an integral part of the versatile smith's technique repertoire.

David LaPlantz has developed a container shape by the *angle raising* process which he combined with a forged handle. Angle raising, one of several raising procedures, is so called because the metal disc is held at an angle against the T raising stake. The forming is accomplished by trapping the metal between the hammer and the T-stake.

David prefers to use as great an angle as possible to push the maximum amount of metal down with each hammer blow. In an object that requires hundreds of hammer blows, each blow counts. In this way he can arrive at a shape faster and continue to enjoy the raising process without the frustration of the long outlay of time and energy.

The demonstration includes riveting and soldering procedures which can be adapted to all metalwork; they illustrate the similarities and

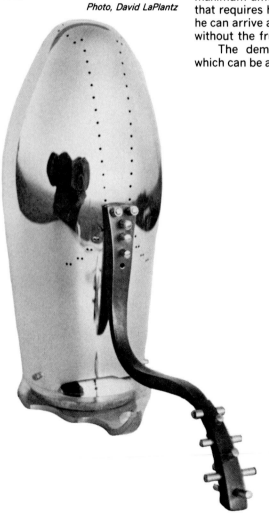

WONDER BOX WITH STUDS. By David La-Plantz. Raised brass, forged mild steel handle, fabricated copper and brass base and rivets. 7½" high, 3½" wide, 8" deep. The container is created by raising and riveting the raised pot to a steel handle. The full demonstration for creating this form follows.

Photo, David LaPlantz

differences between the silversmiths' and the blacksmiths' working methods.

David LaPlantz is well accomplished in both white- and blacksmithing procedures. He says, "I prefer to work with cold annealed metal so I can hold it in my hands, but I do use tongs for hot work. My philosophy in metalwork is to create objects that sometimes have a function such as a container, rattle, and so forth. But more often simply to make forms which relate to a visual, tactile experience. I like making folks happy, to put the laugh back into metalsmithing with my things. We do not grow up, but just change the size and value of our toys. My own works, I hope, will be viewed as objects to handle, fondle, touch, experience, with the hands and fingers. Those really interested will find the hidden surprises —somewhat like those who search a bit further into what life is and find IT. Happiness is looking deeper at all there is all around us."

The demonstration that follows illustrates the tools used in angle raising, how to begin from a prepared blank or disc, raising, finishing, riveting, soldering, and finalizing.

The metal used is a 10-inch disc of 18-gauge brass which has been annealed. Before cutting the disc from the large sheet form with metal shears, or a jeweler's saw, the center point was punched into the metal to indicate the center of the disc which is used to accurately measure the work throughout the raising process.

Demonstration by David LaPlantz
All demonstration photos by Shereen LaPlantz

Tools used to prepare, raise, and rivet the form: metal shears, compass with pencil, clear plastic ruler, mushroom stake (made from an old trailer hitch) and a stake extension holder; #90 round stake. T-stake in a stakeholder attached to a small movable workbench.

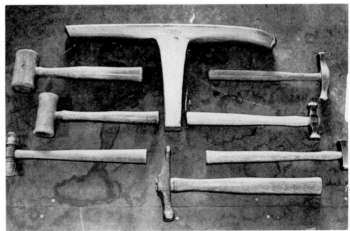

Assorted hammers used for raising, bouging, planishing (*right*); rawhide mallets and plastic hammers (*left*) used for bouging. The T-stake serves as the support. Tools used in each demonstration should be noted carefully for their specific function in the process.

Photos, David LaPlantz

PREPARING AND RAISING

The annealed brass disc is planned with a series of concentric circles about 1/2 inch apart. These will serve as a guide to keep it uniform during the angle raising process. Each course of raising will include: A) annealing the disc and pickling, B) compass layout of circles, C) angle raising on T-stake, D) bouging (moving) the metal to remove surface irregularities which will lead to the final planishing and other surface treatments; bouging is usually accomplished with the rawhide or wood mallet.

A

Circles are drawn on the annealed brass disc.

B

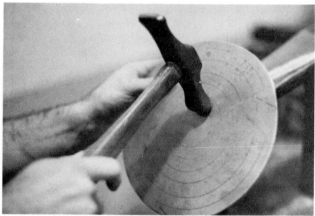

Raising begins by placing the disc against the T-stake and hammering with the cross peen hammer about 2 inches from the die center point.

C

The disc is pushed down upon the T-stake, the metal is moved inward and the bowl shape begins to take form.

D

The raising process continues toward the outer edge. Always stop about 3/8 inch from the outer edge of the disc so the original thickness remains throughout the raising process.

The bouging process is accomplished with a rawhide mallet to correct irregularities in the form over a mushroom stake held in a stake-holder.

Bouging continues on a larger mushroom stake held in a vise to yield a smooth surface.

Often bouging takes place on the T-stake, used in conjunction with the mushroom stake. The biggest problem in raising is to find proper stakes for bouging and final finishing and to discover the best order in which to use them to obtain continuity of form.

The disc is annealed in a pan filled with pumice stones, using a soft feathery flame until the metal is a consistent dull red. It is then immersed in a pickle solution of 1 part sulfuric acid added to 10 parts of water. Pickling cools down and cleans off the disc. Dry. The formerly work-hardened metal is again soft and ready for the next course of raising.

RAISING (continued)

At this point the shape is at course #12, which means the shaping and annealing process has been done 12 times from the same position on the disc as at the beginning.

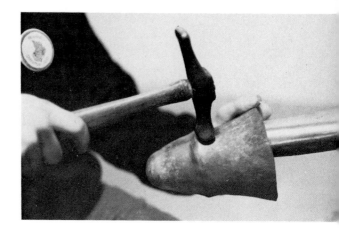

Above, right:
In this course, the raising proceeds from a new position beginning from about 4 inches from the disc's center point and continues until the necessary shaping and reannealing is done.

Right:
By this course, #29, the raising again proceeds from a new position about 5 inches from center; the outer diameter of the disc is shaping up and inward.

By course #34, the raising position is done 4 inches from the outer edge; this is the most difficult part since the metal becomes thicker at the edge with each course.

Course #39 . . . only one more to go. The finished pot required 40 courses; it is a time-consuming process that cannot be rushed.

FINISHING

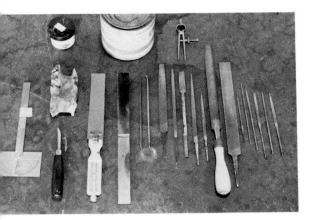

Above, left:
Finishing is accomplished with some of the tools already shown plus those illustrated above: bluing cream and motorcycle polish, dividers, protractor, buffing compound, burnisher, sanding stick, hard felt stick, and various files.

Above:
The bouging technique involves smoothing out irregularities on a T-stake held in a vise and/or over a mushroom stake using the rawhide mallet.

Left:
Rough planishing employs the rounded head of a planishing hammer to raise the low areas and push down the high areas. You can leave a faceted appearance, as shown, or final-planish by the following steps. When planished properly, the final filing and sanding will be minimal. It is followed by buffing and polishing.

Final fine planishing with the flat face of the planishing hammer.

Rough filing using a sandbag to support the piece.

Sanding with a plastic sanding stick.

RIVETING

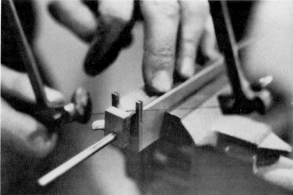

Above:
Riveting the handle and final finishing utilizes some of the planishing and chasing hammers plus a vise, bench pin, tube or wire holding jig, and the jeweler's saw with blade.

Above right:
Copper wire and brass tubing spacers, which will be used for rivets, are cut with a jeweler's saw with the wire and tubing held in the jig in a vise.

Right:
The forged iron handle is fitted with the rivets. The handle already has brass and copper tubing spacers in the handle for decoration. A light riveting hammer and steel block are used.

Right:
Now the rivets in the opposite end are tested to see that they will line up with holes in pot; the pot is supported by a T-stake held in a vise during the riveting procedure.

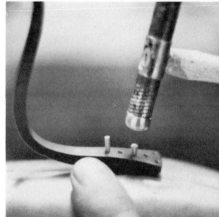

More of the final finishing must be done; the piece is sanded with #600 wet-dry sandpaper in circular motions, followed by buffing with a white diamond compound and a hard felt stick. Then a motorcycle semichrome polish with a soft T-shirt material is used.

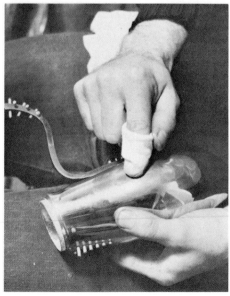

ASSEMBLING

Left:
A design on both sides of the handle is created using a flexible shaft to drill the holes. The object is held tightly close to the body; a full face safety shield is worn.

Above:
Next a double ring insert will be fitted into the neck of the container and soldered and the base will be fitted. Everything is lined up, ready for final assembly.

FINALIZING

Left:
The ring is soldered to the base that will slip into rings riveted to the raised form.

Above:
The flexible shaft tool is used to drill holes in the double rings which fit into the raised form; they are riveted together from the inside.

FINALIZING (continued)

The rivet is set on the outside of the double rings held on a T-stake in a stakeholder. Refer back to page 250 for the finished container form.

Holes are drilled in the raised form which will accept the double rings and rivets to be attached to container base.

David LaPlantz sets the rivets into the handle . . .

. . . and finishes hammering them into place with the light riveting hammer.

Demonstration by David LaPlantz
All demonstration photos by Shereen
LaPlantz

BUCK TOOTH BOX or BANANA LAND CON-
TAINER. David LaPlantz, Raised sheet (brass)
stock, fabricated teeth. 10" long, 2½" high.
Photo, artist

BAND ON THE RING. Container by David
LaPlantz. Fabricated and forged brass and
copper, filed and engraved textural treatment.
Hinged 3/8-inch brass rod (square) with slight
twist. 2⅜" high, 4½" wide, 8" long.
Photo, artist

Wine cup. By William E. Leth. Silver, steel forged handle, pearls. A problem established in combining different materials has an interesting solution.

Right:
Radio cabinet detail. By Max Segal. Sheet iron. Repoussé and chased over a lead plate.

Sugar and spooner. By Michael Spencer. Hot forged from sheet steel. 5" high, 10½" wide.
Photo, Peter Barrs

Spatula, ladle and slotted spoon. Rick Cronin.
Utensil bowls may be shaped within a hollow of
a tree trunk or in a sandbag.
Photo, Alida Fish Cronin

Handles from ladles (*details*) by Barry Berman.
Hammered copper facing and brass rivets over
steel for exquisite detailing.

Grouping of plate armor by Beau Hickory.
Deep drawn from sheet metal worked hot and
cold.

Photo, Larsen

Remington derringer. By Beau Hickory. Engraved and chiseled.

Photo, Larsen

Table. By C. Fletcher Coddington. Forged copper base with queechee wood top.

Photo, artist

Christopher Ray with some of his MAN-
SECTS which are made completely of
forged and welded iron and steel parts.

13

Sculpture

THE sculptor in iron and steel today has no precedents and few antecedents for the forms he wishes to convey. In the total history of world art,
the use of steel has been recognized as a serious expressive medium only
since the mid-1940s. Even then, it was slow to gain attention from art
collectors and museum curators.

Sculptors working today in metals may intuitively use techniques of
the ironsmith, but not to the extent that they might if they consciously
studied and applied them. An example might be a fabricated direct metal
sculpture where some hammering and shaping has been employed for
individual parts. But if the sculptor were aware of the varied detailing he
could accomplish by drawing out, upsetting, twisting, and so forth, he
could conceivably enhance a joint or other portion to result in greater
variety, more exciting areas of interest, and perhaps a heightened personal challenge.

Artists who consciously employ blacksmithing techniques have developed an approach that carries with it certain nuances not necessarily
seen in other works of art. In these, one discovers shapes and designs
with unique linear characteristics and a feeling of solidity and strength
that the metal implies. In addition, steel invites such a variety of surface
embellishments that its potential is limited only by the imagination and
by the artist's technical virtuosity.

Christopher Ray of Philadelphia has been consciously utilizing blacksmithing methods for his sculptures for many years. He experimented
with combinations of other metals with steel, but consistently returned
to forms that he felt were pure in concept.

He says, "I don't consider myself a blacksmith. First of all I am a
sculptor, simply because the intent of my work is to express my concepts
in a form consistent with what I have to say. For me that form is best
shaped in iron. However, I'll bastardize the conventional tradition and
innovate wherever necessary for the sake of the statement. I feel that the
forging of iron is in a sense a physical song, and what transpires from
the beginning of a concept to the poignant silence at the end is a new
drama that is self-renewing and a constant adventure. As all individual
worlds are, mine is ultra real, shaded with whimsy. I find a constant
delight living in the world around me, inside and out. I try to express the
essence and the spirit of some particular aspect of my perceived world,

BEACH SCENE. David Smith. Steel shaped and welded . . . some with portions drawn out, split, and upset.

Collection: The Art Institute of Chicago; Gift of Society for Contemporary American Art

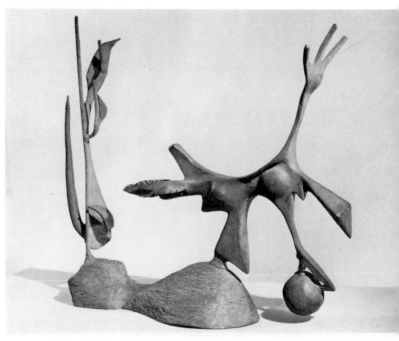

Dogon *Nommo* figure seated on a staff and holding in each hand a lance pointed at the sky. Figure only 12" high.

From the Wunderman Collection, New York

Photo, Lester Wunderman

and the form that best conveys the concepts for me is usually a phantasmagorical creature."

He refers to his Mansect series as an expression of the common life traits and characteristics that all of the living creatures share: "All of our joys and sorrow, the mundane and the profound, madcapacity and the macabre, living and dying, it all goes on and on and on and on and on. So revel in the fact that we are part of the past, the now and, historically, the future."

Among the beauties of iron, for the sculptor, is that like clay, it is both subtractive and additive, but with the permanency of bronze and stone. The sculptor can approach his design in many ways. He may sketch the form and develop it in clay or wax as a small concept. If it is to be monumental, he can enlarge it. Or he may build up the form directly by shaping the metal as he works from a vision he has in his minds' eye.

Neither does one have to be a purist about technique. The sculptor has at his disposal, the complete range of mechanical tools. Modern welding equipment is particularly important. Forge welding may be adequate for small objects, but having to forge-weld large pieces of steel would make the time, effort, and fabrication problems almost prohibitive.

Joe Nyiri's sketchbook is rich in ideas for steel forms large and small. He is able to interpret these visual perceptions in a special approach to the medium. He fabricates portions of an object until he has

THE SHAMAN'S DREAM (*detail*). Michael McCleve. Cast-iron found objects combined with hot forged steel bar and plate. 58" high, 40" wide.

Photo, Ted Bissell

achieved the combinations he seeks.

Michael Malpass covers a range of images, many of which are based on the sphere shape. He has worked through traditional blacksmithing techniques, making animal heads, dragons, and the "usual range of blacksmithed" items. But he has developed a unique interpretation for steel in the sculptures shown in the following pages.

Bruce Newell's forms are inspired by the armor of the thirteenth and fourteenth centuries and by animal imagery. He prefers to work sheet metal using repoussé techniques. Unlike the armor maker of the Romanesque period, Bruce uses an electric shear, grinders, and whatever else will help bring the flat metal to the desired shape and finish. Generally, though, his method for shaping the metal is done with hammers and anvil.

Simon Benetton of Italy works steel into monumental abstract sculptures using both hand hammering and a giant trip-hammer to help achieve the rich forms and the plasticity in the surface areas. Mauro De Biasio's sculptures rely heavily on the figure for inspiration. Though not so large in scale as Benetton's, they are imposing in concept.

The sculptures and techniques shown are offered as points of departure for you who may be seeking new expressions and innovations with a material that offers a richness, strength, and versatility not found in many other contemporary materials.

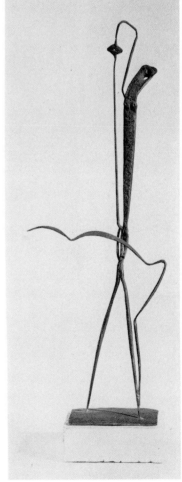

PERSONAGE. Reg Butler. 1950. Iron. 16¾" high.

Collection: Smith College Museum of Art, Northampton, Mass.

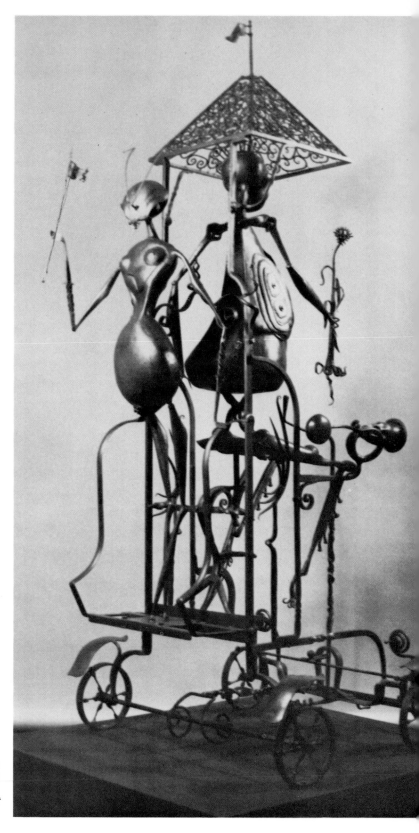

MANSECTS. Christopher Ray. Different forms in the species, with details. This page and opposite.

Courtesy, artist

MANSECT playing a wind instrument. By
Christopher Ray. With structural details.
Courtesy, artist

FLYING MANSECT. Christopher Ray.
Courtesy, artist

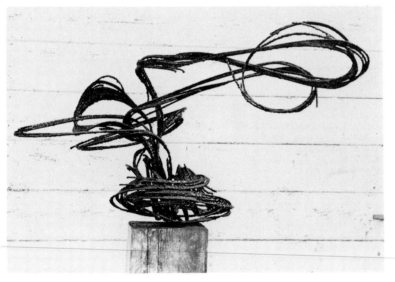

CONTINUUM. E. A. Chase. Forged and welded steel. A study in innovations on a closed loop. 55" wide.
Courtesy, artist

Sketches for sculpture are often made in a notebook by Joe Nyiri, then worked out in pencil or large brush and ink.

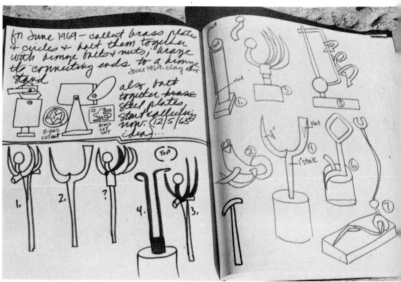

Left to right: Joe Nyiri
UNICYCLE #2. 18" high, 9" wide, 3" deep.
Collection, Mr. Ken Parsons, San Diego

HOMAGE TO APOLLO. 1969. Cast iron and forged steel, laminated mahogany and ash. 37" high, 14" wide, 6" deep.
Collection, Mr. and Mrs. Joseph Hoyle, San Diego

TENSOR SNAIL #2. Steel and cast iron. Burned pine. 30" high, 10" wide.
Courtesy, artist

AMPHIBIAN. By Joe Nyiri. Steel. 28" high, 10" wide, 10-inch diameter.
Courtesy, artist

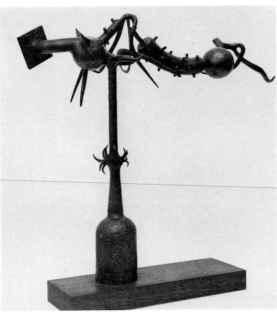

FORKED SCULPTURE. Joe Nyiri. 30" high, 20" wide, 6" deep.
Courtesy, artist

DRAGON. Michael Malpass. Forged sheet iron
shaped over a round stake. 6-inch diameter.

SPHERE. By Michael Malpass. Found objects,
cut and forged shaped pieces welded together.
See demonstration, *opposite*.

Courtesy, artist

A

To create his unique open and closed Spherical Sculptural Forms, Michael Malpass employs a variety of forging techniques using a small gas forge. He combines pieces of junk pile material which he heats, cuts, and bends to shape, with new pieces of steel depending upon his needs and availability.

A. A piece is heated and hammered to straighten it out . . .

B. . . . then lightly curved on the anvil.

C. It is tested for fit within the growing spherical form.

D. Another shape is heated and curved on the anvil.

E. They are all pieced together for final arc or oxyacetylene welding.

F. The pieces above are fabricated to another portion of the sculpture.

Demonstration: Michael Malpass

B

C

D

E

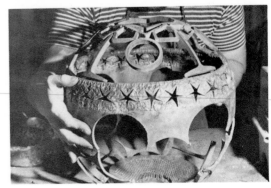

F

RABBIT. By Bruce Newell. Forged and shaped sheet steel. Sixteen-gauge sheet steel, cut, hammered, and welded. The weld is ground smooth; stove polish is applied and buffed into the surface for the finish. Welding by oxyacetylene.

Courtesy, artist

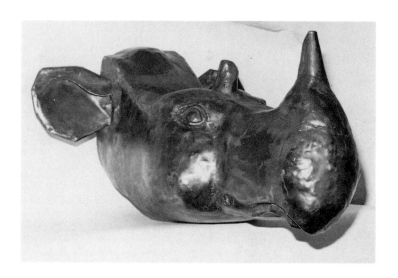

RHINOCEROS. By Bruce Newell. Eighteen-gauge steel using the same procedure as above. 33" wide, 27" deep.

ARMOR SCULPTURE

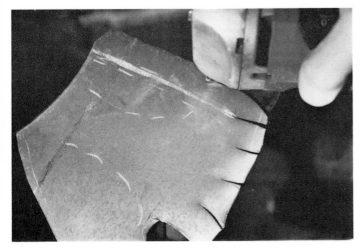

Bruce Mitchell demonstrates his techniques for forming sheet steel into sculpture.

Eighteen-gauge cold rolled sheet steel is worked cold and cut with an automatic metal nibbler.

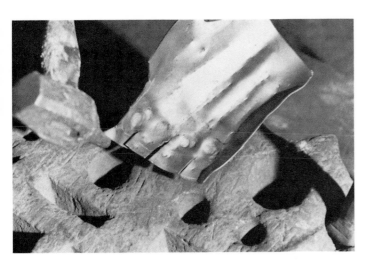

The hand details are cut over the swage block so the sheet is shaped simultaneously.

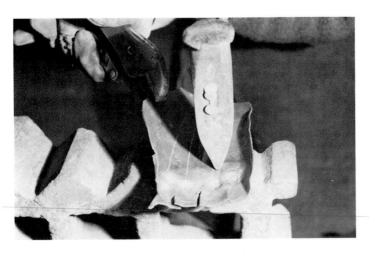

The fingers are cut. Note that the sheet is held with a vise grip; the force of the cutting blow is too hard to hold it by hand.

The finger shapes are hammered within the ridges of the swage block.

Shaping continues by folding the steel over.

The fingers are welded to the hand.

The whole hand.

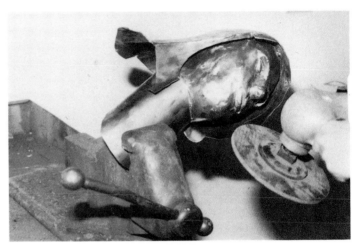

The head form is ground with an electric grinding wheel. The head is secured in the vise.

The body shaped and ready to receive the head.

The finished sculpture. By Bruce Newell. The inspiration for the figures is taken from Romanesque armor ... but there is no need to finish the interiors as armor is finished, for it will not be worn by anyone.

Demonstration by Bruce Newell

REACHING MAN. Anita Riley. Forged iron. 37"
high, 10" wide.

Courtesy, artist

TORSO. Anita Riley. Forged steel strips electric
welded. 32" high, 18" wide.

Courtesy, artist

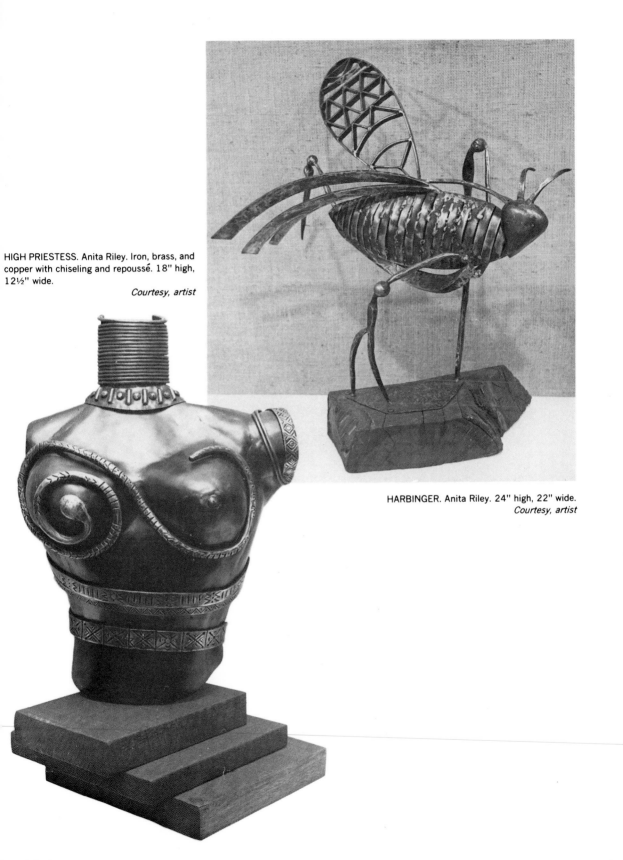

HIGH PRIESTESS. Anita Riley. Iron, brass, and copper with chiseling and repoussé. 18" high, 12½" wide.

Courtesy, artist

HARBINGER. Anita Riley. 24" high, 22" wide.
Courtesy, artist

ARGOMENTO. Simon Benetton. Monumental
sculptures, combining traditional forging techniques with welding and contemporary industrial procedures, are accomplished in the
Treviso, Italy, workshop of the artist.

Collection Antonecci-Fano
Photos, courtesy, artist

Opposite: Cranes and other types of industrial
equipment are employed to fabricate the large-
scale sculptural forms by Simon Benetton.
Some of the plate steel is retrieved from the
bulkheads of ships. The pieces are 13' to 16'
high.

Courtesy, artist

Photo, Stephen Bondi

Sculptures by Simon Benetton show some of
the possible forms one can create in steel.
A. APODITTICO
B. ORIGINE
C. FUGA
D. FORZA
E. DRAMMA
F. ELEMENTS FOR A TOMB. By the Benetton
Studios.

Photos, courtesy, Simon Benetton

A

B

C

E

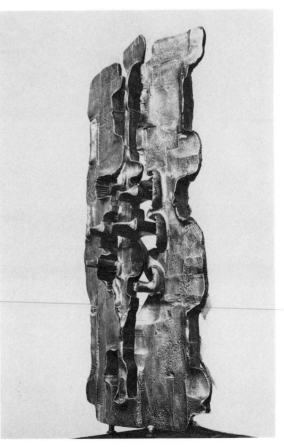

F

FIGURE WITH CROSS. Mauro De Biasio. 1971.
12½" high.

Courtesy, artist

SEA MONSTER. Mauro De Biasio. 1973. 20"
high.

Courtesy, artist

COMPOSITION #2. Mauro De Biasio. 1974.
21½" high.
Courtesy, artist

CHRIST. Mauro De Biasio. 1970. 23½" high.
Courtesy, artist

FIGURE. Mauro De Biasio. 1970. 12½" high.
Courtesy, artist

ULYSSES. Mauro De Biasio. 1974. 13" high,
21½" wide.
Courtesy, artist

MAN WITH MACHINE GUN. Mauro De Biasio.
1974. 39" high.

Courtesy, artist

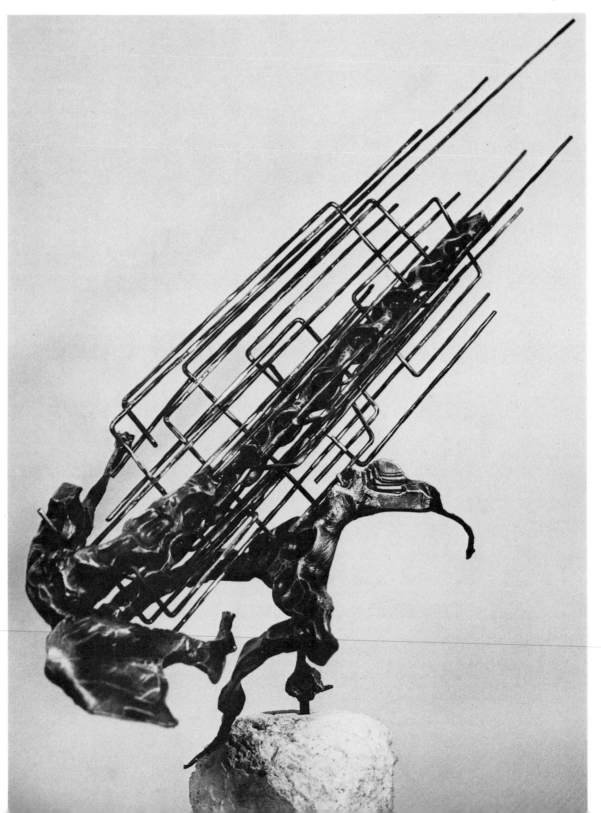

By Samuel Yellin

14

A Gallery of Details

IT is always difficult to reject material that does not fit into a given chapter heading, especially when the author knows the examples illustrate what the readers would like to see. As photographs for this book accumulated, it was soon obvious that they could not all be squeezed into one volume. Therefore, several details by master ironworkers, past and present, have been selected for this mini-gallery for whatever stimulus they may offer.

It would be impossible to draw the structure of each detail so the smith could emulate it exactly. Rather it is hoped that you will welcome the opportunity to analyze how they were done and perhaps accept the challenge of trying to copy them and, preferably, develop an original detail that will be as exciting to you as to the viewer.

Details, exquisitely crafted, are the components of an overall work of art. Whether you visualize a finished form in its skeletal structure and flesh it out, or work from minute portions upwards, each inch of the iron must be thought out and worked while decisions are made quickly and surely.

Solutions to design and technical problems, and much more, may be gleaned from the following examples. To do so effectively, the smith must study them with an open mind and an artist's eye and visualize new ideas and forms for a craft entrenched in antiquity. He should recognize that no art is static, no absolute answers exist simply because something has been part of a culture for centuries.

Art history has proven that each generation has within it the ability to ask new questions and blossom out with revised answers to man's same situations, to burst into bloom at any time with explosive, expressively beautiful statements that are indigenous to the times, the environment, and the medium. With iron, a medium whose potential is ageless and infinite, the craftsman is able to walk along the exciting precipice of originality that may eventually lead to personal discovery and satisfaction.

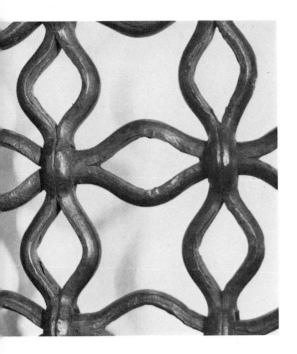

All the details on these pages are by Samuel Yellin. Photographed at the Yellin Museum, Philadelphia, Pa., by Dona Meilach.
Opposite top: Front and back of one detail. Many of Yellin's pieces appear intricately formed; yet the study of their construction reveals logical, easy solutions. Some are movable for various functional reasons.

Detail from a gate. By Samuel Yellin.

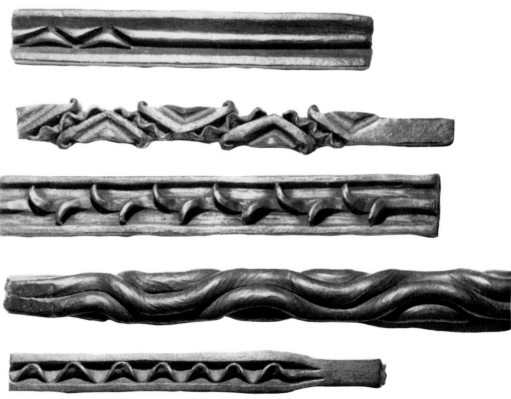

Exercise with a bar. By Samuel Yellin.
*Photographed at the Yellin Museum,
Philadelphia*

Floral details. By Samuel Yellin.

By Samuel Yellin.

By Winthrop H. Hall.

By Allesandro Mazzucotelli.

By Thomas Markusen.

By Thomas Markusen.

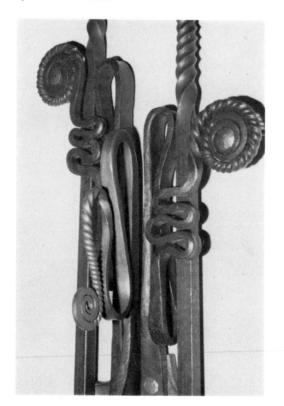

By Max Segal

By George Martin.

By Thomas Markusen.

Details of the work of Samuel Yellin from about 1928 to 1933 photographed at the Washington Cathedral, Washington, D.C., by Dona Meilach, with the exception of the animal head in the spiral-leafed stem (*top right*), taken at the Yellin Museum.

Appendix–Weight Charts

POUNDS PER FOOT FOR IRON AND CARBON STEEL BARS

Diameter or Thickness—Inches	1/8	3/16	1/4	5/16	3/8	7/16	1/2	5/8	3/4	7/8	1	1–1/4	1–1/2
Rounds—Diam. Inches	.042	.094	.167	.261	.376	.511	.668	1.04	1.50	2.04	2.67	4.17	6.01
Flat Bars: Width 1/8 In.	0.053												
3/16 In.	0.080	0.120											
1/4 In.	0.106	0.160	0.213										
5/16 In.	0.133	0.200	0.266	0.322									
3/8 In.	0.159	0.239	0.319	0.398	0.478								
7/16 In.	0.186	0.279	0.372	0.464	0.558	0.651							
1/2 In.	0.212	0.319	0.425	0.531	0.637	0.744	0.850						
5/8 In.	0.266	0.398	0.531	0.664	0.797	0.930	1.062	1.328					
3/4 In.	0.319	0.478	0.637	0.797	0.956	1.116	1.275	1.594	1.912				
7/8 In.	0.372	0.558	0.748	0.930	1.116	1.302	1.487	1.859	2.231	2.603			
1 In.	0.425	0.637	0.850	1.062	1.275	1.487	1.700	2.125	2.550	2.975	3.400		
1–1/4 In.	0.531	0.797	1.062	1.328	1.594	1.859	2.125	2.656	3.187	3.719	4.250	5.312	
1–1/2 In.	0.638	0.956	1.275	1.594	1.913	2.231	2.550	3.188	3.825	4.463	5.100	6.375	7.650
1–3/4 In.	0.744	1.116	1.488	1.859	2.231	2.603	2.975	3.719	4.463	5.206	5.950	7.438	8.925
2 In.	0.850	1.275	1.700	2.125	2.550	2.975	3.400	4.250	5.100	5.950	6.800	8.500	10.200
2–1/2 In.	1.063	1.594	2.125	2.656	3.188	3.719	4.250	5.313	6.375	7.438	8.500	10.625	12.750

WEIGHTS OF SHEET AND WIRE, PLATE OR ROD

Inch, fractions	Carbon steel sheet		Carbon steel wire		Copper sheet		Copper wire		Sterling silver sheet		Silver sheet	Sterling silver wire	
	Thickness in.	Wt./sq. ft.	Diam. in.	Wt. lbs./ft.	Thickness in.	Wt. lbs./sq. ft.	Diam. in.	Wt. lbs./ft.	Thickness	Wt. Troy oz./sq. in.	Sq. in./Troy oz.	Diam. Thickness	Troy oz./ft.
5–1/2	.500	20.400	.500	.668	.500	23.21	.500	.763					
3/8	.375	15.300	.375	.376	.375	17.40	.375	.429					
1/4	.250	10.200	.250	.167	.250	11.60	.250	.191					
3/16	.212	7.650	.212	.094	.212	8.71	.212	.108					
1/8	.125	5.100	.125	.042	.125	5.81	.125	.048					
1/16	.062	2.550	.062	.0104	.062	2.90	.064	.012					
8 gauge	.164	6.875	.162	.0700	.128	5.94	.128	.050	.128	.704	1.42	.128	.852
10 gauge	.134	5.625	.135	.0486	.102	4.733	.102	.0314	.102	.558	1.79	.102	.536
12 gauge	.105	4.375	.105	.0297	.081	3.758	.081	.0198	.0818	.443	2.26	.081	.337
14 gauge	.075	3.125	.080	.0171	.064	2.970	.064	.0124	.064	.351	2.85	.064	.212
16 gauge	.060	2.500	.062	.0104	.051	2.366	.051	.0078	.051	.278	3.60	.051	.133
18 gauge	.048	2.000	.047	.0060	.040	1.858	.040	.0049	.040	.221	4.52	.040	.084
20 gauge	.036	1.500	.035	.0033	.032	1.485	.032	.0031	.032	.175	5.71	.032	.053
22 gauge	.030	1.250	.027	.0022	.025	1.160	.025	.0019	.025	.139	7.19	.025	.033
24 gauge	.024	1.000	.023	.0014	.020	0.929	.020	.0012	.020	.110	9.09	.020	.021

NOTES: Steel sheet U.S. Standard gauge; Steel wire, Washburn & Moen gauge; Copper sheet, Brown & Sharpe gauge; Copper wire, Brown & Sharpe gauge. Brass weighs about 5 percent less than copper; 18/8 Cr/N Stainless steel weighs about 1–1/2 percent more than carbon steel; Pure Silver weighs 1 percent more than Sterling Silver.

Courtesy, George Martin

Bibliography

Blacksmithing

Aston, James. *Wrought Iron: Its Manufacture, Characteristics and Applications*. Pittsburgh: A. M. Byers Co., 1939.

Basic Handtools. Bureau of Naval Personnel Navy Training Course, NAVPERS 10085-A. Washington, D.C.: Government Printing Office, 1963 Revised.

Bealer, Alex W. *The Art of Blacksmithing*. New York: Funk & Wagnalls Co., 1969.

Bollinger, Joseph W. *Elements of Wrought Iron*. New York: Bruce Publishing Co., 1948.

Butler, Doug. *Horseshoeing Iron and Forge Work*. Available from Centaur Supply, Burlington, Wisc. 1965.

Casterlin, Warren S. *Steelworking and Tool Dressing*. New York: M. T. Richardson, 1914.

Cathcart, W. H. *The Value of Science in the Smithy and Forge*. London: Charles Griffin & Co., 1937.

Council for Small Industries in Rural Areas. (See Welsh, Peter C.)

Crowe, Charles Phillip. *Forgecraft*. Columbus, Ohio: R. G. Adams & Co., 1913.

Dines, Glen. *Bull Wagon*. New York: The Macmillan Co., 1963. (Young Adult Book)

Drew, James Meddick. *Blacksmithing*. St. Paul, Minn.: Webb Book Publishing, 1935.

Friese, John F. *Farm Blacksmithing*. Peoria, Ill.: Manual Arts Press, 1921.

Hasluck, Paul N. *Smith's Work*. London, New York: Cassell & Co., 1912.

Hogg, Garry. *Hammer & Tongs: Blacksmithing Down the Ages*. London: Hutchinson, 1964.

Holford, H. *The 20th Century Toolsmith and Steelworker*. Chicago: Frederick Drake & Co., 1912.

Holmstrom, J. G. *Modern Blacksmithing and Horseshoeing*. New York: Frederick J. Drake & Co., 1971. Facsimile Reprint: 1904 edition.

————. *Standard Blacksmithing, Horseshoeing and Wagon Making*. Chicago: Webb Publishing Company, 1907.

Hommel, R. P. *China at Work*. Cambridge, Mass.: MIT Press, 1937.

Horner, Joseph Gregory. *Smithing and Forging*. Manchester, Eng.: Emmott & Co., Ltd., 1920.

The Horseshoer: War Department Technical Manual No. 2–220. San Luis Obispo, Calif.: El Corral College Bookstore. Facsimile Reprint: 1941 edition.

Jones, Lynn Charles. *Forging and Smithing*. New York and London: The Century Co., 1924.

Kays, D. J. *The Horse*. New York, Toronto: Rinehart & Co., 1953.

Liestøl, A. *Blodrefill og mal*. New York: Viking Press, 1951.

Lillico, J. W. *Blacksmith's Manual Illustrated*. London: 1960. 4th impression.

Lungwitz, A., and John W. Adams. *A Textbook of Horseshoeing*. Corvallis, Ore.: Oregon State University Press, 1966. Facsimile Reprint: 1913 edition.

Miller, J. K., and John H. Sekera. *Shop Equipment—Hand Forging—Tool Dressing*. Scranton, Pa.: International Textbook Co., 1936, 1935, 1940; bound as one volume.

Naujoks, Waldemar, and Donald C. Fabel. *Forging Handbook*. Cleveland, Ohio: American Society for Metals, 1939.

Pehoski, Joe. *Blacksmithing for the Home Craftsman*. Grand Island, Nebr.: Stuhr Museum, 1973.

Richards, William Allen. *Forging of Iron and Steel*. New York: D. Van Nostrand Co., 1915.

Richardson, M. T. *Practical Blacksmithing*, Volumes I, II, III, IV. New York: M. T. Richardson Co., 1890.

Robins, F. *The Smith: The Traditions and Lore of an Ancient Craft*. London, New York: Rider and Co., 1953.

Sallows, James Francis. *The Blacksmith's Guide*. 1st Edition J. F. Sallows. Brattleboro, Vt.: The Technical Press, 1907.

Schwarzkopf, Ernst. *Plain and Ornamental Forging*. New York: John Wiley & Sons; London: Chapman & Hall, 1916.

Selvidge, R. W., and Allton, J. M. *Blacksmithing.* Peoria, III.: The Manual Arts Press, 1925.

Smith, H. R. Bradley. *Blacksmith's and Farrier's Tools at Shelburne Museum.* Shelburne, Vt.: Shelburne Museum, Inc., 1966.

Smith, John R. *Manual of Blacksmithing.* Chicago: M. A. Donohue & Co., 1902.

Smith, Robert E. *Forging and Welding.* Bloomington, III.: McKnight & McKnight, 1967.

Stevenson, James Arthur Radford. *The Din of a Smithy.* London: Chapman & Hall, 1932.

Sturt, George. *The Wheelwright's Shop.* London: Cambridge University Press, 1963.

Watson, Aldren A. *The Village Blacksmith.* New York: Thomas Y. Crowell Co., 1968.

Watson, John. *Tables for the Use of Blacksmiths and Forgers.* London: Longmans, Green & Co., 1966. New impression.

Welsh, Peter C. *The Blacksmith's Craft.* Council for Small Industries in Rural Areas, 35 Camp Road, Wimbledon Common, London SW 19, England, 1964. 4th impression.

_____. *Decorative Ironwork.* COSIRA, 1966. Reprint.

_____. *Fabricating Simple Structures.* COSIRA, 1952.

_____. *Metals for Engineering Craftsmen.* COSIRA, 1952.

_____. *Wrought Iron Design Catalog.* COSIRA, 1952.

_____. *Wrought Ironwork.* COSIRA, 1963. 4th impression.

Weygers, Alexander G. *The Making of Tools.* New York: Van Nostrand Reinhold Co., 1973.

_____. *The Modern Blacksmith.* New York: Van Nostrand Reinhold Co., 1974.

Metal Technology

American Society for Metals. *The History of Metals.* Metals Park, Ohio.

_____. *Man, Metals and Modern Magic.* Metals Park, Ohio.

_____. *Metals Handbook.* Metals Park, Ohio, 1939, 1948, 1974.

_____. *The Nature of Metals.* Metals Park, Ohio.

Bacon, John Lord. *Forge-Practice and Heat Treatment of Steel.* New York: John Wiley & Sons, Inc., 1919.

Bethlehem Steel Corporation, *Modern Steels and Their Properties.* Bethlehem, Pa., 1972.

_____. *Quick Facts about Alloy Steels.* Bethlehem, Pa. #2873–A.

_____. *The Tool Steel Trouble Shooter Handbook.* Bethlehem, Pa., 1952.

Brick, Gordon, Phillips. *Structure and Properties of Alloys.* New York: McGraw-Hill, 1965.

Clark, Donald S., and Wilbur R. Varney. *Physical Metallurgy for Engineers.* New York: American Book Co., & Van Nostrand Reinhold, 1962. 2nd edition.

Digges, Rosenberg, and Geil. *Heat Treatment and Properties of Iron and Steel.* NBS Monograph 88. Washington, D.C.: Government Printing Office, 1966. 35¢.

Feldmann, H. D. *Cold Forging of Steel.* New York: Chemical Publishing Co., Inc., 1962.

Fisher, Douglas Alan. *Steel from the Iron Age to the Space Age.* New York: Harper & Row, Publishers, 1967.

Haedeke, Hanns-Ulrich. *Metalwork.* New York: Universe Books, 1970.

Jensen, Jon E. *Forging Industry Handbook.* Cleveland, Ohio: Forging Industry Association, 1970.

Kennedy, Gower A. *Welding Technology.* Indianapolis, Ind.: Howard A. Sams & Co., Inc., 1974.

Ludwig, Oswald A. *Metalwork Technology and Practice.* Bloomington, III.: McKnight & McKnight Publishing Co., 1975.

McGannon, Harold E. (ed.). *The Making, Shaping and Treating of Steel.* Pittsburgh: U.S. Steel Corporation, 1971. 9th edition.

Pender, James A. *Welding.* Toronto, Ontario, Can.: McGraw-Hill Co. of Canada, Ltd., 1968.

Preheating for Welding (Reprint from *The Welding Journal*). TEMPIL: Hamilton Blvd., S. Plainfield, N.J. 07080.

Rose, Augustus F. *Copper Work.* New York: Atkinson, Mentzer & Co., 1908.

Rusinoff, Samuel. *Forging and Forming Metals.* Chicago: American Technical Society Publication, 1952.

Schwartz, Mel M. *Modern Metal Jointing Techniques: Welding and Brazing.* New York: John Wiley & Sons, 1969.

Seabright, Lawrence H. *The Selection and Hardening of Tool Steels.* New York: McGraw-Hill Book Co., Inc., 1950.

Shrager, Arthur M. *Elementary Metallurgy and Metallography.* New York: Dover, 1949/1969.

Smith, Cyril Stanley. *A History of Metallography.* Chicago and London: University of Chicago Press, 1960. Revised 1965.

———. *Stereology.* Proceedings of Second International Congress for Stereology, Chicago. New York: Springer Verlag, 1967.

U.S. Steel Corporation. *The Making, Shaping and Treatment of Steel.* U.S. Steel Corporation, 600 Grant, Pittsburgh, Pa. 15219, 1971. 9th edition.

Union Carbide Corporation. *TheOxy-Acetylene Handbook.* New York: Union Carbide Corporation, 1968. 18th printing.

Untracht, Oppi. *Metal Techniques for Craftsmen.* Garden City, N.Y.: Doubleday, 1968.

Walker, John R. *Modern Metalworking.* South Holland, Ill.: The Goodheart-Willcox Company, Inc., 1973.

History—Aesthetics

Ayrton, Maxwell. *Wrought Iron and Its Decorative Uses.* New York: Country Life Ltd. & Scribner's, 1929.

Blanc, Louis. *Le Fer Forge.* (in French) Paris: G. Van Oest, 1958.

Bolanier, Georges, and Jacques Maquet. *Dictionary of Black African Civilization.* New York: Leon Amiel, 1974.

Bridge, Paul, and Austin Crossland. *Designs in Metal.* London: B. T. Batsford Ltd., 1966. Distributed by Sportshelf, P.O. Box 634, New Rochelle, N.Y. 10802.

Byne, Arthur, and Mildred Stapley. *Spanish Ironwork.* Hispanic Society Publications No. 89, 1915.

Christian, Marcus. *Negro Ironworkers of Louisiana 1718–1900.* Gretna, La.: Pelican Publishing Co., 1972.

Cortes, Antonio. *Hierros Forjados.* (in Spanish) Talleres Graficos del Museo de Arquelogia, Historia y Etnografia, 1935.

D'Allemagne, Henry René. *Decorative Antique Ironwork, A Pictorial Treasury.* New York: Dover, 1968.

Espinosa, R. A. *Hierros Colonialses en Zacatecas.* (in Spanish) Mexico, D.F.: Imprenta Universatria Mexico, 1955.

Ferrari, Giulio. *Il Ferro Nell 'Arte.* (in Italian) Milano: Italiana Urico Hoepli, 1950.

Forbes, Robert J. *Studies in Ancient Technology.* Volumes VIII and IX. Leiden, Netherlands, 1964.

Frank, Edgar B. *Old French Ironwork.* Cambridge, Mass.: Harvard University Press, 1950.

Geerlings, Gerald K. *Wrought Iron in Architecture.* New York, London: Charles Scribner's and Sons, 1929. (Bonanza edition)

Googerty, Thomas F. *Handforging and Wrought Iron Ornamental Work.* Chicago: Popular Mechanics Co., 1911.

Goodwin-Smith, R. *English Domestic Metalwork.* I. Lewis Publ. Ltd., Tithe House, London, England. Legi on Sea, Essex, 1937.

Harris, John. *English Decorative Ironwork.*

Hawthorne, John G. *On Divers Arts, The Treatise of Theophilus.* Chicago: The University of Chicago Press, 1963.

Höver, Otto. *Wrought Iron Encyclopedia of Ironwork.* New York: Universe Books, 1962. 2nd American edition.

Jenkins, J. Geraint. *The English Farm Wagon Origins and Structure.* Pakwood Press, Longfield Surrey, England. The Museum of English Rural Life, University of Reading, 1961.

Kauffman, Henry J. *Early American Ironware Cast and Wrought.* Rutland, Vt.: Charles E. Tuttle Co., 1966. 2nd printing.

Kaye, Myrna. *Yankee Weathervanes.* New York: E. P. Dutton & Co., Inc., 1975.

Klamkin, Charles. *Weather Vanes.* New York: Hawthorn Books, Inc., 1973.

Knauth, Percy, and Editors. *The Metalsmiths.* New York: Time-Life Books, 1974.

Krauss, Rosalind E. *Terminal Iron Works: The Sculpture of David Smith.* Cambridge, Mass., and London: MIT Press, 1971.

Krom, Edward F. *Handwrought Ironwork.* Milwaukee: The Bruce Publishing Co., 1946.

Kuhn, Fritz. *Stahlgestaltung.* (in German) Tubingen, Berlin, Ger.: Alle Rechte vorbehalten, 1956.

———. *Wrought Iron.* Translated from the German by Charles B. Johnson. New York: Architectural Book Publishing Co., 1969. 2nd English edition. (Orig. in German, Harrap, London, 1967.)

Laude, Jean. *African Art of the Dogon.* New York: The Viking Press & The Brooklyn Museum, 1973.

Lindsay, John Seymour. *An Anatomy of English Wrought Iron.* New York: Taplinger Publishing Co., 1965.

Lister, Raymond. *Decorative Wrought Ironwork in Great Britain.* Boston: Charles T. Branford Co., 1957.

Lorenz, Paul. *La Ferronnerie Italienne.* (in French) Paris: G. M. Perrin, 1969.

Lynch, John. *Metal Sculpture.* New York: The Viking Press, 1957.

Maryon, Herbert. *Metalwork and Enamelling.* London: Chapman & Hall, Ltd., 1959. Dover Publications, Inc., New York.

Mazzucotelli—The Italian Art Nouveau Artist of Wrought Iron. Tubingen: Verlag Ernst Wasmuth, 1971. Edizioni il Polifilo Milano via Bernonuovo 2, Italy.

Meilach, Dona Z., and Donald Seiden. *Direct Metal Sculpture.* New York: Crown Publishers, Inc., 1966.

Murphy, B. S. *English and Spanish Wrought Iron Work.* London: Batsford, 1900.

Preece, John, and Mario Callegari. *Gates of Veneto.* London: John Baker, 1968.

Schubert, H. R. *History of the British Iron and Steel Industry to A. D. 1775.* London: 1957.

Seiber, Roy. *African Textiles and Decorative Arts.* New York: The Museum of Modern Art, 1972.

Simon Benetton. Genoa, Italy: Immordine Editore.

Smetana, Gunther. *Entwurfe fur Kunstschmiedearbeiten.* (in German) Stuttgart, Ger.: Julius Hoffmann, 1955.

Smith, David. *David Smith.* ed. Cleve Gray. New York: Holt, Rinehart and Winston, 1968.

Sonn, A. H. *Early American Wrought Iron.* New York: Chas. Scribner's Sons, 1928.

Trowell, Margaret. *African Design.* New York, Washington: Frederick A. Praeger, 1960.

Tunshall, Small, and Christopher Woodridge. *English Wrought Ironwork.* London: Architectural Press.

Underwood, Austin. *Creative Wrought Ironwork.* Princeton, N.J.: D. Van Nostrand, 1965.

Wallace, Phillip B. *Colonial Ironwork in Old Philadelphia.* New York: Dover Publications, Inc., 1970.

Welsh, Peter C. *Arms and Armor.* New York: Guide to the Collections, Metropolitan Museum of Art, 1962.

_____. *The Metropolitan Museum of Art Bulletin.* Volume XXVIII. No. 4. New York, December 1969.

Wrought Iron Railings, Doors and Gates. Architect's "detail" Library. Volume 1, London: Iliffe Books Ltd., 1964.

Zimelli, Umberto, and Giovanni Vergerio. *Decorative Ironwork.* London: Paul Hamlyn, 1966.

Books—Guns, Swords and Knives

Akehurst, Richard. *The World of Guns.* London, New York: The Hamlyn Publishing Group Ltd., 1972.

Angier, R. H. *Firearms Bluing and Browning.* Harrisburg, Pa.: The Stackpole Co., 1936.

Dunlap, Roy F. *Gunsmithing.* Harrisburg, Pa.: The Stackpole Co., 1963.

Hayward, J. F. *The Art of the Gunmaker.* 2 volumes. New York: St. Martin's Press, 1962.

Hughes, B. R. *American Handmade Knives of Today.* Union City, Tenn.: Pioneer Press, 1972.

_____, and Jack Lewis. *The Gun Digest Book of Knives.* Chicago: Follett, 1973.

Johnson, Major Thomas M. *Collecting the Edge Weapons of the Third Reich.* Columbia, S.C.: Thomas M. Johnson, 1975.

Latham, Sid. *Knives and Knifemakers.* New York: Winchester Press, 1973.

Peterson, Harold L. *American Indian Tomahawks.* New York: Museum of the American Indian, Heye Foundation, 1965.

_____. *American Knives, The First History & Collector's Guide.* New York: Charles Scribner's Sons, 1958.

_____. *Daggers and Fighting Knives of the Western World from the Stone Age Until 1900.* New York: Walker and Co., 1968.

_____. *Encyclopedia of Firearms.* New York: E. P. Dutton, 1964.

_____. *A History of Body Armor.* New York: Charles Scribner's Sons, 1968.

_____. *A History of Knives.* New York: Charles Scribner's Sons, 1966.

Rawson, P. S. *The Indian Sword.* London: Herbert Jenkens, Ltd., 1968.

Robinson, B. W. *The Arts of the Japanese Sword.* Rutland, Vt.: Chas. E. Tuttle Co., 1967.

_____. *A Primer of Japanese Sword-Blades.* Paragon Book Reprint Corporation, 1967.

_____. *A Short History of Japanese Armor.* London: Her Majesty's Stationery Office, 1965.

Russell, Carl P. *Firearms, Traps and Tools of the Mountain Men.* New York: Alfred A. Knopf, 1967.

Wilkenson, Frederick. *Antique Firearms.* Garden City, N.Y.: Doubleday & Co., Inc., 1969.

Yumoto, John M. *The Japanese Sword.* Rutland, Vt. and Tokyo, Japan: Charles E. Tuttle Co., 1958.

Exhibition Catalogs

Davis, Myra Tolmach. *Sketches in Iron: Samuel Yellin. American Master of Wrought Iron 1885–1940.* The Dimock Gallery.

The George Washington University, Washington, D.C., March 6–25, 1971.

Iron-Art of the Blacksmith in the Western Sudan. Gallery II, Creative Arts Department, Purdue University, Bloomington, Indiana, 1975. (Museum Catalog)

Made of Iron. University of St. Thomas, Art Department, Houston, Texas, 1966.

Metalsmithing: Ebendorf, Jerry, Markusen. Syracuse University, Lubin House, New York, April 17–May 18, 1973.

Smithing '73. State University of New York, Brockport College, Art Department, April 14–May 15, 1973.

Watson, Aldren A. *The Bulletin of the Cleveland Museum of Art,* Volume 51, No. 4, April 1964.

———. *The Metropolitan Museum of Art Bulletin.* January 1963.

———. *The Metropolitan Museum of Art Bulletin,* April 1964.

———. *Made in Iron.* September–December 1966, Available from Art Department, University of St. Thomas, Houston, Texas.

Welsh, Peter C. *American Folk Art.* Smithsonian Institution, Washington, D.C., 1965.

Suppliers

These suppliers responded to requests for information so at this writing they are valid sources; but names, numbers, addresses can change quickly. (No endorsement is implied.) Your best up-to-date sources are the blacksmith publications and searches on the Internet for blacksmithing, iron, metal and the type of equipment desired. The Artist-Blacksmith's Association (ABANA), Anvil Fire (see resouce listing, Magazines) and other publications provide relatively up-to-date supplier listings.

A Cut Above
16512 Arminta St.
Van Nuys, CA 91406

Bonded and coated abrasive supplies
www.acutabove.com
800-444-2999 (free brochure)

Bayshore Metals, Inc.
P.O. Box 882003
San Francisco, CA 94188-2003

Metals
Fax: 415 -285-5759
800-533-2493
or 415-647-7981

Bob Bergman
8126 N. Postville Rd.
Blanchard, WI 53516

KA-75 air hammer
888-535-6320

Bohler Steel
2340 S. Arlington Hts. Rd.
Arlington Hts. IL 60005

Stock steel
St. 200 http://
www.bohlersteel.com
847-228-7370

J.G. Braun Company
8145 River Drive
Mornton Grove, IL
60053- 2645

Steel, bronze, stainless supplies
http://www.JGBraun.com
Fax:847-663-0667
800-323-4072

Brian Russell Designs
10385 Long Rd.
Arlington, TN 38002

Sahinler Air Hammers
http://www.
powerhammers.com
901-867-7300

Carolina Glove Co.
PO Drawer 820
Newton, NC 28658

Kevlar gloves in pairs or lefts only
Fax: 828 464 1710
800-438-6888

Centaur Forge, Ltd
P.O. Box 340 AFN
117 N. Spring St.
Burlington, WI
53105-0340

Tools, equipment, books
Call or write for catalog
http://www.anvilfire.com/centaur
414-763-9175   Email:
CF340.aol.com

Cleveland Steel Tool Co.
474 E. 105th St.
Cleveland, OH 44108

Steel punches
http://
www.clevesteeltool.com
800-446-4402

Crucible Material Corp.
5639 W. Genesee St.
Camillus NY 13031-0991

Complete listing of tool steels
http://www.
crucibleservice.com
800-365-1185

E&C Machine, Inc.
1174 Ember Rd.
Lexington, NC 27292

Trip Air Hammers
336-249-4482 or
336 475-6760

Firedesign
9 Reed Street
Asheville, NC 28803

Grainger
Call for catalog

Glendale Forge Tools
Monk St.
Thaxted, Essex CM6 2NR
England

Iron Age Antiques
Ocean View, DE 19970

Kayne & Son Custom Hdwe., Inc.
100 Daniel Ridge Rd.
Candler, NC 28715-9434

Lawler Foundry Corp.
PO Box 320069
Birmingham, AL 35232-00069

Meier Steel
Daryl Meier
75 Forge rd.
Carbondale, Ill. 62901

NC Tool Company
6568 Hunt Road
Pleasant Garden, NC 27313

Nimba Forge
353 Glen Cove Road
Port Townsend, WA 98368

Norm Larson Books
5426 Hwy. 246
Lompoc, CA 93436

Off Center Products
2311 Ross Way
Tacoma, WA 98421-3402

Postville Power Hammers
Blanchardville,WI 53516

Sculpt Nouveau
PO Box 460459
Escondido, CA 92046

Tennessee Fabricating company
2025 York Ave.
Memphis, TN 38104

Valley Forge & Welding
280 Franklin Ave.
Willits, CA 95490

Wallace Metal Work
R.D. 1 Blacksmith Lane
Kempton, PA 19529

Bull air hammers
www.bullhammer.com
Phone and fax: 828-277-6000

Hand tools, motors and supplies
800-473-3473 ext.1053

Mfgrs. Equipment and supplies . http://www.armoury.damon.co.uk/glendale
Fax: 011-44-1371-831419
        011-44-1371-830466

Used tools, books
302-539-5344

Air hammers, tools (catalog)
Fax: 828 665-8303
828-667-8868

Ornamental components & accessories
Fax: 205-595-0559
        205-595-0559

Pattern-welded steel.
Prices available
Fax: 618-549-6239
darylmeier@usa.net
618-549-3234

Gas forges and tools
800-446-6498

Anvils
nimba@olympus.net
Fax/Phone 360-385-7258

Books and more books
larbooks@impulse.net
805-735-2095

Mfgrs. of hammers and tools
gnsjr@worldnet.att.net
253-274-0276

KA hammers; new & used eqpt.
888-565-6320

Metals dyes and finishing kits.
Sculptor@home.com
800-728-5787

Cast iron components
tenthfab@memphison line.com
800-258-4766

tools and supplies
jere@sabornet
800-367-5357

Peddinghaus anvils,
new & used equpt.
610-756-3377

Resources
2nd Edition

Organizations

American Craft Council (ACC) Information Center
72 Spring St
New York, NY 10012
212-274-0630

ABANA - Artist-Blacksmith's Association of North America
PO Box 206
Washington, MO 63090
314 390-2133
http://www.abana.org

Australian Blacksmiths Association
RMB 1155 Tongala
Victoria, Australia 3621
03-58-5900736
wake@river.net.com.au

BABA - British Artist Blacksmiths Association
111 Main Street
Ratho, Newbridge, Midlothian. EH28 8RS.
Scotland
        E-mail phil@rathobyres.demon.co.uk
        Fax: 01-31-333-3354
http://www.baba.org

Crafts Council of Great Britain
44a Pentonville Road
Islington
London N1 9BY, England
United Kingdom
0171-278-7700
http://www.craftscouncil.org.uk

Irish Blacksmith Organization
Anna O'Donoghue
21 Healy Terrace
Bellina Co. Mayo, Ireland
Fax: 353-96-72666
        Tel: 353- 96 70998

Additional Internet Resources

These sites provide links to a variety of other related sites, host chat and discussion groups, current events, photos of work, artist listings, and more.

The Anvil Fire, http://www.anvilfire.com

ArtMetal Village, http://www.artmetal.com

Metal Web News
www.mindspring.com/~wgray1

Winikoff's Virtual Junkyard For Blacksmiths
http://www.seanet.co,/~neilwin/index.htm

University of Georgia Center for Continuing Education. Forge & Anvil: a television series on blacksmithing 1966.
http://www.gactr.uga.edu/forge/

Amazon Books: Search using the words: blacksmithing, ornamental ironwork
http://www.amazon.com

Museums

Many museums have collections of ironwork; but the following is the only museum devoted to the art form and medium.

The National Ornamental Metal Museum
374 Metal Museum Drive
Memphis, TN 38106-1539
901-774-6380
http://memphisguide.com/NOMN.html

Education Opportunities

ABANA Journeyman Program (See ABANA above)

International College of French Wrought Ironwork,
Maison des Compagnons du Devoir,
Chemin de Reims,
51140 Muizon, France.
Fax 01033 26029639
01033 26020931

John C. Campbell Folk School
One Folk School Rd.
Brasstown, N.C. 28902-9603
800-FOLK-SCH. http:www.grove.net/~jccfs

NOMMA (National Ornamental and Miscellaneous Metals Association)
804-10 Main St. Ste. E
Forest Park, GA 30050
404-363-4009 Email: nommainfor@aol.com

Ozark School of Blacksmithing
Box 5780
Potosi, MO 63664
573-438-4725

Penland School of Crafts
PO Box 37
Penland, NC 28765-0037
828-765-2359 Email: http://www.penland.org

Peters Valley Craft Education Center
19 Kuhn Rd.
Layton, NJ 07851
201-948-5200 Email: http://pvcrafts.org

Turley Forge
RR 10 Box 88C
Santa Fe, NM 87501
505-471-8608

The Venice European Centre for the Skills of Architectural Heritage Conservation.
AI DIRETTORE
Del Centro Europeo di Venezia per i Mestieri, della Conservazione, del Patrimonio Architettonico,
Isola di San Servolo,
Casella Postale 676, I-30100
VENEZIA

Magazines

The Anvils Ring- published by ABANA (see organizations, above)
Hammer's Blow - published by ABANA (see organizations, above)

Anvil Magazine
P.O. Box 1810
Georgetown, CA 95634
800-94-ANVIL

Blacksmith's Journal
P.O. Box 193
Washington, MO 63090
800 944-6134
http://www.blacksmithsjournal.com

Index

Page numbers in italics indicate illustrations.